GRETTIR'S SAGA

GRETTIR'S SAGA

Translated by Denton Fox and Hermann Pálsson

UNIVERSITY OF TORONTO PRESS
Toronto   Buffalo   London

© University of Toronto Press 1974
Toronto   Buffalo   London
Printed in Canada

Reprinted 1977, 1981, 1985, 1988, 1990, 1993, 1996, 1998,
2001, 2005

ISBN cloth 0-8020-1925-0
ISBN paper 0-8020-6165-6
LC 72-90746

Printed on acid-free paper

Photographs by James Rupert Norquay

University of Toronto Press acknowledges the financial assistance to
its publishing program of the Canada Council and the Ontario Arts
Council.

University of Toronto Press acknowledges the financial support for its
publishing activities of the Government of Canada through the Book
Publishing Industry Development Program (BPIDP).

Contents

Introduction

Grettir's Saga is the last of the great Icelandic sagas: it was probably written about 1325, some thirty or forty years after *Njal's Saga*, and at the end of the hundred years during which most of the important sagas were written. Its author was evidently a man of great knowledge and sophistication; the saga shows that he had mastered both the matter and the literary techniques of the earlier sagas.[1] *Grettir's Saga* is one of the longest, most profound, and most unorthodox of the sagas.

This work has sometimes been thought of as a crude folktale filled with monsters and blind violence, an example of the sort of rough and popular material which must have lain behind *Beowulf*. But in fact it is more like *Beowulf* itself; although some of the elements of the saga are the kind of stuff one finds in folktales, the structure of the work is highly wrought, and its meaning intricate. Its art is self-concealing; in particular, its structure seems, deceivingly, to be rambling and naïve, a chronicle of a series of disconnected events. The author, however, planned his work with great care;

---

1 The saga writer's borrowings from earlier sagas can be seen from the references he makes to them in the text itself. He mentions *Laxdœla Saga* (chapter 10), *Bandamanna Saga* ('The Saga of the Confederates,' chapter 14), *Bjarnar Saga Hítdœlakappa* (chapter 58), *The Saga of Bodmod, Grimolf, and Gerpir* (chapter 12), and *Earl Eirik's Saga* (chapter 19). Also there is ample evidence to show that the author was heavily indebted to a number of other sources, though he fails to acknowledge them. The first eight chapters are freely adapted from *Landnámabók* ('The Book of Settlements'), and a great deal of other genealogical detail is derived from that source. Chapters 25-7 are based on *Fóstbrœðra Saga* ('The Sworn-Brothers' Saga'). Other works used by the author include *Heiðarvíga Saga, Eyrbyggja Saga, Kristni Saga, Hungrvaka, Íslendingabók* ('The Book of the Icelanders'), *Egil's Saga, Njal's Saga, Vatnsdœla Saga, Kormak's Saga*, and finally some version of the story of Tristram and Iseult. See Guðni Jónsson's introduction to his edition of *Grettir's Saga* in the Íslenzk Fornrit series.

perhaps the best way to grasp the meaning of the saga is to look briefly at the way it is put together.

The saga falls into three unequal parts: a prologue of thirteen chapters; the main body of the saga, seventy-one chapters describing Grettir's life and death; and an epilogue of nine chapters. The prologue, like the epilogue, appears at first to have only a slight relevance to the central part of the saga but, again like the epilogue, it is in fact an organic part of the whole. On the level of plot, the excuse for the prologue is that it describes some of Grettir's ancestors, and tells how his family moved from Norway to Iceland. These chapters also help us to understand Grettir's character, because some of the salient features in his make-up are inherited from his forebears. His recalcitrance, for example, reminds us of his father as a young man. But, on a thematic level, the prologue is much more significant. The central action in this part of the story is the exodus from Norway, where the newly established kingdom seemed increasingly oppressive, to the anarchic and completely individual-istic violence of viking life, and finally to the virgin country of Iceland, a country which offered the possibility, at least, of men living together in an organized society while still preserving their individual freedom. The central character, and the one who epito-mizes this part of the saga, is Onund Tree-Foot, whom we discover later to be Grettir's great-grandfather. After a turbulent and chaotic life he settled in Iceland: the journey cost him a leg, and, as he says, he traded his cornfields in Norway for icy Kaldbak ('Cold-Ridge'), but he never flinched or compromised.

The author of the saga looks back from the fourteenth century, when Iceland was no longer an independent country, to the violent and lawless time of the vikings in the ninth century, then to the period of settlements in Iceland, and finally to the first half of the eleventh century, the time of the central part of the saga. The saga continually reveals the author's concern with the conflict between man's desire for individual freedom and the restrictive bonds imposed by society. The flight from Norway to Iceland, from sub-jection and confinement to a perilous freedom beset both by the external hazards of a new land and by the internal hazards of loneliness and pride, is partly a parallel of the main action of the saga, Grettir's escape to freedom and destruction. But the prologue closes at the time when Christianity was being introduced into Iceland, and here a new element enters. Onund's career, as a heroic and individualistic warrior in a chaotic world, had its own propriety; Grettir's character is like a larger version of Onund's, but he is born too late, and into a Christian and civilized world, where the heroic virtues are no longer sufficient. For the rest of the saga, the conflict between the Christian world and the survival of the pagan world, as sorcery or as heroic pride, is a recurrent theme.

Grettir is introduced with these words: 'As a child he was self-willed, taciturn and harsh, sardonic and mischievous. His father was not very fond of him, but his mother loved him dearly.' These sentences are the preface to a series of anecdotes about Grettir's childhood, when time and again he defies, violently, cruelly, and wittily, the authority of his father, and is shielded by his mother. But they also foreshadow Grettir's whole life: he constantly rebels, often with self-destructive wilfulness, against the powers and authorities of the masculine world he lives in, but also, up to the very end, he keeps the closest of relationships with a few other humans.

The anecdotes about Grettir at the age of ten are in several ways a paradigm of the saga. They indicate, for instance, the narrative technique: where a modern novelist might take a single incident or a single day, and linger over it to extract all the meaning possible, the saga-writer's method is sparse and quick narrative. Instead of describing one incident from a dozen different aspects, he describes a dozen similar but different incidents. This technique is particularly appropriate for the theme of the saga: Grettir must repeatedly fight the same battle, over and over again. He wins each one, except the last, but his victories never last long, since his defeat of one threat to his autonomy only breeds another threat.

Although the author, with immense skill, varies the circumstances of Grettir's battles so that the saga is anything but monotonous, Grettir emerges as an obsessional character, repeating time and again the same actions. He is a romantic hero viewed unromantically: he is above other men in that he is stronger than they are, and he has higher goals, but he is also beneath them, not only because he is an outlaw, but also because he is lacking in some of the ordinary human qualities which make for survival.

His childhood comes to an abrupt end with his first killing, when he is only sixteen. It is typical of the author's subtle way of unfolding Grettir's character that we are not told unequivocally whether or not his first victim was guilty of stealing his food-bag. But whether or not he is partially justified, here as elsewhere in the story, Grettir's actions are violent, immoderate, and have drastic consequences. As a child, he was a member of his father's household, but rebelled against his authority; his first crucial act, when he leaves the confines of his home to go out among men, is to act violently against society and kill a man. This time the context in which he lives is no longer his father's farm but society at large. Instead of being chastised or disciplined by the harsh paternal hand ruling his home, he now has to pay the penalty demanded by a justice-seeking society, where there is no maternal interference to mitigate the severity of the punishment. As a result of his first killing, he is made an outlaw, perhaps his natural state, and forced to leave Iceland for three years.

Grettir's life falls neatly and symmetrically into five acts: the first act, which ends with Grettir's first killing, is set in Iceland; the second in Norway, the third back in Iceland, the fourth recounts his second trip to Norway, and the final act shows his last years in Iceland. The second act centres on four hostile encounters, each one of a different type. These encounters, which presage Grettir's later life, show him, typically, taking on all possible enemies: the supernatural, the non-human natural world, and human antagonists in their two possible forms – as an impersonal massed force, or as a single personal enemy. The first of them, a fight against the supernatural, comes when Grettir breaks into the grave-mound and grapples with the undead mound-dweller. He is successful, but the circumstances of the fight suggest his arrogant urge to seek out superhuman adversaries. This urge, which keeps being manifested throughout the saga, is commendable, in that it comes from Grettir's desire to do battle with the profoundest of evils, but also dangerous, in that it comes from Grettir's obsessional feeling that he must be superior to everything, and must keep proving this superiority. Grettir's second fight is against a band of violent criminals: he completely defeats the berserks who come to a supposedly undefended farm in order to rob and to rape. This fight shows Grettir in his best aspect, as a man who uses his formidable courage, strength, and intelligence to protect the weak. Throughout the saga, Grettir shows himself constantly as a protector of others – though never of himself. The third fight is against a natural force, the bear. The bear is the non-human equivalent of the berserks (a term probably derived from 'bear' + 'sark'), a force which threatens peaceful society, and here again Grettir shows himself as the protecting hero who can succeed singlehanded where a group of men had failed. The fourth fight, or series of fights, is against an individual, Bjorn ('Bear'), who threatens Grettir's honour. Bjorn is, at first sight, a much less formidable antagonist than the earlier ones, and Grettir has, in fact, no trouble in killing him. But this fight is, as it turns out, more dangerous than the earlier ones, because Bjorn is protected by his friends and kinsmen, and they are in turn protected by society, in the person of the earl. Grettir cannot stand alone against all society, and he is saved only by his brother. This fight foreshadows the future fights in which Grettir is protected, and finally avenged, by his family, but it also foreshadows Grettir's downfall: he can conquer any single enemy, but he cannot stand alone against the whole world.

At the beginning of the third act, when Grettir returns to Iceland, he is without any serious difficulties. He has served his sentence of three-years' outlawry, and his successes in Norway have brought him fame, if perhaps also pride. But almost immediately he becomes tangled in the web of family feuds, largely because of his refusal to tolerate anything which can be construed as an insult. The most important episode in this act, and one of the climaxes of the saga, is Grettir's fight with Glam. On the one hand this is a laudable act; Glam is an evil and dangerous spirit who should be destroyed. On the other hand, Grettir is warned against undertaking the fight, he is motivated largely by his own pride, and he must pay for his hubris. Just before Glam is killed, he curses Grettir: '... from now on outlawry and slaughter will come your way, and most of your acts will bring you ill luck and misfortune. You will be made an outlaw and forced to live by yourself. I also lay this curse on you: you will always see before you these eyes of mine, and they will make your solitude unbearable, and this shall drag you to your death.' The rest of Grettir's life is a realization of this curse. The curse is ambiguous: it can be seen as an actual supernatural interference which changes the course of his life; it can also be seen, and perhaps more usefully, as a literary device, and a manifestation of Grettir's own character. Grettir has gone too far on a path that takes him inexorably apart from other men; he cannot live in society, yet he cannot bear living away from it. He is doomed to find himself in an impossible situation where his only option is to choose between two equally unacceptable courses of action: to live in society as a hunted animal or else to escape into the wilderness where solitude is his great and constant enemy. This third act of Grettir's tragedy ends with Grettir being hailed for his achievement. Everyone agreed 'that no man in the entire country was Grettir Asmundarson's equal in strength, in courage, or in accomplishments.' But the curse is also taking effect: 'He had become so frightened of the dark that he did not dare go anywhere alone after nightfall, because all kinds of phantoms appeared to him then.'

When Grettir goes back to Norway, at the beginning of the fourth act, he goes seeking a society in which it is possible for him to live. There has been a change of rulers in Norway; the new king is distantly related to Grettir and can be expected to give Grettir a good place among his retainers. And his first deed in Norway, when he swims across the icy channel to fetch fire for his shipwrecked and freezing companions, is also a humane and social act. But, like so many of Grettir's deeds, it is ambiguous, in both its motives and its results. He undertakes the enterprise even though he has a premonition that it will turn out badly; he is moved by compassion, but perhaps also by pride. And, in Grettir's over-strong hands, the fire does in fact turn from an agent of warmth and life to an agent of destruction: the house that he breaks into is burnt down, and the brothers inside are killed. The same sort of ambiguity appears when Grettir is given a chance to undergo an ordeal and so prove that he cannot be blamed for the burning. A boy, or, as is tentatively suggested, 'an unclean spirit,' mocks Grettir, and Grettir, although inside a church, hits him, thus nullifying the ordeal. The mocker can be seen as an aftereffect of Glam's curse; it is still true, however, that Grettir's loss of patience, and his inability to tolerate any affront to his honour, is what keeps him from passing the ordeal. And so he is exiled from Norway, as he was earlier exiled from Iceland; from now on he is confined to Iceland, and the net is closing in on him.

The fifth and final part of Grettir's life story is the longest and most important one. When he arrives in Iceland he learns, in one moment, that he has been made a permanent outlaw because of the Icelanders burnt in Norway, that his father has died, and that his brother Atli has been killed. The loneliness and alienation that is so heavily stressed here keeps increasing, so that the whole act is a study of isolation. But surprisingly, this part of the saga is also one of the most varied in mood. We see Grettir in all lights: as an avenger of his brother, as the temporary captive of terrified peasants, as the guest of a friendly half-ogre in a magical valley in the middle of a glacier, as a resourceful predator and ogress-killer, as a genial humorist. But all the same, Grettir's growing alienation is the constant theme. He is almost always in motion: he may settle down briefly in one part of Iceland, but always his enemies make it impossible for him to stay there, and he is harried all over Iceland. At last, he goes home to his mother, and says farewell to her: her speech makes it clear that it is his farewell to the world, and not just to her: 'Now you are going, my two sons, and you are fated to die together, and no one can escape the destiny that is shaped for him. I shall never again see either of you ... '

His last days are on the inaccessible rocky island of Drang, a geographical symbol of the plight to which he has been reduced. The island is the place of ultimate isolation; he finds there the protection and the freedom from society which he wants, but these things turn out to be identical with confinement and incarceration. And, at the end, all of the forces which he defeated in the first act of the saga combine to overcome him: the supernatural (the sorceress); natural forces (the storm); hostile marauders (Ongul's men), and the individual trying to avenge his honour (Ongul).

At the time of his death, Grettir has attained a surprisingly high stature. The author has never tried to romanticize him, and we have seen him, at various times, as a cruel child, as a juvenile delinquent, and as a sulky and touchy figure not unlike the gun-happy villain of a western. But, by the end, Grettir's trials seem to have purified him; he still never gives way, but he seems motivated more by bravery and intelligence, and less by pride. Although it is largely his own doing that he has become an isolated individual standing against the world, he accepts the inevitable, and makes the best of it. The change in him can be seen by his relationship with others: he is closer to his brother, Illugi, than he has ever been to any man, and he states explicitly his dependence: 'Bare is his back, who has no brother.' He even treats Glaum, the despicable buffoon, with great tolerance. Another indication of his change is his attitude towards animals. As a boy he committed several startling acts of cruelty towards geese and horses; later he steals and kills animals to survive; but in the last part of the saga he shows his sympathy for the ewe in Thorisdale whose lamb he has slaughtered, and on Drang Isle the grey-bellied ram becomes a kind of companion.

The epilogue brings a change of tone, and even a change of genre; we seem to move from the realistic saga world into a world of ballad or folk song, even comic opera. Everything becomes black and white: Ongul, as Grettir's killer, and in his turn an outlaw, should be Grettir's successor, but in fact he is shown as entirely and uncomplicatedly evil, while Thorstein, Grettir's brother, is absolutely good. Love was hardly mentioned in the main body of the saga, except for maternal love, but in the epilogue love is central, first the romantic love of Thorstein and Spes (Latin for 'hope'), and then their love for God. The necessary vengeance for Grettir is taken, and then, with this matter settled finally, Thorstein and Spes become Grettir's true successors. They are successful where he failed: they live happily and honourably in society, and when, at the end of their lives, they reject the world to live as hermits, they find peace in their solitude.

A note on the translation

Grettir's Saga survives in four vellum manuscripts from the fifteenth century, as well as in a number of later paper manuscripts. Our translation is based on Guðni Jónsson's edition in the Íslenzk Fornrit series (Reykjavik 1936). We have usually relegated the genealogies in the saga to footnotes, where they are printed in italics; we have occasionally added notes of our own (in roman) commenting on them. The saga contains many scaldic stanzas composed in an intricate metre and in a highly artificial diction. In our rendering of these untranslatable poems, we have tried to save their sense, though we have necessarily sacrificed their metre and diction.

We are very indebted to Professor Roberta Frank, who read our translation in manuscript and made many helpful suggestions.

Grettir's Saga has been translated into English twice before: by Eiríkr Magnússon and William Morris (London 1869), and by George Ainslie Hight (London 1914).

Publication of this volume is made possible by a grant from the Humanities Research Council of Canada, using funds provided by the Canada Council.

GRETTIR'S SAGA

Bjarg
in Midfjord
site of Grettir's birth

Tvidægra Moor
looking south from Bjarg
(see pages 29-30, 100)

Arnarwater Moor
where Grettir supported himself by fishing
(see chapters 55-7)

Sælingsdale
a hot spring known as Grettir's Bath
(not mentioned in the saga)

A gorge in Vatnsdale
near where Thorhall lived in Thorhallsstead
(see chapters 32-5)

Forsæludale
where Grettir fought Glam
(see chapters 32-5)

Eiriks Glacier
overlooking Thorisdale
(see chapter 61)

Gudlaugsvik
driftage, an important source of firewood
(see pages 153, 161-2)

Bjarg
a rock known as Grettir's Lift

Glaumbæ
where Glaum joined Grettir on his way to Drang Isle
(see pages 144-5)

Drang Isle
where Grettir died
from Reykir

Drang Isle
from an airplane
(see chapters 69-82)

1

There was a man called Onund[1] who was an Oplander on his mother's side, but his father's family were mostly from Rogaland and Hordaland. Onund, who was a notable viking, used to go across the North Sea to plunder. On one expedition, he was with Balki Blængsson of Sotaness, Orm the Wealthy, and a man called Hallvard. They had five ships, all of them well manned.

They were raiding in the Hebrides, and when they came to the Barra Isles they met a certain King Kjarval, who also had five ships.[2] They attacked him, and there was a fierce battle, for Onund's men pushed on relentlessly. Many were killed on both sides, but at last King Kjarval fled with a single ship. Onund and his men seized the other ships and also a great deal of loot. They stayed in the Isles the next winter, and then for three summers they raided around Ireland and Scotland. After that they went home to Norway.

2

At that time there was no peace in Norway: Harald Thick-Hair, the son of Halfdan the Black, was fighting his way to the throne. He was already a king in the Oplands. He went to the north of the country where he fought many battles, always successfully. After

---

1 *Onund's father was Ofeig Club-Foot, the son of Ivar Prick. Onund's sister was Gudbjorg, the mother of Gudbrand Hump, who was the father of Asta, the mother of St Olaf* (who was king over Norway from 1015 to 1030, and who figures later in this saga).

2 Kjarval (Irish *Cearbhall*) was king of Ossory, in southern Ireland, and died c. 888.

that he fought his way south through the land and imposed his authority on every region he visited. When he reached Hordaland, a great many men came against him, led by Kjotvi the Wealthy, Thorir Long-Chin, and King Sulki with his South Rogalanders. Geirmund Hell-Skin, who was king in Hordaland, was abroad in the west at the time, so he was not at the battle.

That was the same autumn that Onund and his companions sailed back from the west. When Thorir Long-Chin and King Kjotvi heard that, they sent messengers to ask for their help, and to offer them a good return for it. They decided to join Thorir and Kjotvi, for they were eager to prove themselves, and they said they wanted to be wherever the battle was the hardest.

The fight with King Harald was at Hafrsfjord in Rogaland. Each side had a large force and this battle was one of the greatest ever fought in Norway. It is mentioned in many sagas, for they always say much about great historic events.[1] Men came there from all over the country, and many from other lands, as well as a great number of vikings.

Onund laid his ship alongside Thorir Long-Chin's, in the very middle of the battle. King Harald attacked Thorir's ship, for Thorir was a berserk and a great warrior. They fought fiercely on both sides, but then the king ordered his own berserks to advance – they were called Wolf-Skins and iron could not bite into them – and when they raged forward no one could withstand them.[2] Thorir resisted with great valour, but was killed in his ship. The ship was then cleared from stem to stern and the fastenings cut, so it drifted back among the other ships.

Then Onund's ship was attacked by the king's men, but Onund stood in the prow and fought courageously. One of the king's men said, 'That man in the prow is doing very well. We must give him something to remember the battle by.' Onund had one foot on the gunwale and was striking at a man when he himself received a thrust. As he warded it off he bent his knee a little, and just then one of the king's forecastle-men struck at his leg below the knee, severing the leg. After Onund was disabled, most of his men were

1 Here as elsewhere in the story it is obvious that the author is well read
   in saga-literature. Although his main source for this episode was probably
   Landnámabók, he seems also to have known some of the Kings' Sagas
   which describe King Harald Thick-Hair's rise to power and how he earned
   his later nickname 'Fine-Hair'.
2 Berserks ('bear-shirts') were warriors valued for their capacity to run
   amuck and fight with murderous frenzy, impervious to pain. They figure in
   the sagas as stock villains, and may indeed have existed more in literature
   than in history.

killed, and Onund himself was carried aboard a ship belonging to a man called Thrand,[3] who was fighting King Harald; his ship lay on the other side of Onund's.

After that there was a general rout; Thrand's men and the other vikings escaped as best they could and sailed west across the sea. Onund, Balki, and Hallvard went with Thrand. Onund's life was saved, but ever after he walked with a wooden leg, so that he was called Onund Tree-Foot for the rest of his life.

3

At that time there were many great men across the sea in the west who had fled from their estates in Norway because King Harald had made all those who fought against him outlaws and had confiscated their property.

When Onund was healed of his wounds, Thrand and he went to see Geirmund Hell-Skin, who was then the most famous viking in the west. They asked him if he did not want to return to his kingdom in Hordaland, and they offered him support, for they were anxious about their own estates – Onund was rich and well born. Geirmund said that King Harald's power had become so great that he thought there was little hope of their getting anything back by fighting, in view of their earlier defeat, at a time when most of the best men in the land had taken a stand together. He added that he had no inclination to become the slave of a king and to beg for his own property. He was no longer a youth, and he thought it better to consider other prospects. Onund and Thrand went back to the Hebrides, where they met many of their friends.

There was a man called Ofeig Grettir.[1] He had fled west across the sea to escape from King Harald, and so had his kinsman,

3 *Thrand was the son of Bjorn, and the brother of Eyvind the Easterner.*
1 *Ofeig was the son of Einar, who was the son of Olvir Child-Sparer. Ofeig's brother was Olaf the Broad, the father of Thormod Skapti. Another son of Olvir Child-Sparer was Steinolf, the father of Una, who married Thorbjorn the Salmoner.*
   A third son of Olvir Child-Sparer was Steinmod, the father of Konal, who who was the father of Alfdis of the Barra Isles. Konal had a son called Steinmod, the father of Halldora, who married Eilif, the son of One-Armed Ketil.

Thormod Skapti. Both had brought with them all their households. They plundered in Scotland and in many other parts of the west.

Thrand and Onund Tree-Foot decided to go west to Ireland to see Thrand's brother, Eyvind the Easterner, who was in charge of the defences of Ireland.[2]

The father of Thrand and Eyvind was a man called Bjorn.[3] He had fled from Gautland, because he had burnt alive Sigfast, King Solvi's brother-in-law, in his own house. He had gone to Norway that summer and had spent the next winter with the chieftain Grim.[4] But Grim wanted to murder Bjorn for his money. So Bjorn went to Ondott Crow, who lived at Hvinisfjord in Agder. Bjorn was taken in gladly, and so he stayed there during the winters and went raiding in the summers until his wife Hlif died. After that Ondott gave his daughter Helga to Bjorn for a wife, and Bjorn gave up his expeditions. Eyvind had taken over his father's warships and had become a great chieftain west over the sea.[5]

When Thrand and Onund arrived in the Hebrides they met Ofeig Grettir and Thormod Skapti, and they became very close friends, for when someone met a man who had stayed behind in Norway during the worst of the fighting, he felt as if that man had been brought back from the dead.

Onund was very withdrawn, and when Thrand saw that he asked what was on his mind. Onund replied with this verse:

I've never seen happiness
since that murderous axe
maimed me in battle:
mishaps come always too soon.
Now I fear no one will think me
the man I once was,
and that is what has killed
all my happiness.

Thrand replied that Onund would be thought a brave man wherever he went. 'What you should do is to find yourself a wife

> *Ofeig was married to Asny, the daughter of Vestar, who was the son of Hæng; Ofeig and Asny had two sons who were called Asmund the Beardless and Asbjorn, and three daughters called Aldis, Æsa, and Asvor.*
> 2 *Eyvind's mother was Hlif, the daughter of Hrolf, the son of Ingjald, the son of King Frodi. Thrand's mother was Helga, the daughter of Ondott Crow.*
> 3 *Bjorn was the son of Hrolf of Ar.*
> 4 *Grim was the son of Kolbein Snub.*
> 5 *Eyvind was married to Rafarta, the daughter of King Kjarval of Ireland. Their sons were Helgi the Lean and Snæbjorn.*

and settle down. I will help you in every way I can, once I know where your mind is turned.'

Onund said that Thrand had spoken like a true friend, but added that he had once been in a better situation for finding a good wife than he was now.

Thrand said, 'Ofeig has a daughter called Æsa, and we can make our try there if you would like.'

Onund willingly agreed.

Then they discussed the matter with Ofeig who gave them a fair answer, saying that he knew Onund was of good family and had much money. 'But I think his estates are of little value, while it also seems to me that he himself is not entirely in sound shape, and my daughter is still a child.'

Thrand said that Onund was more vigorous than many who had two legs. And with Thrand's backing the agreement was reached, that Ofeig would give his daughter away with money as her dowry, because neither he nor Onund was willing to pay anything for the estates in Norway.

A little later Thrand became betrothed to the daughter of Thormod Skapti. Both marriages were to be put off for three years. Thrand and Onund went raiding in the summers, and stayed in the Barra Isles in the winters.

4

There were two Hebridean vikings called Vigbjod and Vestmar, who stayed out at sea summer and winter. They had eight ships and raided mostly in Ireland, where they committed many atrocities until Eyvind the Easterner took charge of the country's defences. Then they fled to the Hebrides and raided there and on the west coast of Scotland.

Thrand and Onund set out to confront them, and heard that they had sailed to the island of Bute, so Thrand and Onund went there with five ships. When the vikings saw their ships and realized how few they were, they thought that they themselves had plenty of men, and so they seized their weapons and sailed towards them.

Onund told his men to bring their ships into a deep narrow channel between two cliffs. Then they could only be approached from one direction, and the channel was just wide enough for five ships abreast. Onund, who was a shrewd man, had the five ships brought into the channel in such a way that they could quickly pull back whenever they wanted, for there was plenty of deep water behind them. There was a small island on one side of the channel, and he had one of his ships lie in its lee. Then they brought a great number of stones to the edge of the cliff above, where they could not be seen from the ships.

The vikings came on very boldly, thinking the others were in a trap. Vigbjod asked who these men were who were so penned in. Thrand replied that he was the brother of Eyvind the Easterner, 'and here is my companion, Onund Tree-Foot.'

Then the vikings laughed, and said:

May trolls take you, Tree-Foot,
May trolls break you all.

'It is quite a novelty for us to see men going to battle who are so utterly helpless.'

Onund said they could not be sure of that until it had been put to the test.

After that they brought their ships together, and a fierce battle began, with both sides fighting well. When the battle was in full swing Onund let his ship drift towards the cliff, and as soon as the vikings noticed this they thought he was trying to escape, and so they closed on him and came under the cliff as quickly as they could. At that moment the men who had been left on the cliff came forward to the edge. They hurled such big stones down at the vikings that no resistance was possible. Many of the vikings were killed and others hurt and put out of the fight. They wanted to get away but were unable to, because their ships were then in the narrowest part of the channel. They were caught by the other ships and the heavy current. Onund and his men vigorously attacked Vigbjod's ship while Thrand set on Vestmar, but they could achieve very little.

When the crew on Vigbjod's ship dwindled, Onund and his men attempted to board her. Vigbjod saw this and urged on his men fiercely. Then he turned towards Onund and many retreated before him. Onund, who was a powerful man, told his followers to observe how it would turn out for the two of them. They pushed a log under his knee so he stood solidly. The viking came aft along the ship until he reached Onund. Then he struck at him with his sword, hitting the shield and slicing a piece off, but the sword ran into the log under Onund's knee and stuck fast. Vigbjod stooped to jerk the sword free, and just then Onund struck at his shoulder, cutting off his arm, and the viking was out of the fight.

When Vestmar saw that his companion had fallen he leapt into the ship that lay furthest out and fled away, and so did all who could. After that Onund and his men searched among the dead. Vigbjod was at the point of death. Onund went up to him and said:

> Watch your wounds bleed
> and think if you've ever
> seen me flinch. On a single leg,
> I dodged the blows you dealt me.
> Some men are full of boasts,
> brainless though they be.
> The axe-breaker's courage failed
> when it came to the test of battle

They took much loot there, and returned to the Barra Isles in the autumn.

5

The next summer Thrand and Onund made ready to go west to Ireland. But Balki and Hallvard decided to sail west to Iceland, since there were good reports of the land. Balki settled in Hrutafjord and lived on two farms, both of which are called Balkastead. Hallvard took possession of Sugandafjord and Skalavik as far as Stigi, and lived there.

Thrand and Onund went to see Eyvind the Easterner, who welcomed his brother warmly. But when he found out that Onund was with him, he became furious and wanted to attack him. Thrand asked him not to do that, saying it was not proper to fight with Norsemen, and least of all with those who were not causing any trouble. Eyvind replied that Onund had caused trouble before, when he fought King Kjarval, and that he must now pay for it. The brothers went on arguing about this until Thrand said he would share the same fate as Onund. Then Eyvind relented.

They stayed in Ireland for most of the summer, and went on some raids with Eyvind, who thought Onund a very brave man. In the autumn they went back to the Hebrides. Eyvind assigned to Thrand all of their inheritance, should Thrand outlive their father Bjorn. They remained in the Hebrides until they married, and for several years after.

6

What happened next was that Thrand's father Bjorn died, and when the chieftain Grim heard this, he went to see Ondott Crow and laid claim to Bjorn's possessions. Ondott said that Thrand was his father's heir. Grim replied that Thrand was now abroad in the west, and also that Bjorn had been a Gautlander by birth, and the king had the right to inherit from all foreigners. Ondott said he intended to keep the property for his grandson Thrand. Grim went away and did not get any of his claim.

Thrand heard of his father's death and set out at once from the Hebrides, together with Onund Tree-Foot.

But Ofeig Grettir and Thormod Skapti went out to Iceland with their households. They made land at Eyrar in the south, and stayed the first winter with Thorbjorn the Salmoner. Then they took possession of Gnupverjahrepp, Ofeig taking the western part between Thver River and Kalf River – he lived at Ofeigsstead near Steinsholt, and Thormod taking the eastern part – he lived at Skaptaholt.[1]

We now return to Thrand and Onund, who sailed east across the sea to Norway before a good wind, so that there was no news of their voyage until they came to Ondott Crow. He welcomed Thrand warmly and told him about the claim which the chieftain Grim had made to Bjorn's property.

'It seems to me better, kinsman, for you and not the king's slaves to inherit from your father. You had a lucky start, since no one knows about your voyage. But I suspect that Grim will issue a summons against either of us if he can, so I want you to take charge of the inheritance and then get into another country.'

Thrand said he would do this. He took over the possessions and made ready to leave Norway in a hurry. Before he put out to sea

1 *Thormod's daughters were Thorvor, the mother of Thorodd the Priest of Hjalli, and Thorve, the mother of Thorstein the Priest, the father of Bjarni the Wise.*

he asked Onund Tree-Foot if he did not want to go to Iceland. Onund said he would like first to see his kinsmen and friends in the south of the land.

Thrand said, 'Then we must now separate. But I would like you to keep my kinsmen in mind, because it is on them that vengeance will be taken if I manage to get away. I am going out to Iceland, and I hope that you will go there too.'

Onund gave his promise, and they parted the best of friends. Thrand went out to Iceland, and was welcomed warmly there by Ofeig and Thormod Skapti. Thrand lived at Thrandarholt, west of Thjors River.

7

Onund went south to Rogaland and met there many of his kinsmen and friends. He stayed there in secret, with a man called Kolbein.

Onund heard that King Harald had confiscated his property and allotted it to a man called Harek, who was the king's steward. Onund set out one night and took Harek by surprise in his house, and had him put to death. Onund seized all the valuables that he and his men could lay their hands on, and then they burnt the house. For the rest of the winter Onund stayed in various places.

This autumn the chieftain Grim killed Ondott Crow, since he had failed to get hold of the inheritance on the king's behalf. But Signy, Ondott's wife, brought all their valuables aboard a ship the same night, and with her sons, Asmund and Asgrim, sailed to her father Sighvat. A little later she sent her sons to her foster-father,[1] Hedin of Soknadale, but it was not long until they became discontented and wished to go back to their mother. So they left at Christmas and went to Ingjald Tryggvi of Hvin. He took them in at his wife Gyda's request, and they stayed with him for the rest of the winter.

In the spring Onund went to the north of Agder, for he had heard that Ondott was dead, and how he had been killed. When he found Signy he asked her what kind of support she and her sons

---

1 It was common practice, in early Scandinavia as elsewhere, for a man to send his child to be brought up by a foster-father, sometimes his social inferior.

would accept from him. She replied that they would gladly take vengeance on Grim for the killing of Ondott. Then Ondott's sons were sent for, and when they met Onund Tree-Foot they all joined forces, and he had a watch kept on Grim's activities.

In the summer Grim was going to hold a large ale-feast, and he had invited Earl Audun. When Onund and Ondott's sons heard this they went to Grim's farm. They arrived without warning, set fire to the house, and burnt to death the chieftain Grim and nearly thirty other people besides. They seized many valuable treasures. Onund went into the woods, but the brothers took a boat that belonged to their benefactor Ingjald and rowed to a hiding-place not far from the farm.

Earl Audun came for the feast as had been arranged, and found his friends missing. He collected some men and stayed there for several days, but nothing was heard of Onund or the others.

The earl slept in a loft with two other men. Onund, who knew everything that happened on the farm, sent for the brothers. When they met, Onund asked whether they would prefer to keep a watch on the house or to attack the earl. They chose to attack the earl. They rammed the loft door with a beam and broke in the door. Then Asmund seized the earl's two companions and flung them down so hard that they were almost dead. Asgrim leapt at the earl and told him to pay him compensation for his father's death, because the earl had aided and abetted Grim when Ondott was killed. The earl said he had no money with him and offered to pay later. Then Asgrim put the point of his spear against the earl's chest and told him to pay immediately. The earl took off a necklace and three gold rings and a velvet cloak. Asmund took the treasures and nicknamed the earl Audun Nanny-Goat.

When the farmers and the men of the district learned of the fighting, they went there, intending to support the earl. There was a fierce battle, as Onund had a considerable force, and many important farmers and retainers of the earl were killed.

Then the brothers came up and told about their dealings with the earl. Onund said it was too bad that the earl had not been killed. 'That would have been some revenge on King Harald for the property and kinsmen we have lost because of him.'

They replied that what had happened was a greater disgrace for the earl.

Then they went over to Surnadale to Eirik Ale-Lover, who was a landed man,[2] and he put them all up for the winter. They had

2 See appendix, page 193.

12

drinking parties that Christmas with a man called Hallstein Horse. It was Eirik's turn first to be the host, and he entertained well and truly. Then it was Hallstein's turn, and at that feast there was a disagreement between them, and Hallstein struck Eirik with a drinking horn. Eirik could not get revenge and went home.

Ondott's sons were very displeased at this. A little later Asgrim went over to Hallstein's farm, walked into the house alone, and gave Hallstein a great wound. The men who were there inside jumped up and made for Asgrim. He defended himself bravely and got out of their hands in the darkness, but they thought they had killed him.

Onund and Asmund, who heard this, assumed that Asgrim was dead, and they thought there was nothing they could do about it. Eirik advised them to go to Iceland. He said that it would do them no good to be in the country once the king turned his mind to this matter.

So they took his advice and made ready to sail for Iceland, each in his own ship.

Hallstein, who lay wounded, died before Onund and Asmund left Norway. Kolbein, who was mentioned earlier, sailed with Onund.

8

Onund and Asmund put to sea when they were ready, and they kept their ships close together. Onund had spoken this:

Time was when warriors felt
I was fit for the raging battle,
when the fierce shower of spears
came storming at Hallvard and me.
But now I must hobble
on one leg aboard this ship,
bound for a land of ice.
I'm not the man I was.

They had a difficult passage and ran into strong south winds, so they were driven north off their course. They sighted Iceland, and when they were able to orient themselves they were north of Langaness. The two ships were then so close together that they could talk back and forth. Asmund said they should sail towards Eyjafjord, and that was agreed on. They beat towards the land, but then a gale blew up from the south-east, and when Onund tried to sail close to the wind the boom broke, so they had to lower the sails and they were driven out to sea.

Asmund got into the lee of Hris Island, and waited there until he had a fair wind to take him up Eyjafjord. Helgi the Lean gave him the whole of Kræklingahlid. He lived at a farm called South Gler River. His brother Asgrim came to Iceland several years later and lived at North Gler River.[1]

9

Now we return to Onund Tree-Foot. He was driven out to sea for several days but then the wind shifted to the north, and he sailed towards the land. The men who had made the voyage before realized that they had drifted west of Skagi, and so they sailed up Stranda Bay, close to the South-Strands.

Then six men in a ten-oared boat rowed out to them and called up asking who was in charge of the ship. Onund named himself, and asked where they were from; they said they were servants of Thorvald of Drangar. Onund asked whether all the land in the Strands had been claimed, and they replied that there was a little still unclaimed in the Inner-Strands, but nothing so far north.

Onund asked his crew which they would prefer: to explore the land to the west first, or to take what had been pointed out to them. They chose to explore the land first. Then they sailed up the bay and into the creek off Arness, put out a boat and rowed ashore.

At that time, a wealthy man called Eirik Snare was living there. He had claimed possession of the land between Ingolfsfjord and Ofæra in Veidileysa. As soon as Eirik knew that Onund had arrived he offered to give him anything he wanted, and added that there was not much land still unclaimed. Onund said he would like first to see what land was available. So they went south across the fjords, and when they reached Ofæra, Eirik said, 'Now you can

1 *Asgrim was the father of Ellida-Grim, who was the father of Asgrim.*
This Asgrim Ellida-Grimson plays an important role in *Njal's Saga*, and his son Thorhall is mentioned in chapter 53 below.

have a look at it. From here on the land is unclaimed up to Bjorn's settlement.'

A great mountain jutted out on that side of the fjords, white with snow. Onund looked at the mountain and spoke this stanza:

The seafarer must suffer
weather fair and foul.
He wins and then he loses
his land and his wealth.
Now I've fled my estates,
my friends, and my family,
but the worst of it is, I've bartered
my grainfields for icy Kaldbak.[1]

Eirik replied, 'Many have lost so much in Norway that they can never be compensated. I think that almost all the land in the main districts has been claimed, so I cannot urge you to leave this place. I will keep my promise that you can have from my land what you need.'

Onund said he would accept that, and then he took possession of the land between Ofæra and Kaldbak Cliff, including the three inlets, Byrgisvik, Kolbeinsvik, and Kaldbaksvik. Afterwards Eirik gave him the whole of Veidileysa and Reykjarfjord and all Reykjaness on his side. The driftage rights were not reserved, for driftwood was so plentiful then that everyone could take what he wanted.[2]

Onund built a farm at Kaldbak, and had many men there. After his wealth had begun to grow, he set up another farm at Reykjarfjord. Kolbein lived at Kolbeinsvik. For several years Onund stayed at home in peace.

10

Onund was so brave that few men with two legs could stand up to him. He was also famous all over the land because of his lineage.

What happened next was that a feud arose between Ofeig Grettir

1 Kaldbak, literally 'Cold-Ridge,' is the name of a mountain south of Kolbeinsvik.
2 Driftage rights along the coast of Iceland were considered a great asset, because of driftwood and stranded whales.

and Thorbjorn Earls'-Man, and in the end Thorbjorn killed Ofeig at Grettisgeil near Hæl. Ofeig's sons gathered a large body of men to prosecute the slayer. They sent for Onund Tree-Foot, and in the spring he rode south. On the way he spent a night at Hvamm with Aud the Deep-Minded; she welcomed him very warmly because they had known each other in the British Isles.

Her grandson Olaf Feilan was then a fully grown man, and Aud was much worn by old age. She mentioned to Onund that she wanted to find a wife for her grandson Olaf, and would like him to ask for the hand of Alfdis of the Barra Isles, who was the cousin of Æsa, Onund's wife. Onund thought this a good idea, and Olaf rode south with him.

When Onund met his friends and his wife's relatives they asked him to stay. Then they discussed the lawsuit, and it was referred to the Kjalarness Assembly, for this was before the Althing was instituted.[1] The case was settled by arbitration, and a large award was agreed upon, while Thorbjorn Earls'-Man was sentenced to outlawry.[2]

Thrand invited Onund and Olaf to stay and so did Thormod Skapti. They carried Olaf's offer of marriage, and it was readily accepted, since everyone knew what an outstanding woman Aud was. When the agreement had been made, everything was settled, and Onund and Olaf rode back home. Aud thanked Onund for helping Olaf. In the same autumn Olaf married Alfdis of the Barra Isles, and then Aud the Deep-Minded died, as is related in *Laxdœla Saga*.

1 The Kjalarness Assembly was one of thirteen local assemblies in early Iceland; it was founded some time before the Althing ('General Assembly') was instituted in 930.

2 *His son was Solmund, the father of Kari the Singed. They lived abroad for a long time afterwards.*

   Thorbjorn's grandson, Kari Solmundarson, 'the Singed', plays an important role in *Njal's Saga*. His nickname is explained by the fact that he managed to escape from the famous burning of Bergthorsknoll where his father-in-law, Njal, and other members of his family were killed. See *Njal's Saga*, chapter 129.

11

Onund and Æsa had two sons; the elder was called Thorgeir, and the younger Ofeig Grettir.[1] A little later Æsa died, and after that Onund married a woman called Thordis.[2] He had a son by her called Thorgrim, who quickly grew up to be tall and strong, a good farmer and an intelligent man.

Onund lived at Kaldbak until he was an old man, and died from an illness. He lies buried in Treefoot's Mound. He was the most valiant and deft of all the one-legged men who have been in Iceland.

Thorgrim was the most outstanding of Onund's sons, although the others were older. By the time he was twenty-five his hair had turned grey, and so he was called Greyhead. His mother Thordis married again, to Audun Shaft of Vididale, and their son was Asgeir of Asgeirs River. Thorgrim Greyhead and his brothers owned jointly a great deal of property and did not divide it between them.

Eirik Snare lived at Arness, as has already been mentioned. He had a wife called Alof,[3] and they had a son called Flosi; he was a promising man, and had many friends.

Three brothers came out to Iceland, Ingolf, Ofeig, and Eyvind, who claimed the three fjords that are called after them, and spent the rest of their lives there. Eyvind had a son called Olaf who lived first at Eyvindarfjord, but later at Drangar, and was a capable man.

As long as the older men lived there were no disagreements in the district, but after Eirik's death Flosi thought that the Kaldbak men had no legal right to the land that Eirik had given Onund. Because of this a serious quarrel arose between them, but Thorgrim and his brothers held their ground. It became impossible to hold common games.

Thorgeir, who was in charge of the brothers' farm at Reykjarfjord, often went fishing, for the fjords were then full of fish.

---

1 He is the grandson of the Ofeig Grettir who was killed in the last chapter.
2 *Thordis was the daughter of Thorgrim of Gnup in Midfjord, and related to Midfjord-Skeggi.* Midfjord-Skeggi figures in several sagas, including *Laxdœla Saga, Kormak's Saga*, and *Thord's Saga*.
3 *Alof was the daughter of Ingolf of Ingolfsfjord.*

Now Flosi and his men made their plans. There was a man called Thorfinn who was a servant of Flosi at Arness, and Flosi sent him out to kill Thorgeir. Thorfinn concealed himself in the boat-house and in the morning Thorgeir made ready to row out to sea with two other men, one called Hamund and the other Brand. Thorgeir walked in front, carrying on his back a leather flask containing sour whey for drinking. It was still very dark, and when he was walking down from the boat-house Thorfinn leapt at him and struck him with an axe between the shoulders; the axe sank in, making a squelchy noise. Thorfinn let go of the axe, because he thought that the wound would be fatal, and because he wanted to get away as quickly as he could.

Thorfinn ran all the way north to Arness and arrived there before full daylight. He announced that Thorgeir had been killed and said that he needed Flosi's protection. He also said the only thing now was to offer a settlement: 'That is the best thing we could possibly do now, after all that has happened.'

Flosi said he wanted first to know what had actually happened. 'I can see that you are scared stiff by this great achievement,' he added.

Now we return to Thorgeir. He had turned quickly when the blow came, and the axe went into the flask but did not wound him at all. They did not look for the assailant because it was dark, but rowed out across the fjords over to Kaldbak and told the people there what had happened. They made great fun of this and nick-named him Thorgeir Flask-Back, a name which stuck for the rest of his life.

Then this stanza was composed:

Time was when famous warriors
bathed their shining swords
in deep pools of warm blood.
But now that wretched coward
has drowned his axeblade
in cold sour whey.

12

At that time in Iceland there came such a hard famine that another like it has never happened. Almost no fish were caught, and nothing drifted ashore. This lasted for several years.

One autumn some merchants in a sea-going ship were driven off course and they wrecked their ship near Vik. Flosi took in four or five of them, including their captain, Stein, while the others stayed in various places around Vik. They tried to build a new ship out of the wreckage, but they had a hard time of it, and the new ship had a narrow stem and stern but was broad in the beam.

In the spring a strong gale blew up from the north and lasted for almost a week. When the storm ended the farmers went looking for driftage. There was a man called Thorstein who lived at Reykjaness. He found a whale drifted ashore out on the headland, at a place called Rif Skerries. It was a big finback, so he at once sent a man to tell Flosi of Vik and then the neighbouring farmers.

There was a man called Einar, a tenant of the Kaldbak men, who lived at Gjogur and was supposed to look after the driftage on his side of the fjords. As soon as he knew about the stranded whale, he took his boat, rowed across the fjord to Byrgisvik, and sent a man over to Kaldbak. When Thorgrim and his brothers heard about the whale they hastily made ready and set out twelve strong in a ten-oared boat. Ivar and Leif, the sons of Kolbein, also went with them, and brought four more men. All the farmers who could manage it came along to the whale, as well.

In the meantime Flosi had sent for his kinsmen north in Ingolfsfjord and Ofeigsfjord, and also for Olaf Eyvindarson who lived at Drangar. Flosi and the men of Vik, who were the first to arrive, at once started cutting up the whale and hauling the pieces up on dry land. There were nearly twenty of them in the beginning, and soon more came.

Then the Kaldbak men arrived in four boats, and Thorgrim laid claim to the whale and forbade the Vik men to cut it up, divide it, or take it away. Flosi told him to show that Eirik had given Onund Tree-Foot the driftage rights in definite terms, for otherwise he would defend his position with force. Thorgrim thought he had too few men, so he decided not to attack.

Just then a boat approached from the south across the fjord, with men rowing furiously. Soon they came up, and it was Svan of Hol in Bjarnarfjord with his servants. He at once told Thorgrim not to let himself be robbed, and offered him his support, for they were good friends. Thorgrim and his brothers said they would accept that, and then they made a bold attack.

Thorgeir Flask-Back was the first to climb on the whale, and he attacked Flosi's servants. Thorfinn, who was mentioned earlier, was standing in a foot-hold cut into the whale just behind its head and was busy carving up the whale. Thorgeir said, 'I give you back your axe.' Then he struck at Thorfinn's neck, taking his head off.

Flosi was standing on the beach when he saw this, and he urged his men to strike back. They fought for a long time, and the Kaldbak men had the best of it. Few of the men had any weapons except for the axes and cleavers with which they had been cutting up the whale. The men of Vik abandoned the whale and retreated up the foreshore, but the Norwegian merchants were armed with proper weapons and were dangerous opponents. Stein, the captain, cut off Ivar Kolbeinsson's leg, but Ivar's brother Leif struck one of Stein's companions dead with a whale-rib. They fought with everything they could lay their hands on, and men were killed on both sides. Then Olaf of Drangar arrived with many boats and backed Flosi, so that the Kaldbak people found the odds against them rather too heavy. They had already loaded their boats, and Svan told them to get aboard. They moved back down to the boats, with the Vik men in pursuit, and when Svan reached the water he struck at Stein, wounding him badly, and then leapt into his boat. Thorgrim gave Flosi a serious wound and then made his escape. Olaf struck at Ofeig Grettir and gave him a fatal blow. Thorgeir caught Ofeig up in his arms and leapt with him into a boat. Then the Kaldbak men rowed south across the fjords, and so they parted. This was composed about the encounter:

I've heard how the steely
weapons were used,
when whale-blubber was wielded
at Rif Skerries.
The fighters kept exchanging
lethal whale-meat missiles.
That's how these boors
play the game of battle.

Afterwards a truce was arranged between them, and they referred the dispute to the Althing. Thorodd the Priest and Midfjord-Skeggi and many other people in the south helped the Kaldbak men. Flosi and many of those who had been with him were sentenced to outlawry, and he paid out a great deal of money because he insisted on settling all the fines by himself.

Thorgrim and his brother could not prove that they had paid money for the land and the driftage rights which Flosi had laid a claim to. So Thorkel Moon, who was then the Lawspeaker, was asked to arbitrate the matter. He said that to him the legal position seemed to be that payment had been made for the land, even though it had not been a full price. 'That is what Steinunn the Old did when she accepted from my grandfather Ingolf all of Rosmhvalness and gave him in return a many-coloured cloak with a hood.[1] That transaction has never been invalidated, and yet there was much more at stake there. My opinion is that the disputed land should be divided evenly between the two parties and that it should be made law that each shall have the driftage on his own land.'

This was done, and the land was so divided that Thorgrim and his brother had to give up Reykjarfjord and all the land on the other side of it, but they retained Kamb. A large sum of money was paid in compensation for the killing of Ofeig, but none for the killing of Thorfinn; Thorgeir received compensation for the attempt on his life. And so they were reconciled.

Flosi made preparations to sail to Norway with Stein, and sold his farms in Vik to Geirmund the Shifty, who lived there for the rest of his life. The ship that the merchants had built was very broad, so it was called the Tub, and from this ship the inlet takes its name.[2] Flosi put to sea in it, but was driven back to Oxarfjord, and the events that followed are told in the *Saga of Bodmod, Grimolf, and Gerpir*.[3]

1   Thorkel Moon was the Lawspeaker of the Althing from 970 to 984. His grandfather, Ingolf, was the first settler in Iceland and is supposed to have made his permanent home there in 874. The principal sources of information about Ingolf's settlement are *Íslendingabók* ('The Book of Icelanders') and *Landnámabók* ('The Book of Settlements'). The story of how Steinunn paid for her land with the token payment of a single garment is told in *Landnámabók*.

2   The inlet is named Trékyllisvík, from *Trékyllir*, 'wooden tub' and *vík*, 'inlet.'

3   This saga is no longer extant, but it was known to the compilers of *Landnámabók*, from which this reference is taken.

13

After that the brothers Thorgrim and Thorgeir divided their property, Thorgrim taking the money, and Thorgeir the land. Then Thorgrim moved south to Midfjord, and at Skeggi's suggestion bought the farm at Bjarg. Thorgrim married a woman called Thordis,[1] and they had a son called Asmund. He was a tall strong man, and very intelligent; he had an exceptionally fine head of hair, which turned grey when he was still young, and for that reason he was called Grey-Locks or Grey-Bush.

Thorgrim became a very serious farmer, and kept all the people on the farm working hard. But Asmund would not do much work, and so he did not get on well with his father. Matters continued in this way until Asmund reached manhood, and then he asked his father for money to go abroad, but Thorgrim said he could have very little; however he gave him a few marketable goods. Asmund went abroad and was soon making a lot of money. He sailed to various countries and became an important and very wealthy merchant. He was a much-liked and dependable man, with many well-born kinsmen in Norway.

One autumn he went east to stay in Oslofjord with a well-born man called Thorstein, by origin an Oplander. He had a sister called Rannveig, who was an exceptionally fine woman. Asmund asked for her hand, and his proposal was accepted on her brother Thorstein's advice. Asmund settled down there for a time, and men thought very highly of him.

Asmund and Rannveig had a son called Thorstein. He was a strong and extremely handsome man, tall, and with a fine voice, but appeared to move rather slowly, so he was nicknamed the Galleon. When Thorstein was still very young, his mother fell ill and died, and after that Asmund was not happy in Norway, so Rannveig's family took care of the boy and his inheritance, but Asmund started voyaging again and became a famous man.

Once Asmund brought his ship into Hunavatn. At that time Thorkel Krafla was chieftain in Vatnsdale, and when he heard that

---

1 *Thordis was the daughter of Asmund of Asmundargnup, who was the original settler of the Thingeyrar District.*

Asmund had come from abroad, he rode down to the ship and invited Asmund to come home with him. Thorkel lived at Masstead in Vatnsdale, and Asmund stayed there for a while. Thorkel was the son of Thorgrim, the Karns River priest, and a very shrewd man.

At this time Bishop Fridrek and Thorvald Kodransson had already come to Iceland, and they were then living at Lækjarmot. They were the first to preach Christianity in the north of the country; Thorkel and many others were given preliminary baptism.[2] The bishop had many dealings with the men of the north, but these events do not concern this saga.[3]

There was a woman called Asdis[4] who had been brought up by Thorkel. She was unmarried and was considered to be an excellent match on account of both her family and her wealth. Asmund was growing tired of seafaring and wanted to settle in Iceland, and so he made up his mind and asked for her hand. Thorkel knew a good deal about him and realized that he was a wealthy man and skilful in handling money, so it came to pass that Asdis was married to him. Asmund became an intimate friend of Thorkel, and an excellent farmer, a man skilled in law, and an ambitious man.

A little later Thorgrim Greyhead of Bjarg died; Asmund was his heir and lived at Bjarg for the rest of his life.

14

Asmund established a splendid farm at Bjarg with a large household, and he had many friends. These were his children by Asdis:

2 *Prímsigning: Prima signatio* – the sign of the Cross was made, but there was no baptism. These catechumens would be allowed to associate with Christians and attend church.

3 The fullest account of the introduction of Christianity into Iceland is to be found in *Kristni Saga*, which was used by the author of *Njal's Saga*. There is also an account of Thorvald's missionary activity (*þorvalds þáttr Viðförla.*)

4 *Asdis was the daughter of Bard, who was the son of Jokul, the son of Ingimund the Old, the son of Thorstein, the son of Ketil Raum. Asdis' mother was Aldis, the daughter of Ofeig Grettir, as has been related already.* (Cf footnote on pages 5-6.)

Ingimund the Old and his sons and grandsons are the leading characters in *Vatnsdæla Saga*, one of the sagas known to the author of *Grettir's Saga*.

Atli was the oldest; he was an honest and quiet man, gentle and peaceable, whom everyone liked.

Their second son was Grettir. As a child he was self-willed, taciturn and harsh, sardonic and mischievous. His father was not very fond of him, but his mother loved him dearly. Grettir Asmundarson was a good-looking child, with a square face, and freckles, but he developed slowly.

One of Asmund's daughters was Thordis, who later married Glum,[1] and the other was Rannveig, who married Gamli.[2]

Grettir grew up at Bjarg, and when he was ten years old he began to take on strength. Asmund told him he would have to get to work; Grettir replied that he was not well suited for that, but still he asked what he was supposed to do.

Asmund replied, 'You are to look after my geese.'

Grettir said, 'A shabby little job.'

Asmund said, 'Do it well, and then we shall get on better.'

Grettir took charge of the geese; there were about fifty of them, as well as many goslings. It was not long before he found them difficult to herd, and the goslings slow. He became very angry at this, since he was not the best-tempered of men. A little later some vagrants found goslings lying about dead, and geese with their wings broken. This was in the autumn. Asmund was not at all pleased, and he asked if Grettir had killed the birds. Grettir grinned, and said:

When winter comes
I wring the goslings' necks,
and I can also vanquish
fully-grown birds.

'You are not to vanquish any more of them,' said Asmund.

' "He is my friend who keeps me from evil," ' said Grettir.

'Another task will be found for you,' said Asmund.

' "The more one tries, the more one knows," ' said Grettir, 'and what am I to do now?'

Asmund said, 'You are to rub my back by the fire, just as I always have it done.'

---

1   *Glum was the son of Ospak Kjallaksson of Skridinsenni. The son of Glum and Thordis was Ospak, who quarrelled with Odd Ofeigsson, as is related in 'Bandamanna Saga.'*

2   *Gamli was the son of Thorhall the Vinlander. Gamli and Rannveig lived at Melar in Hrutafjord, and had a son called Grim.* Thorhall the Vinlander is mentioned in *Eirik's Saga,* where he is supposed to have sailed to Vinland c. 1002.

'That must be hot on the hand,' said Grettir, 'and it is a shabby job.'

Grettir performed this task for some time, but as the autumn passed Asmund could stand the heat much better and kept urging Grettir to rub his back harder. At that time it was the custom on farms to have large halls where the household used to sit by long fires in the evenings. Tables were put up for meals, and afterwards the people would sleep alongside the fire. Also women used to work at the wool there in the daytime.

It happened one evening, when Grettir was to scratch Asmund's back, that the old man said, 'Get the laziness out of your bones, you coward.'

Grettir said, ' "It is rash to goad a reckless man." '

Asmund said, 'You have no spirit in you.'

Grettir saw wool combs lying on the bench and he picked up one and ran it down Asmund's back. Asmund jumped to his feet in a fury, and tried to hit Grettir with his stick, but he ducked away. Then Asdis came up and asked what was going on between them. Grettir replied with this verse:

My generous father wants
to see my hands singed.
I feel the heat
burning me.
Now we both shall suffer
for his stupid plan:
I'll use my nails on him
and watch the blood flowing.

It displeased Asdis that Grettir should have played this trick, and she said he would never be a very cautious man. The incident did not improve matters between Asmund and Grettir.

Some time later Asmund said to Grettir that he was to look after the horses, and Grettir replied that it would suit him better than back-rubbing by the fire.

'Then you must do as I tell you,' said Asmund. 'I have a fawn-coloured mare, which I call Kengala, and she is so wise about the weather and the rain that a storm invariably follows when she refuses to go out to graze. If she does this, you are to stable the horses, but otherwise keep them grazing up north on the ridge, once winter sets in. I think it is important that you do better with this job than you did with the other two I gave you.'

Grettir said, 'This is a cold job and one worthy of a man, but I don't like trusting in the mare – no one has done this before that I know of.'

Grettir took charge of the horses, and all went well until after Christmas, but then it became cold and snowy with poor grazing. Grettir was thinly clad and not yet fully hardened, so he began to feel the cold bitterly, but Kengala grazed away in the most exposed places during the worst of the weather. No matter how early she went out to graze, she would never come back before night, and Grettir thought he would find some dirty trick to repay her in full for her excursions.

Early one morning Grettir came to the stable and opened the door. Kengala was standing by the crib, because she used to keep to herself all the fodder that was given to her and the other horses. Grettir got on to her back; he had a sharp knife in his hand and he slashed her across the shoulders and then back all along both sides of her spine. The mare, who was both fat and restive, shied violently, and lashed out so that her hooves crashed against the wall. Grettir fell off, but as soon as he got to his feet, he tried to get on her back again. There was a fierce struggle, but in the end he succeeded in cutting loose her back skin all the way to her loins, and then he drove the horses out to pasture. But Kengala's only grazing was to bite her back, and soon after midday she started off and ran back to the stable, and Grettir shut the door and went home. Asmund asked where the horses were, and Grettir told him he had stabled them as usual. Asmund said that a blizzard must be near, since the horses did not want to stay in the open in this fine weather.

Grettir said, ' "Wisdom can fail in the wisest of men." '

The night passed and no storm came. Grettir drove out the horses, but Kengala could not bear to graze. Asmund thought it most strange that the weather did not break. On the third morning he went to the horses, and when he came to Kengala he said, 'I think the horses have done very badly for such a mild winter, but at least your back will be in good condition, Kengala.'

'What is expected happens,' said Grettir, 'and so does the unexpected.'

Asmund stroked the mare's back and the hide came away with his hand. He was bewildered at this, and then he said that Grettir must be responsible. Grettir grinned and did not answer. Asmund went home swearing violently, and when he walked into the hall he heard his wife say, 'My son's horse-tending must have been a success.'

Asmund said:

Women always talk too much,
but now you must listen:
Grettir has flayed the hide
off my trusted Kengala.
This bright son of mine
has taught me one lesson:
Never shall I give him
another command.

His wife said, 'I don't know which I dislike less, the way you always give him jobs, or the way he always does them.'

'I will put an end to that,' said Asmund. 'But Grettir shall not be so well treated now.'

'Then neither of us must find fault with the other,' said Grettir. And for a while nothing happened. Asmund had Kengala killed.

Grettir had many other escapades which are not included in this saga. He became very big, and no one was sure how strong he was, for he did not wrestle. He often composed verses and poems which were thought somewhat libellous. He was not in the habit of lying by the fire in the large hall, and he usually did not have much to say.

15

At that time there were many young men in Midfjord. Skald-Torfa was living at Torfustead, and she had a son called Bersi, who was an unusually accomplished poet. The brothers Kormak and Thorgils were living at Mel, and also a man called Odd the Orphan-Poet, who had been brought up with them and was their dependent. Then there was a man called Audun who had grown up at Audunarstead in Vididale; he was an honest and kind-hearted man, and the strongest man of his age in the north of the land. Kalf Asgeirsson and his brother Thorvald were living at Asgeirs River. Grettir's brother Atli, who was then turning into a strong man, was an exceptionally gentle person who was loved by everyone.

All these men used to play ball together on Midfjord Lake, and the people of Midfjord and Vididale came to the games, as well as many others from Vesturhop and Vatnsness and even from Hrutafjord. The ones who had come far found themselves places to stay near the games.

These games were so arranged that players of equal strength were matched against each other, and the sport was a great entertainment during the autumns. When Grettir was fourteen years old, his brother Atli asked him to come to the games. The players were matched against each other, and Grettir was told to play against Audun, who was several years older. Audun struck the ball over Grettir's head so he could not catch it, and it went far away over the ice. This infuriated Grettir, and he thought Audun was trying to make a fool of him. He fetched the ball, came back, and when he was close to Audun, he struck his forehead with the ball and broke the skin. Audun hit back at Grettir with the stick he had in his hand but hardly touched him because Grettir dodged the blow, and then they clinched and wrestled. The onlookers soon realized that Grettir was stronger than they had thought, for Audun was a powerful man. They fought for a long time, but in the end Grettir fell and then Audun jumped on him and roughed him up. Atli, Bersi, and many others ran in and separated them. Grettir said there was no need to hold him as if he were a wild dog. ' "Only a slave avenges himself at once; and only a coward never," ' he said.

This incident was not allowed to grow into a serious disagreement, for the brothers Kalf and Thorvald wanted them to be reconciled, and also Audun and Grettir were related to each other. So the game was continued as before, and nothing further happened to cause friction between them.

16

Thorkel Krafla, who was a powerful chieftain in Vatnsdale, was now becoming very old. He and Asmund Grey-Locks were good friends, as befitted their relationship, and it was Thorkel's custom to ride over to Bjarg on a visit every spring. So in the following spring Thorkel rode over and Asmund and Asdis welcomed him with open arms. He stayed there for three days and the two men talked about a good many things. Thorkel asked Asmund how he thought his sons would turn out, and whether they were going to be successful. Asmund said he thought that Atli would become an excellent farmer, and would be careful and prosperous.

Thorkel said, 'A useful man, just like yourself. But what do you say about Grettir?'

Asmund answered, 'This can be said: he will be a strong and ungovernable man. He has a mind of his own, and he has been difficult for me to deal with.'

Thorkel said, 'This does not sound very promising, Asmund. What shall we do about our riding to the Althing this summer?'

Asmund said, 'I'm getting rather too old for travelling and would like to stay home.'

'Do you want Atli to go in your place?'

'I don't think I can spare him,' said Asmund, 'considering all the work and arrangements on the farm, but Grettir will not work, and he is intelligent enough, I think, to take care of my legal business for me, with your guidance.'

'You can arrange matters that way, then,' said Thorkel.

When he was ready he rode home, and Asmund sent him away with good gifts.

A little later Thorkel made ready to go to the Althing and set off with sixty men, for all the farmers who supported him went with him. He called at Bjarg, and Grettir joined him there. They went south across Tvidægra Moor, and they rode fast across the high country, since the grazing was poor there, and then they came down to the settled district beyond. When they rode down to Fljotstongue, they thought it was time to sleep, so they unbridled the horses and let them graze with their saddles on. The men slept until late in the day, and when they woke up they started looking for their horses which had strayed away in all directions – some of them had been rolling on the ground. Grettir was the last to find his horse, and he found him with the saddle under his belly and the food-bag gone. (It was the custom in those days for people to bring their own food with them to the Althing, and most of them used to carry food-bags on their saddles.) Grettir went to look for the bag and could not find it, but then he saw a man running and asked him who he was. The man replied that his name was Skeggi and that he was a servant at As in Vatnsdale. 'I'm travelling with Thorkel Krafla,' he added, 'but I've been careless and lost my food-bag.'

Grettir said, ' "Misery loves company." I've lost my food-bag too, so let's search together.'

Skeggi agreed gladly. They walked around for a while, and then Skeggi unexpectedly ran off over the moor and snatched up a food-bag. Grettir saw him bend down and asked what he had picked up.

'My food-bag,' said Skeggi.

'Who will vouch that it is yours?' asked Grettir. 'Let me see it, anyhow, for many things look alike.'

Skeggi said no man was going to take away from him what was his own. Grettir caught hold of the bag, and they both pulled at it, for neither of them would give in.

'You seem to have the strange idea,' said the servant, 'that just because all men are not as rich as you are in Midfjord that for that reason they won't dare to hold their own against you.'

Grettir said it had nothing to do with his standing, but that everyone should have what belonged to himself.

Skeggi said, 'Audun is too far away now to strangle you as he did at the ball-game.'

'That is all very well,' said Grettir, 'but you are certainly not going to strangle me, whatever may have happened then.'

Then Skeggi seized his axe and struck at him, but when Grettir saw that he caught the axe handle with his left hand just above Skeggi's grip, and violently wrenched it free. Then he drove the axe into Skeggi's head so that it went straight into his brain, and he dropped down dead. Grettir took the bag, slung it across his saddle, and rode after his companions.

Thorkel was riding in front, not knowing what had happened, but other members of the party were looking for Skeggi, and when Grettir caught up with them, they asked what he knew about him. Grettir replied with this stanza:

I think that a bloodthirsty ogress
has just attacked Skeggi:
in a murderous mood
she went for his blood.
Over his head she stood gaping,
hard-mouthed with ruthless fangs,
then she split open his skull:
I witnessed it myself.

Thorkel's men jumped up and said that trolls were not likely to have attacked the man in broad daylight. Thorkel was silent at first, but then he said, 'It's not a question of that, for Grettir must have killed him. But what happened?'

Grettir then told the whole story of their argument. Thorkel said, 'This is most unfortunate, for Skeggi came as my follower and belonged to a good family. But this is what I intend to do about the matter: I myself shall pay whatever compensations may be awarded, but I can do nothing about the possible penalty of outlawry. You have a choice, Grettir: you can go to the Althing and take your chance on what may happen there, or you can turn back now.'

Grettir chose to go to the Althing, and so he went. A charge was laid on behalf of the dead man's heirs, and Thorkel pledged himself to pay the compensation, but Grettir was also sentenced to three years' outlawry abroad.

When the Althing broke up, the leading men journeyed together for a while before they parted, and they stopped for a rest under Sleda Ridge. It was on that occasion that Grettir lifted the boulder which still lies there in the grass and is now called Grettir's Lift. Many of the men came up to look at the boulder, and everyone thought it very remarkable indeed that so young a man could lift so huge a rock. Then Grettir rode home to Bjarg and told about his travels. Asmund was not very pleased, and he said that Grettir would turn out to be a brawler.

17

There was a man called Haflidi, who lived at Reydarfell in Hvitriverside. He was a seafarer and owned a trading ship, which at this time was laid up at Hvit River. There was a man on his ship called Bard, who had a young and beautiful wife.

Asmund sent a messenger to Haflidi to ask him to take Grettir in and look after him. Haflidi said he had been told that Grettir was rather wild, but for the sake of his friendship with Asmund he took him on, and then he made his ship ready for a voyage abroad.

Asmund sent Grettir off with nothing but provisions for the voyage and a little homespun cloth. Grettir asked his father for some sort of weapon, but Asmund said, 'You have not been very obedient to me, and I don't know that you are likely to do anything useful with a weapon, so I shall not provide one.'

Grettir said, 'What is not given needs no thanks.'

After that father and son parted with little affection. Many people wished Grettir a safe journey, but few a happy return. His mother saw him off, and before they parted she said, 'You are not as lavishly fitted out, my son, as I should wish so well-born a man to be. What is most lacking, I think, is that you have no weapon which could be of any use, and my heart tells me that you will need one.'

Then she took from under her cloak an inlaid sword, a most valuable weapon, and said, 'This sword belonged to my grandfather Jokul and to others of Vatnsdale in the past, and it brought them many victories. Now I want to give it to you, and may it serve you well.'

Grettir thanked her for the gift, and said he thought it better than anything else, however valuable. Then he went on his way, and Asdis wished him the best of luck. Grettir rode south across the moor, and did not break his journey until he arrived at the ship. Haflidi welcomed him and asked about his outfit, and Grettir said:

That wealthy man
fitted me out
poorly, I think,
when I left home.
But his good wife's gift
proved the saying,
'For a child,
mother is best.'

Haflidi said it was obvious that she was the one who cared the most for him.

They put out to sea when they were ready and when the wind was fair; after they got out of the shallows they hoisted the sail. Grettir made a den for himself under the ship's boat and would not stir, either to bail or to tend to the sail, or to do any of the other work which was supposed to be shared equally among the crew. And he refused to buy himself off from working.

They sailed south around Reykjaness and then south from the coast, and when land was out of sight they were caught by a driving gale. The ship was leaky and ill suited for running before the wind, and the crew became worn out by the cold and the wet. Grettir flung his lampoons about, which infuriated the others. One day the weather was cold and stormy, and the men called out asking Grettir to be of some use, 'for our fingers are numb with the cold.' Grettir looked up and said:

A lucky thing
if every finger
of all these numbskulls
is numbed to death.

They got no work out of him and were even less pleased than before. They said he was going to pay with his skin for his lampooning and his other offences, 'You find it more pleasant,' they said, 'to stroke the belly of Bard's wife than to do your duties on board, and we won't stand for that.'

The weather grew worse and worse, and they stood bailing day and night, and threatening Grettir. When Haflidi heard about this he went up to where Grettir lay, and said, 'I don't like what's going on between you and the men. You don't fulfill your obligations, and then in addition you lampoon them, so now they are threatening to throw you overboard. This situation is becoming impossible.'

'Why shouldn't they do what they want?' said Grettir. 'But I hope that one or two of them will have joined me by the time I go overboard.'

'That must never happen,' said Haflidi. 'Matters will never turn out well if this is your attitude, but I can give you some advice.'

'What is that?' said Grettir.

'They blame you for lampooning them,' said Haflidi, 'and so I would like you to compose an insulting verse about myself, for it may be that this will make them tolerate you the better.'

'I will never make verses about you,' said Grettir, 'unless they be honest ones. I'm not going to put you on a level with these numbskulls.'

Haflidi said, 'You can make the verse in such a way that it seems abusive at first sight although it is in fact complimentary when it has been studied closer.'

'That's easy to manage,' said Grettir.

Haflidi went up to the men who were bailing, and said, 'Hard is your toil, and one might guess that you have no love for Grettir.'

'We find his lampooning even worse than everything else,' they said.

Haflidi said in a loud voice, 'It will turn out badly for him in the end.'

When Grettir heard Haflidi blaming him, he said:

How different it was
when shrill-voiced Haflidi
was eating curds
back home at Reydarfell.
Then he ruled his roost;
but now this elegant fighter,
morning and night, eats only
a sailor's breakfast.

The merchants disliked this, and said that Grettir could not slander Haflidi without paying for it.

Haflidi said, 'Grettir thoroughly deserves that you should disgrace him in some way or other, but I will not have my honour staked against his ill-natured thoughtlessness. We will not avenge this now while we are in such danger, but bear it in mind when you get ashore, if you want to.'

They said, 'Can we not suffer this as well as you? Why should his verses sting us more than they do you?'

Haflidi said they were right, and after that the crew cared much less about Grettir's verses.

The voyage was long and hard; the ship began to leak more, and the crew became exhausted with work. Bard's young wife often sat beside Grettir and basted up his sleeves for him,[1] and the sailors taunted him about it. Haflidi went up to where Grettir was lying, and said:

Get out of your cosy corner!
The ship keeps on ploughing
a deep furrow through the sea,
as you brag to the woman.
Now she's basted up your sleeves
for comfort, and she'd like you
to be brave, for once,
while there's no land in sight.

Grettir stood up at once, and said:

The ship pitches hard,
but I will stand up.
I know the woman will grieve
if I lie here idle.
She, chaste and fair,
will take it badly,
if I let others
do my duty.

Then he ran aft to the men who were bailing and asked what they wanted him to do, but they said he would not be able to do much good.

Grettir said, 'One man's help is better than nothing.'

---

1 The sleeves of tunics and shirts were very wide, and without buttons, so for warmth the sleeves had to be basted up at the wrists every time a garment was put on.

Haflidi told them not to refuse his offer. 'Perhaps he thinks that all he needs is just to offer his help.'

At that time there were no pumps in ships, but the crew had to bail with casks or tubs; it was a wet and exhausting job. Two buckets were used, and one was carried down while the other was being carried up. The men asked Grettir to fill the buckets, and said they would now find out what he could do. He said they would soon see. He went below and began to fill the buckets, and they got two men to empty the buckets for him, but before long they were completely exhausted. Then four men took over, and the same happened to them. Some people say that eight men were bailing against him in the end, and then the ship was made dry. After that the merchants spoke very differently to Grettir, for they saw what he was capable of with all that strength. And from then on he worked very hard, whenever he was needed.

Afterwards, they drifted eastward, and a dense fog came on, until one night without warning the ship ran on to a rock, so that the lower part of the prow broke off. They put out the ship's boat and rescued the women and all the loose goods. There was a small island near by, and during the night they ferried there as much as they could of their belongings. When it began to get light, they talked about where they had come, and the men who had made the crossing before recognized that they had reached South-More in Norway. There was another island a short distance away, between them and the mainland, which was called Harams Isle. There were many people living on that island, and also there was the estate of a landed man.

18

The landed man who had the farm was named Thorfinn; he was the son of Kar the Old, who had lived on the island for a long time. Thorfinn was a great chieftain.

When it was broad daylight some people on the island noticed the merchants in distress, and told Thorfinn about it. He started off at once and launched a large boat of his which had sixteen oars on either side. There were nearly thirty men on board, so they rowed very quickly, and they managed to save the merchants' cargo, but the ship went down and a lot of valuable gear was lost with it. Thorfinn brought all the shipwrecked people to his home, and they stayed there for a week drying out their goods. Then the merchants went to the south of the country, and there is nothing more to tell of them.

Grettir, who stayed on with Thorfinn, kept in the background and had little to say most of the time. Thorfinn gave him shelter, but otherwise took little notice of him. Grettir did not keep him much company, and would not go out with him during the day, and that displeased Thorfinn, who, however, did not grudge him his food. Thorfinn was a very hospitable and cheerful man who liked to have happy people about him. Grettir was often away from the house, visiting the other farms on the island.

There was a man called Audun, who lived at a place called Vindheim. Grettir went there every day and became a good friend of his. Grettir would often sit there for a long time, and it happened late one evening, when he was getting ready to go home, that he saw a huge fire burst forth on the headland below Audun's farm. Grettir asked what was happening, but Audun said there was no need for him to worry about it.

'If such a thing were seen in my country,' said Grettir, 'it would be said that the flame came from a buried treasure.'

The farmer said, 'The owner of this fire, I think, is one whom it is better not to enquire about.'

'Still, I wish to know,' said Grettir.

'There on the headland stands a gravemound,' said Audun, 'and Thorfinn's father, Kar the Old, was buried in it. At one time only a single farm belonged to Kar and his son, but after Kar died he so haunted the place that he drove away all the farmers who owned land there, and now the whole of the island belongs to Thorfinn, but no one who is under Thorfinn's protection comes to any harm.'

Grettir said he had done well to tell him. 'I shall be back tomorrow, and then you must have digging tools ready for me.'

'I warn you not to do this,' said Audun, 'for I know this will make Thorfinn your enemy.'

Grettir said he would take that risk. The night passed, and when Grettir came back early next morning the digging tools were ready, and the farmer went with him to the mound. Grettir began to break open the mound, and worked hard without stopping until he reached the rafters, late in the afternoon. Then he tore them up. Audun did his best to discourage him from entering the mound. Grettir told him to watch the rope, 'for I am going to find out what inhabits the barrow.'

Then Grettir went into the mound. Inside it was dark, and the air not very sweet. He groped about to find out how things were arranged. He came upon some horse bones, then he knocked against the carved backpost of a chair, and he could feel someone sitting in it. A great treasure of gold and silver was gathered together there, and under the man's feet was a chest full of silver. Grettir took all the treasure and carried it towards the rope, but as he was making his way through the barrow he was seized fast by someone. He let go of the treasure and turned to attack, and they set on each other mercilessly, so that everything in their way was thrown out of place. The mound-dweller attacked vigorously, and for a while Grettir had to give way, but finally he realized this was not a good time to spare himself. Then they both fought desperately, and moved towards the horse bones, where they had a fierce struggle for a long time. Now the one and now the other was forced to his knees, but in the end the mound-dweller fell backwards, and there was a great crash.

Then Audun ran away from the rope, thinking that Grettir must be dead. Grettir drew his sword – Jokul's Gift – and struck with it at the mound-dweller's neck so that it cut off his head. He placed the head against Kar's buttocks and brought the treasure over to the rope: he found Audun gone, so he had to climb up the rope, hand over hand. He had tied the treasure to the rope and he hauled it up afterwards.

Grettir, who was very stiff after his dealing with Kar, made his way back to Thorfinn's farm, carrying the treasure. All the people there were at the table; Thorfinn gave Grettir a sharp look when he entered the hall and asked him what urgent business had made him forget good manners.

Grettir said, 'Many a small thing happens late at night.' Then he put out on the table all the treasure he had taken from the mound. There was one thing which Grettir kept gazing at: a short sword, so excellent a weapon that he said he had never seen a better one. That was the last thing he handed over. Thorfinn's eyes lit up when he saw it, for it was an heirloom which had always belonged to his family.

'Where did you get these treasures?' said Thorfinn.

Grettir said:

I've been misled
by the buried treasure.
Men will soon learn
about the hoard in the mound.

Yet I can see this:
few warriors would willingly
go there alone
in search of gold.

Thorfinn said, 'You do not frighten easily. No one before has ever been eager to break into the mound. I know that treasure is wasted which is hidden in the earth or put into mounds, so I will not blame you, especially since you have brought it back to me. And where did you get hold of that fine sword?'

Grettir replied with a verse:

I took this short sword
from the hellish darkness,
a weapon which makes
wounds flourish in men.
The undead was defeated.
This precious deadly destroyer
of helmets, if it were mine,
would stay in my hand.

Thorfinn said, 'That was well asked, but you must do something worthy of fame before I give you the sword, for I myself could never get it from my father as long as he lived.'

Grettir said, 'No one knows whom in the end it will benefit the most.'

Thorfinn took the treasure and kept the sword by his bed. The winter passed on until Christmas without anything else happening.

19

The summer before, Earl Eirik Hakonarson had left the country and sailed west to England to visit his brother-in-law, King Canute the Great. He left the rule of Norway to his son Hakon, who was still a boy, and so was to be under the guidance and authority of Earl Svein, Eirik's brother. Before he sailed abroad, Earl Eirik, who was an efficient ruler, summoned the landed men and the rich farmers, and they discussed at length the laws and the government.

They thought it was an evil custom in the land, that raiders or berserks could challenge important men to duels for the sake of their wealth or their women and that whoever was killed by the other did not have to be atoned for. Because of this many suffered disgrace and loss of money, or even lost their lives, and so Earl Eirik made all duels illegal in Norway and outlawed all robbers and berserks who caused trouble. Thorfinn Karsson of Harams Isle took part in bringing about this change, for he was a wise man and a close friend of the earl.

Two brothers were named as the worst offenders; one was called Thorir Paunch and the other Ogmund the Evil. They came from Halogaland, and were bigger and stronger than other men. They used to go about in a berserk's fury, and they spared no one when they were angry. They would take away the wives and the daughters of farmers, keep them for a week or two, and then send them back to their husbands or fathers; wherever they went they used to steal or make other trouble. Earl Eirik made them outlaws everywhere in Norway, and it was Thorfinn who had most to do with bringing this about, so the brothers felt that he had fully earned their enmity. After that the earl went abroad, as is related in his saga,[1] and Earl Svein had the authority and power in Norway.

Thorfinn went back to his farm and stayed mostly at home until Christmas, as was said before, but then he made ready to go to a place called Slysfjord on the mainland, to visit another farm that belonged to him. He invited there many of his friends. Thorfinn's wife could not go with him because their daughter, a young woman, was in bed ill, so the two of them stayed home. Grettir also remained behind and eight of the servants. Thorfinn went to the Christmas feast with thirty free men, and they had great feasting and mirth.

On Christmas Eve the weather was bright and calm, and Grettir was outside for most of the day, watching the ships passing north and south along the coast, for people were going to the various places where feasts were being held. By then, the farmer's daughter had recovered, so that she could go about with her mother.

Towards the end of the day Grettir saw a ship coming towards the island; it was rather small, with a line of overlapping shields from stem to stern, and all the wood above the water line was painted. The men were rowing fast and making for Thorfinn's boat shed. As soon as the ship grounded they jumped overboard; Grettir counted twelve of them. They did not strike him as being very peaceable. They lifted their ship and carried it on to dry land, and

1 *Earl Eirik's Saga* is no longer extant.

39

then they ran to the boat shed where Thorfinn's big ship was standing. It had always taken at least thirty men to launch it, but these twelve pulled it at once to the shingle. Then they lifted their own ship and carried it into the shed.

Grettir saw that they were intending to offer themselves hospitality, so he went down to meet them, welcomed them warmly, and asked who they were and what the name of their leader was. The man he spoke to answered quickly, saying that he was called Thorir Paunch and that his brother was called Ogmund, while the others were their companions. 'I presume,' said Thorir, 'that Thorfinn, the master of this farm, will have heard of us. Is he at home, by the way?'

Grettir said, 'You must be men of great luck, since you have arrived at such an opportune time, if you are the men I take you to be. The farmer has gone away with all the free men and is not due back till after Christmas, but his wife and daughter are both at home. If I thought that I had any grudge to repay, this is exactly how I would have wished to come, for here is everything you need, both ale and other pleasures.'

Thorir had been silent while Grettir talked on, but then he said to Ogmund, 'Hasn't everything turned out just as I guessed? I had it in mind to take vengeance on Thorfinn for having had us outlawed. This man has good news to tell us, and we don't have to drag every word out of him.'

'Every man chooses his own words,' said Grettir, 'and I shall give you such assistance as I can; now come with me.'

They thanked him and said they would do as he asked. When they came up to the house Grettir, who was being very talkative, took Thorir by the arm and led him into the hall. Thorfinn's wife was in the hall, hanging up tapestries and decorating the room. When she heard Grettir she stood still on the floor and asked him whom he was welcoming so wholeheartedly.

Grettir answered, 'It is proper, lady, to welcome our guests. Farmer Thorir Paunch has arrived with eleven companions and they plan to stay over Christmas, which is an excellent thing, since there were so few of us here.'

She said, 'I do not reckon these people among farmers or good men, for they are the most evil of robbers and criminals. I would gladly have given most of my possessions not to have them come here at this time. You repay Thorfinn badly for taking you destitute from a shipwreck and keeping you here this winter as a free man.'

Grettir said, 'It would be better now to help the guests off with

40

their wet clothes instead of reproaching me; there will be an opportunity for that later.'

Then Thorir said, 'Don't be upset, lady. You won't be any the worse off for your husband's absence, since you'll get a man in his place – and so will your daughter and all the other women, too.'

'Spoken like a true man,' said Grettir. 'The women will have no cause for complaint.'

Then all the women rushed away, weeping in despair. Grettir said to the berserks, 'Let me take care of everything you want to put aside, your weapons and wet clothes. We shall not find the people very pliable as long as they are terrified.'

Thorir said that he did not worry about women fussing. 'But we should treat you very differently from the rest of the household. I think we should take you completely into our confidence.'

'That is for you to decide,' said Grettir. 'But I myself do not treat all men alike.'

Then they put aside most of their weapons. Grettir said, 'I think it would be a good idea to sit down at the table and have something to drink, for you must be thirsty after all your rowing.'

They agreed eagerly, but said they did not know where the cellar was. Grettir asked if they would trust him to look after them and manage matters, and the berserks said they would gladly do so. He went to fetch ale and gave it to them. They were exhausted and drank heavily, but he kept them provided with the strongest ale he could find, and this went on for a long time. At the same time he told them a lot of funny stories, so that altogether there was a great deal of noise. The rest of the household showed no desire to intrude.

Then Thorir said, 'I've never met a stranger as friendly as this man. How do you want me and my companions to repay you for your service?'

Grettir said, 'I don't want any reward for the time being, but if we are as good friends when you leave as now seems likely, I should like to join you. I may be less of a man than some of you, but I shall never hold you back from great deeds.'

This pleased them immediately, and they wanted to seal their friendship with vows at once. Grettir disagreed, 'For the old saying is true: "Ale makes another man." This should not be done in a hurry, so let's not go beyond what I have already said. We are not very cool-tempered.' But they said they would not change their minds.

The evening went on, and it was dark when Grettir saw that they were becoming stupefied by the drink. Then he said, 'Don't you think it's time to go to bed?'

Thorir said it was, 'And I shall do what I promised for the lady of the house.'

Grettir walked out of the hall and said in a loud voice, 'Go to your beds, women, for Farmer Thorir will have it so.'.

They cursed him in reply, screaming and crying. At that, the berserks came out, and Grettir said to them, 'Let's go outside, and I'll show you Thorfinn's stores of clothes.'

They agreed, and so they all went to a very large storehouse. It had a secure lock on the door, and the house itself was very strongly built. Beside it there was a large privy, also sturdily built, separated from the storehouse by a partition wall of boards. The storehouse stood on high ground, and there were steps leading up to it.

The berserks, who were making a great riot, began to push Grettir about, but he playfully ducked away, and when they weren't expecting it he skipped out of the building, seized the latch, slammed the door, and put on the lock. Thorir and his men thought at first that the door must have come shut accidentally, and so they paid no attention. They had a light with them, for Grettir had been showing them many of Thorfinn's valuables, and they kept on looking at them for a while.

Grettir hurried back to the farmhouse, and when he came in the door he called out in a loud voice and asked where the housewife was. She kept silent, for she did not dare to answer. He said, 'There is a chance to make a good catch here. Are there any usable weapons about?'

She answered, 'There are weapons here, but I don't know what use you can make of them.'

'Let's talk about that later,' he said. 'Now everyone must do what he can, for we shall not get this chance again.'

The housewife said, 'It would be God's mercy if this situation could be put right now. Above Thorfinn's bed is hung the great barbed spear that used to belong to Kar the Old, and there too is a helmet and a coat of mail and that good short sword. These weapons won't fail you unless your courage does.'

Grettir seized the helmet and the spear, belted on the short sword, and rushed out. The housewife called to her servants and told them to help so brave a man; four of them took up weapons but the other four did not dare to come anywhere near.

Now to return to the berserks. They thought that it was taking Grettir a long time to come back, and they began to suspect treachery. They rushed against the door and found that it was locked; then they tried the wooden partition and made every board creak. In the end they succeeded in breaking through the partition and came out into the passage,[2] and so to the steps. Then their berserks' rage came on them, and they started howling like dogs. At that moment Grettir arrived, and with both hands he hurled the spear at Thorir's waist, as he was starting to come down the stairs, so that it went right through him. The spear had a long broad blade: Ogmund the Evil was walking just behind Thorir and knocked against him when he was hit, so that the spear penetrated Thorir as far as the barbs and went right through his shoulders and into Ogmund's chest. The two men slumped down dead, and then the others came running down the steps, one after the other. Grettir attacked each of them in turn, hewing with his sword and thrusting with his spear, but they defended themselves with logs that lay on the ground and with anything else they could lay their hands on. Because of their immense strength they were perilous men to deal with, even though they had no weapons. Grettir killed two of the berserks from Halogaland there in the yard. The four servants came out then – they had been arguing about which weapon each of them was to have. They attacked the berserks while they were retreating, but when they turned around the servants ran back to the house. Six of the vikings were killed there, all by Grettir's hand. Then the remaining six tried to get away, and made their way down to the boat shed. They went inside and defended themselves with oars; Grettir received some heavy blows and came close to serious injury.

The servants went home then and said much about their own valour. The housewife asked them to find out what had become of Grettir, but they refused to go.

Grettir killed two more in the boat shed, but the remaining four got out past him. They ran in pairs in different directions, and he chased the two who were nearer. The night was very dark. They ran into a grain shed at the farm of Vindheim, which was mentioned earlier. For a long time they fought there, but in the end Grettir killed them both. By then he was stiff and exhausted, most of the night had passed, and it had become very cold with snow falling in drifts, so he did not bother to look for the two who were left, and instead walked back to the farm.

The housewife had lights burning in the windows of the upper rooms, as a beacon, and after he saw them he managed to find his way back. When he came in the door the housewife came to him and welcomed him most warmly. 'You have won great fame,' she said, 'and you have kept me and my household from a great

2 Apparently a balcony or narrow porch which was in front of both the privy, into which they had broken, and the storehouse.

43

disgrace – if you had not saved us, we would never have found any help.'

Grettir said, 'I seem to myself much the same man as I was in the evening, when you were heaping abuse on me.'

The housewife said, 'We had not then found out that you were so valiant a man. Everything is at your command in this house which is fitting for us to give and honourable for you to receive. And I expect that Thorfinn will reward you still better when he comes home.'

Grettir said, 'There is little need to discuss rewards now, but I shall accept your offer until your husband comes back. I think you can sleep in peace, as far as the berserks are concerned.'

Grettir drank little that night, and lay down with his weapons beside him. In the morning, as soon as it was light, the men of the island were summoned together, and they went to look for the berserks who had escaped the night before. They were found late in the day under a boulder, dead from exposure and from their wounds. Then they were taken down to the shore and buried under a heap of stones at the tide-mark.[3] After that the men went home, and all the islanders were glad to have peace. Grettir spoke this verse when he came back to the housewife:

> By the breakers there lie buried
> Twelve warriors with burning swords;
> Alone and gladly I worked it all.
> What act of a man's can now be valued,
> Noble lady, graceful with gold,
> If such a work is counted small?

The housewife said, 'Surely there are few men now alive who are your equal.'

She put him in the seat of honour and treated him well in every way, and so it went on until it was time for Thorfinn to return.

---

3 According to early Norwegian law, everyone was entitled to a Christian burial in consecrated ground, except for criminals, traitors, murderers, truce-breakers, thieves, and suicides; all these were to be buried at the tide-mark.

20

After Christmas Thorfinn made ready to go home. He gave good parting gifts to the many men whom he had invited, and then he set off for home with his companions. They were close to his boat shed when they saw a ship lying on the shore, and they soon realized that this was Thorfinn's large galley. Thorfinn had not heard of the vikings' visit. He told his men to hurry ashore; 'For I suspect,' he said, 'that it is not friends who have been at work here.'

Thorfinn was the first to go ashore, and he went straight up to the boat shed. He saw a ship there, and recognized that it belonged to the berserks. Then he said to his men, 'I suspect that something so serious has happened that I would gladly give the island and everything here for it not to have happened.'

They asked him why. He said, 'Men whom I know to be the worst vikings in all Norway have come here: Thorir Paunch and Ogmund the Evil. They won't have been here for our benefit, and I don't trust the Icelander.' He kept on talking in the same vein to his companions.

Grettir was at home, and it was because of him that people were slow in going down to the beach. He said he did not care if Thorfinn was worried about what had happened, but when the housewife asked his permission he told her that she could go wherever she wanted but that he was not going anywhere. She hurried down to meet Thorfinn and welcomed him warmly. He was delighted to see her and said, 'Thank God that I see you safe and sound, and my daughter too. But how have things gone for you since I left home?'

She said, 'Everything has turned out well, but we came very close to a great shame, and there would have been no help for us if your guest of this winter had not saved us.'

Thorfinn said, 'Now I am going to sit down, but you go on with the story.'

She told him in detail about everything that had happened there, and she praised highly Grettir's courage and valour. Thorfinn said nothing while she was telling her story, but when she had finished he said, 'The saying is true: "It takes time to test a man's worth." But where is Grettir now?'

His wife said, 'He is in the hall at home.'

Then they walked to the house. Thorfinn went up to Grettir, embraced him, and thanked him handsomely for the bravery he had shown. 'And I will tell you,' said Thorfinn, 'what few people will tell their friends, that I hope you will some time be in need of help, and then you will know whether or not I will be a friend. I shall never be able to repay you for what you have done unless you should find yourself in trouble. But you will have hospitality here with me whenever you want to accept it, and you will be held as the foremost of my men.'

Grettir thanked him well, 'And I would have accepted this even though you had offered it sooner.'

Grettir stayed there for the rest of the winter, and was on the best of terms with Thorfinn. He became famous for this affair throughout all Norway, and especially in those places where the berserks had made most trouble.

In the spring Thorfinn asked Grettir what he intended to do, and he said he wanted to go north to Vaagan for the market there. Thorfinn asked him to take as much money as he wanted, but Grettir said that all he needed then was some pocket money. Thorfinn said that this was the least he owed him, and he went down to the ship to see him off. Then he gave Grettir the fine short sword, and Grettir carried it as long as he lived, for it was a most valuable weapon. Thorfinn asked Grettir to come to him whenever he might need any help.

Then Grettir went north to Vaagan, where there was a great crowd of people. Men who had never seen him before welcomed him warmly because of the great deed he had done when he killed the vikings. Many well-born men invited him to visit them, but he said he wanted to go back to his friend Thorfinn. He got a passage in a cargo boat which belonged to a well-born man called Thorkel, who lived at Saltfjord in Halogaland. When Grettir arrived at Thorkel's farm Thorkel welcomed him cordially and urged Grettir at length to stay with him the following winter. So Grettir accepted this and stayed the winter with him, as an honoured guest.

21

There was a man called Bjorn, who was staying with Thorkel, a hot-tempered man, but of good family, and related to Thorkel. He was not popular with most of the people, for he used to mock the men who were with Thorkel, and so he drove many of them away. Grettir and he cared little for each other; Bjorn thought Grettir worth little in comparison with himself, but Grettir would not yield, so there was friction between them. Bjorn was a loud-mouthed and self-assertive man, so many of the young men were attracted to him, and they used to swagger about outside in the evening.

It happened early in the winter that a savage bear came out of its den and became so ferocious that it spared neither man nor beast; it was thought that the bear must have been roused by the noise Bjorn and his companions made. The animal was very hard to deal with and was destroying the farmers' flocks: Thorkel suffered the greatest loss for he was the richest man in the district.

One day Thorkel summoned his men to come with him and search for the bear's den. They found it in some cliffs by the sea: there was an overhanging crag with a cave in it, and a narrow path leading to the cave. Below the cave the cliff dropped down to broken rocks next to the sea. To fall from the path would be certain death. The bear used to lie in its den all day, but it always came out at night. No pen was safe for the sheep against the bear, and dogs were no use. People thought it a great calamity. Thorkel's kinsman Bjorn said that the worst was over since the den had been found. 'And now,' he said, 'I shall find out what sort of sport I will have with my namesake.'[1] Grettir appeared not to notice Bjorn's bragging.

After this Bjorn used to go out every evening when the others were going to bed. One night Bjorn went to the den and found out that the bear was inside, roaring savagely. Bjorn lay down on the narrow path with his shield over him intending to wait until the bear followed its usual custom and came out from the den. But the bear scented a man and delayed for some time. Bjorn became very sleepy where he was lying, and he was not able to keep himself awake. Then the bear came out of its den. It saw where the man was

1 'Bjorn' is the Icelandic word for bear.

47

lying, and clawed at him with its paw, tore the shield off him, and threw it down over the cliff. Bjorn awoke with a great start, took to his heels and ran home, fearing that the bear might catch him.

Bjorn's companions knew all about this, for they had kept an eye on his movements. They found his shield in the morning and made a great mockery of the whole affair.

At Christmas Thorkel himself went to the den, along with Grettir, Bjorn, and five of his own men. Grettir was wearing a fur cloak, but he laid it aside when they were attacking the bear. It was difficult to get at the bear for they could only thrust at it with spears, which the bear warded off with his jaws. Bjorn kept urging the men to attack, but he himself never came so near as to take any risk. When no one was watching he seized Grettir's cloak and threw it into the den towards the bear. They accomplished nothing there and so they turned back late in the day. When Grettir was getting ready to go home he missed his cloak and saw that the bear was lying on it. Then he said, 'Which one of you boys has been joking with me and has thrown my cloak into the den?'

Bjorn answered, 'Someone who is not afraid to admit it.'

Grettir said, 'I don't worry much about trifles like this.'

Then they started home, and after they had walked for a while Grettir's boot-thong broke, and Thorkel told the others to wait for him, but Grettir said there was no need for that.

Then Bjorn said, 'You don't need to think that Grettir will run away and leave his cloak. He will want to win fame and kill the bear single-handed, after the eight of us have run away from it. Then he would be the man he is said to be – but so far he has been slow enough in attacking the bear.'

Thorkel said to him, 'I am not so sure how this will turn out for you, but leave him alone, for you will not be his equal in courage.'

Bjorn replied that he would say whatever he pleased despite either of them.

By then there was a ridge between Grettir and the others, and he turned back to the narrow path on the cliff. This time there was no argument about who should be first to attack. Grettir drew and held the sword Jokul's Gift, but he carried his short sword by a loop attached to the hilt which he slipped up over his hand. He did this because he thought he could manage better if he had a free hand. He at once went along the narrow path, and when the bear saw a man it savagely jumped up and made for him. It struck at him with the paw which was furthest away from the cliff, but Grettir swung his sword and hit the paw above the claws slicing them off. Then the bear tried to strike at him with the paw that was still unhurt, but it tottered when it shifted its weight on to its other leg and found only a stump, so it fell forward and into Grettir's arms. He caught hold of the bear between the ears and held it off, so it could not bite him. Grettir later said that holding the bear off was the hardest test he ever had. But with the bear struggling so hard and the path so narrow, the two of them fell down over the cliff. The bear, being heavier, landed on the rocks first, with Grettir on top, and was badly injured by the fall. Grettir seized the short sword and drove it into the bear's heart, and that was its death. After that he went home, and took with him the cloak, which had been all torn into tatters, and also the piece he had cut off the bear's paw.

Thorkel and his men were drinking when Grettir came in, and they laughed at the torn cloak Grettir had on. He put up on the table the piece he had cut off the paw. Thorkel said,'Where are you now, kinsman Bjorn? I never saw your weapons biting so well, and now I want you to offer Grettir a gift in compensation for the insult you put on him.'

Bjorn said he would be slow to do this, 'And I don't care whether Grettir is pleased or not.'

Grettir said:

The warrior came frightened home
from his visits to the bear
though neither was hurt
on those trips in the autumn.
No one saw me *waiting*
beside the bear's den,
yet I came home safely
after visiting the beast.

' You have certainly acted bravely,' said Bjorn 'and you are giving a very different account of me – for I realize this taunt is aimed at me.'

Thorkel said, 'I should like you, Grettir, not to avenge yourself on Bjorn. I will pay you full reparation on his behalf so that the two of you may be reconciled.'

Bjorn said Thorkel could spend his money on better things than this. 'I think it best that Grettir and I deal with each other. One man's loss will be the other man's gain.'

Grettir said he liked that very well.

'Then,' said Thorkel, 'for my sake, Grettir, you must not harm Bjorn while you are both staying with me.'

'So it shall be,' said Grettir. Bjorn said that he would not be afraid to face Grettir wherever they might meet. Grettir grinned at him, but he would not accept any reparation, and so they stayed there for the rest of the winter.

22

In the spring Grettir went north to Vaagan with Thorkel's men. He and Thorkel parted as good friends. Bjorn went west to England, in charge of Thorkel's ship which was going there. He stayed in England that summer and made for Thorkel the purchases which had been delegated to him. Late in the autumn he sailed back east.

Grettir stayed at Vaagan until the fleet scattered, and then he sailed south with some merchants. They came to a harbour called Garten at the mouth of Trondheim Fjord, and there they put up tents. After they had settled themselves they saw a ship approaching the harbour from the south, and they could soon tell that it was a ship which had been to England. It came to land some distance away and the men went ashore. Grettir and his companions went to meet them, and when they were close Grettir saw that Bjorn was among them. He said, 'It's a good thing that we have met here; we must take up our old argument. I want to find out which of us is the better man.'

Bjorn said that their argument was old and forgotten – 'But if there was anything wrong I should like to make amends, so that you may feel fully satisfied'.

Then Grettir said:

I vanquished the bear,
and won praise for my deed.
The savage beast tore apart
my long cloak of fur.
A shameless man was to blame,
and he must be paid back.
But I've never been boastful
about my own deeds.

Bjorn said that greater matters than this had been compensated for with money. Grettir replied that not many men had played tricks on him, nor had he accepted compensation for them. He said it would be the same in this case – 'And both of us shall not walk away from here unharmed, if I can have my way. I charge you with cowardice if you dare not fight now.'

Bjorn realized that he could not talk himself out of it, so he took his weapons and went on dry land. They rushed together and fought, but it was not long before Bjorn was wounded, and soon he fell dead to the ground. When his companions saw this they boarded their ship and sailed north along the coast to meet Thorkel, and they told him what had taken place. He said that this had happened no sooner than he had expected. A little later Thorkel went south to Trondheim and met Earl Svein there.

After the killing of Bjorn, Grettir went south to More, met his friend Thorfinn and told him what had happened. Thorfinn welcomed him warmly, 'And it's a good thing,' he said, 'that you are in need of a friend. You must stay with me until this affair is brought to an end.'

Grettir thanked him for the offer and said that he would accept it.

Earl Svein was in residence at Stenkjer near Trondheim when he heard about Bjorn's killing. At that time Hjarrandi, Bjorn's brother, was staying with the earl as one of his retainers. Hjarrandi was very angry when he heard that Bjorn had been killed and asked the earl for his help in the affair. The earl promised him this, and then sent messengers to Thorfinn, summoning both Thorfinn and Grettir. They made ready at once to obey the earl's orders and went north to Trondheim to see him. Then the earl held a meeting about the incident, and he asked Hjarrandi to be present. Hjarrandi said he was not going to weigh his brother's death against money. 'I shall either suffer the same fate that he did, or else avenge him,' he said.

When the case was examined it seemed to the earl that Bjorn had been guilty of many offences against Grettir, but Thorfinn offered to pay whatever amount of money the earl would consider an honourable settlement for Bjorn's heirs to accept. He spoke at length about how Grettir had freed the people of the north by killing the berserks, as has already been related.

The earl said, 'What you are saying, Thorfinn, is very true. It was a great riddance and we think it honourable to accept money in compensation, as you suggest. Grettir is now a famous man because of his strength and courage.'

Hjarrandi refused to accept this settlement, and so the meeting came to an end. Thorfinn asked his kinsman Arnbjorn to go with Grettir every day, for he knew that Hjarrandi was waiting for an opportunity to kill him.

23

One day Grettir and Arnbjorn went out for a stroll in the town, and when they passed a certain gate a man rushed out of it, brandishing an axe, and struck at Grettir with both hands. Grettir, who was not prepared for this, reacted slowly, but Arnbjorn, who had seen the man, seized Grettir and pushed him forward so hard that he fell on his knees. The axe caught him in the shoulder, making a gash right down to the armpit, which was a serious wound. Grettir turned round quickly and drew his short sword, and then he saw that this was Hjarrandi. The axe landed in the street and stuck fast there, so Hjarrandi had some difficulty in pulling it free, and at that moment Grettir struck at him, landing a blow on the arm and severing it just below the shoulder. Then Hjarrandi's five companions came rushing forward, and a fight started, but it was soon over. Grettir and Arnbjorn killed the five men who had been with Hjarrandi, except for one who got away and rushed to see the earl to tell him what had happened. The earl was furious when he heard about it, and announced a meeting for the following day.

Thorfinn and Grettir came to the meeting. The earl brought charges against Grettir for the killings; Grettir admitted them, but said he had been defending his very life. 'I have indeed some marks on my body to prove it,' he said. 'And I would have been killed if Arnbjorn hadn't saved my life.'

The earl said it was a pity he had not been killed. 'For you will cause the death of many men if you are allowed to live.'

At the time Grettir's friend and companion Bersi Skald-Torfuson was staying with the earl. He and Thorfinn went before the earl and asked him to spare Grettir's life, and suggested that the earl should decide the whole matter, and that Grettir should be allowed to stay in the country. It was very difficult to persuade the earl to consider a settlement, but in the end he gave in to their appeal, and it was decided that Grettir should be allowed to live in peace until spring. The earl refused, however, to make a final settlement until Gunnar, the brother of Bjorn and Hjarrandi, was present. Gunnar was a landowner in Tonsberg.

In the spring the earl summoned Grettir and Thorfinn east to

Tonsberg, for he wanted to stay there during the height of the shipping season. Grettir and Thorfinn travelled east to Tonsberg, and the earl was already in residence when they arrived. There Grettir met his brother Thorstein the Galleon, who was a land owner in Tonsberg, and who welcomed him warmly and asked him to stay with him. Grettir told him about his troubles; Thorstein listened attentively, and warned him to be on his guard against Gunnar.

And so the spring passed.

24

Gunnar stayed in town and waited for an opportunity to get at Grettir. One day Grettir happened to be drinking in a certain tavern, for he tried to keep out of Gunnar's way. Then, when he was least on guard, the door was rammed so hard that it broke into pieces, and four fully armed men came rushing inside. It was Gunnar and his men, and they at once set on Grettir, who grasped his weapons, which were hanging above him, and backed into a corner to defend himself. He had a shield in front of him, and he kept striking at them with his short sword, so they could make little headway. Grettir landed a blow on one of Gunnar's men, and that did for that man. Then Grettir cleared some space around him, and the others backed up towards the door. Soon Gunnar lost another man, and then he tried to get away with his remaining companion. This companion made it as far as the door when he tripped over the threshold: he lay there on the ground and was slow in getting to his feet again. Gunnar guarded himself with his shield and backed away from Grettir, who kept attacking him hard and fast. Grettir jumped up on the raised platform inside the door; Gunnar's hands, with his shield were still inside the door, and Grettir struck a blow between Gunnar and his shield, cutting through both wrists. He fell backwards out through the doorway, and Grettir gave him his death blow. Gunnar's companion, who was just then scrambling to his feet, went straight to the earl and told him what had happened.

Earl Svein was enraged at his story, and immediately called a meeting in the town. When Thorfinn and Thorstein the Galleon learned about these matters they gathered their kinsmen and friends and came in a crowd to the meeting. The earl was very angry and would not listen to anyone. Thorfinn, who was the first to go before him, said, 'I have come here because I wish to offer you settlement and compensation for the killings which Grettir has committed. It will be for you alone to decide the terms, if only Grettir's life can be spared.'

The earl answered angrily, 'You don't tire easily of begging for Grettir's life, but I don't think you have a good case. Grettir has now killed three brothers, one after the other, and they were all so brave that none of them would weigh his brother's death against money. It is no use now, Thorfinn, to plead for Grettir's life, since I am not going to encourage lawbreaking in this land by accepting compensation for such terrible crimes.'

Next Bersi Skald-Torfuson came forward and pleaded with the earl to accept a settlement. 'I'm willing to give whatever I own for this,' he said. 'Grettir comes from a good family, and is a close friend of mine. You must realize, sir, that it is better to spare the life of one man and receive in return the thanks of many, while at the same time deciding alone the amount of the fine, than to reject an honourable offer and take the chance that you may not be able to seize the man at all.'

The earl answered, 'These words come well from you, Bersi, for you are always showing what a fine man you are. However, I do not intend to break the law of this land by sparing the lives of those who have already forfeited them.'

Then Thorstein the Galleon came forward and greeted the earl; he made offers on Grettir's behalf, using many well-chosen words. The earl asked him what made him plead for this man, and Thorstein told him they were brothers. The earl said he had not known that. 'It is of course noble of you to try to help him, but since we have already decided not to accept money in compensation for these killings, we shall set the same value on all these pleas: we are going to take Grettir's life, whatever the cost, as soon as we can.'

With that the earl jumped to his feet, and refused to consider any of the offers which the three men had made.

Thorfinn and the others went over to Thorstein's house and prepared to make a stand there. When the earl realized this, he told his retainers to arm themselves, and then marched there with all his men in battle order. But before they arrived, the others had already formed up in front of the gate to the house, with Thorfinn, Thorstein, and Grettir in the front, and then Bersi; each of them had many men.

The earl told them to hand Grettir over to him and not make things impossible for themselves. They made all the same offers as before, but the earl refused even to listen to them. Thorfinn and

Thorstein said that the earl would have to go to more trouble if he wanted to take Grettir's life: 'We will all share the same fate, and it will be said that you go to great lengths to destroy one man's life, if we are all to be killed, too.'

The earl said he would spare none of them, and they were then on the point of fighting. But then many well-meaning men approached the earl and asked him not to be the cause of so much trouble; they said he would suffer great losses before the other men were killed. The earl realized that this was good advice, so he calmed down a little, and then preparations were made for a settlement. Thorfinn and Thorstein were both eager for this, provided that Grettir's life would be safe.

The earl said, 'I want you to know that despite the generous compromise I am making here, I do not consider this as a final truce. But I am unwilling to fight my own men, although I can see how little respect you have shown me throughout this whole affair.'

Thorfinn said, 'This does you great credit, sir, and you alone will determine the fines for the killings.'

The earl said that for their sake he would allow Grettir to go in peace to Iceland as soon as ships could sail there, if they would agree. They accepted that, and paid the earl as much money as he wanted; then they and the earl parted with little friendship. But Grettir and his brother Thorstein parted the best of friends, and Grettir went along with Thorfinn, who became famous for the help he had given him in these very difficult circumstances. None of the men who helped Grettir were ever again in the earl's favour, except for Bersi.

This is what Grettir said:

Thorfinn,
the fighters' friend,
was fated to give me
his noble help
when the stealthy
goddess of death
claimed my life
in the town of Tonsberg.

And Thorstein,
this slow-moving
galleon, gave me
a helping hand.
He, more than others,

saved me
from the grasping
clutches of death.

The earl's men thought us
hard to attack,
no easy matter
to overcome us,
when Bersi wanted
to burn out their hearts
with the fire
of our flaming swords.

Grettir went back with Thorfinn and stayed there until Thorfinn found him a place on a ship with some merchants who were going to Iceland. Thorfinn gave him many fine gifts – garments, and a painted saddle with a bridle. They parted in friendship, and Thorfinn asked him to visit him, should he come back to Norway again.

25

Asmund Grey-Locks was still farming at Bjarg while Grettir was abroad, and he was considered the leading man in Midfjord. But Thorkel Krafla died while Grettir was away from Iceland. Thorvald Asgeirsson was then living at As in Vatnsdale and was becoming a great chieftain.[1] Asmund received much support from Thorvald in lawsuits and other matters.

Asmund had brought up a man called Thorgils Maksson, who was closely related to him. Thorgils was a vigorous man, and with Asmund's help he made a lot of money. Asmund had bought for him the farm at Lækjarmot, and he lived there.

Thorgils was a good provider and used to go to the Strands every year for whalemeat and other necessities. He was a very resolute man and often searched all the eastern part of the common shore for driftage.

At that time the sworn-brothers Thorgeir Havarsson and Thormod

1 *Thorvald was the father of Dalla, who married Isleif, who later became*
  Bishop of Skalholt (1056-80; the first native-born bishop in Iceland).

Kolbrun's-Poet[2] had reached the height of their arrogance. They owned a cargo boat which they used when they were raiding in various places, and they were thought to be a great menace.

It happened one summer that Thorgils Maksson found a stranded whale on the common shore, and with the help of his men he started cutting it up at once. When the sworn-brothers heard of this, they went there, and at first they talked with him reasonably enough. Thorgils offered them half of that part of the whale which had not yet been cut up, but they demanded either all the uncut whale, or else that the entire whale – both cut and uncut – should be divided into two equal shares. But Thorgils flatly refused to give up what he had already cut from the whale. Then they started threatening each other, and soon they seized their weapons and fought. Thorgils and Thorgeir fought for a long time without any interference from the others. They were both very resolute and the struggle was long and hard, but in the end Thorgils fell dead.

Meantime, in another place, Thormod was fighting Thorgils' men, and he also won the day, killing three of them. After Thorgils had been killed his companions went back home to Midfjord, taking his body with them; his death was thought a very great loss.

The sworn-brothers took the entire whale, and Thormod mentions the fight in the memorial poem which he composed on Thorgeir.

Asmund Grey-Locks heard that his kinsman Thorgils had been killed. It was his duty to take legal action over the killing, so he set out, named witnesses to the wounds, and then he referred the case to the Althing, for that seemed to be the law, in view of the fact that the killing had taken place in another Quarter. And so time passed.

26

There was a man called Thorstein Kuggason,[1] who shared with Asmund Grey-Locks the duty of taking legal action over the killing of Thorgils Maksson. So Asmund sent word to Thorstein to come

---

2 The two heroes of *Fóstbrǽðra Saga* ('The Sworn-Brothers' Saga),
   which incidentally was the chief model for Halldor Laxness' novel, *The Happy Warriors*.

1 *Thorstein was the son of Thorkel Kuggi, the son of Thord Gellir, the son of Olaf Feilan, the son of Thorstein the Red, the son of Aud the*

to see him. Thorstein was a great fighter and a very aggressive man. He set out at once to see his kinsman Asmund, and they discussed the lawsuit. Thorstein was very firm and said that compensation should not be accepted, for they had sufficient backing to enforce either outlawry or blood-vengeance. Asmund said he would give him his full support, whatever course he chose to take. Then they rode north to see their kinsman Thorvald and asked for his support, which he willingly agreed to give. After that they started proceedings against Thorgeir and Thormod, and then Thorstein rode back home; he lived at Ljarwoods in the Hvamm District. At that time Skeggi[2] was living at Hvamm, and he gave his support to Thorstein in this lawsuit. They rode to the Althing with a large force, and prosecuted their lawsuits vigorously. Asmund and Thorvald rode from home sixty strong, and stayed at Ljarwoods for several days.

27

At that time Thorgils Arason was living at Reykjahills and Thorgeir Havarsson could rely on his firm support because of their close kinship,[1] for Thorgils was the greatest chieftain in the West Quarter. He was so hospitable that he used to give any free man food for as long as he would accept it. Because of this, there were always a number of people staying at Reykjahills. Thorgils ran a magnificent farm, and he was both benevolent and wise.

Thorgeir used to stay with Thorgils in the winter and go to the Strands in the summer. After the killing of Thorgils Maksson he went to Reykjahills and told Thorgils what had happened. Thorgils told him that he was welcome to stay. 'But I think,' he said, 'that

Deep-Minded. Thorstein Kuggason's mother was Thurid, the daughter of Asgeir the Rash, who was an uncle of Asmund Grey-Locks.
Thorstein Kuggason figures also in *Laxdæla Saga* and *Bjarnar Saga Hitdælakappa.*
2 *Skeggi was the son of Thorarin Foal-Brow, the son of Thord Gellir. Skeggi's mother was Fridgerd, the daughter of Thord of Hofdi.*
1 *Thorgils was the son of Ari, the son of Mar, the son of Atli the Red, the son of Ulf the Squint-Eyed who was the first settler of Reykjaness. Thorgils Arason's mother was Thorgerd, the daughter of Alf of the Dales. This Alf had another daughter called Thorelf, who was the mother of Thorgeir Havarsson. So Thorgils and Thorgeir were first cousins.*

they will make the case hard for you, and I'm unwilling to add to these difficulties. I intend to send a messenger to Thorstein and offer him money in compensation for the killing of Thorgils, but if he refuses to accept a settlement I'm not going to worry very much about defending this case.'

Thorgeir said he would accept his reasoning.

In the autumn Thorgils sent a messenger to Thorstein Kuggason to try for a settlement. Thorstein adamantly refused to accept money from Thorgils in reparation for this particular killing, but, as for the other killings, he said he would accept the counsel of wise men. When Thorgils heard this, he called Thorgeir and asked what kind of help he thought best for him. Thorgeir said that if he were outlawed and had any choice left, he would like to go abroad. Thorgils said in that case they should try to arrange for that. There was a ship laid up at Nordur River in Borgarfjord, and Thorgils secretly bought a passage on it for the sworn-brothers. And so the winter passed.

Thorgils heard that Thorstein and the others, who were then at Ljarwoods, were going to the Althing with a large following. So he delayed his departure, for he wanted Thorstein and his men to ride south before he himself set out from home, and this was the way it turned out. The sworn-brothers rode south with Thorgils, and on the journey Thorgeir killed Torfi Bundle at Maskelda, and also Skuf and Bjarni at Hundadale. Thormod describes it this way in *Thorgeir's Poem*:

The warrior forced Thorgils
to pay for his arrogance;
a battle was fought,
and the raven tore at raw flesh.
Later that same sea-warrior
was at the deaths of Skuf and Bjarni.
His deft war-seasoned hand
was eager for battle.

Thorgils made a settlement there and then in the valley over the killing of Skuf and Bjarni, but because of all this his journey took longer than he had intended. Thorgeir travelled to the ship, but Thorgils rode on to the Althing and arrived there when the court was already in session.

Asmund Grey-Locks was just then asking the defence to present its case in the action over the killing of Thorgils Maksson, and Thorstein Kuggason stood near the court with all his men fully armed. Thorgils approached the court and offered compensation for the killing on condition that Thorgeir would then be acquitted. He tried to find some legal grounds for the defence, and asked whether everyone was not equally free to make use of the common driftage. The Lawspeaker was asked if this was the law. Skapti, who was the Lawspeaker at the time,[2] sided with Asmund for the sake of their kinship; he said that this law applied only to men of equal social standing, and added that farmers had greater privileges than men without land. Asmund pointed out that Thorgils Maksson had offered the sworn-brothers an equal share of the uncut portion of the whale when they arrived on the scene; and so the defence argument was quashed. Thorstein and his men followed this up with determination and said that they could not be satisfied unless Thorgeir was outlawed. Thorgils realized that there were only two courses open to him: either to attack them with all his men, although the outcome would be very uncertain, or else let them proceed as they wanted. And since Thorgeir was already safely on board, Thorgils did not try to interfere further. So Thorgeir was sentenced to outlawry, but only a fine was imposed on Thormod, who was then acquitted. It was thought that Asmund and Thorstein had greatly improved their standing by this lawsuit.

Then the men rode home from the Althing. Some of them were saying that Thorgils had not pursued his case with much vigour; he paid no attention to that and let them say whatever they wanted. But when Thorgeir was told that he had been sentenced to outlawry, he said, 'I hope that those who have made me an outlaw will be fully rewarded in the end – if I can only have my way.'

There was a man called Gaut Sleituson, who was a kinsman of Thorgils Maksson, and who had taken a passage on the same ship that Thorgeir was travelling on. He growled at Thorgeir and threatened him; when the merchants saw this, they thought it out of the question to let these two men travel on the same ship. Thorgeir said he didn't care how Gaut scowled at him, but the outcome was that Gaut left the ship and travelled to the north of the land. Nothing else happened between him and Thorgeir on this occasion, but from this there grew a quarrel, as was borne out by later events.[3]

2 Skapti Thoroddsson was the Lawspeaker of the Althing from 1004 to 1030. He plays an important part in *Njal's Saga*.
3 This is an allusion to *Fóstbrœðra Saga*, chapter 15, which describes what happened later when Gaut killed Thorgeir.

28

In the summer Grettir Asmundarson came back to Iceland and landed at Skagafjord. He was then so famous for his strength that no other young man was thought comparable. He rode at once home to Bjarg, and Asmund welcomed him. By this time Atli had taken charge of the farm, and he and Grettir got on well together. Grettir had now become so arrogant that he thought nothing was too great for him.

By this time all the men had grown up who had been young when Grettir took part in the ball-game on Midfjord Lake before he went abroad. One of them was Audun,[1] who was living at Audunarstead in Vididale; he was a successful farmer and a good man. Audun was stronger than anyone else there in the north, but he was also thought to be the most peaceable man in the whole district.

It occurred to Grettir that Audun had once humiliated him in a ball-game, as was described earlier, and so he decided to find out which of them had grown stronger in the meantime. At the beginning of the hay-making season Grettir set off and went over to Audunarstead; he was wearing splendid clothing and riding on the fine painted saddle which Thorfinn had given him. He had a good horse and carried excellent weapons. It was still early in the morning when he arrived at Audunarstead and knocked on the door. There were only a few people about, and Grettir asked if Audun was at home. He was told that Audun had gone to his shieling to fetch some dairy produce.[2] Grettir unbridled his horse; the home meadow had not been mown, and the horse went to graze in the lushest part of it. Grettir entered the hall, sat down on the bench, and soon was fast asleep. A little later Audun came home and saw a horse with a painted saddle grazing in the field. He was bringing home some produce on two horses, and one of them carried milk curds in skin bags which were tied at the neck – these were called curd bags.

1 *Audun was the son of Asgeir, the son of Audun, the son of Asgeir the Rash.*
2 In Iceland, as in some other mountainous countries, it was customary to move the livestock to higher ground in the summer to make the best use of the grazing. The 'shieling' refers to the dairy and the sheds built to accommodate the herdsmen and dairymaids.

61

Audun unloaded the horses and carried the curds in his arms into the house. It seemed dark when he came inside; Grettir stretched out his foot and tripped Audun so that he fell on top of the curd bag, with the result that the band at the neck of the bag came off. Audun jumped to his feet and asked who the devil was there; Grettir gave his name.

Audun said, 'That was a stupid thing to do. What do you want here?'

'I want to fight you,' said Grettir.

'I must see to the food first,' said Audun.

'You do that,' said Grettir, 'if you have no one else you can trust with it.'

Audun stooped down to pick up the curd bag, flung it into Grettir's arms, and told him this was a present for him. Grettir was covered all over with curds and thought this a greater insult than if Audun had wounded him seriously. Then they set on each other, and there was a hard scuffle. Grettir kept going for him with great force, and Audun gave way, for he realized how much Grettir had out-grown him in strength. Everything in their way was thrown out of place as they knocked each other all over the hall. They both fought as hard as they could, but in the end Grettir gained the upper hand, and Audun was forced down, after he had torn all the weapons off Grettir. The struggle continued, and they were making a lot of noise, but then there was also a great din outside. Grettir heard someone riding up, dismounting, and coming quickly into the house, and just then a fine-looking man appeared. The newcomer was wearing a red tunic and had a helmet on his head. He had come into the hall because of all the noise he had heard when they were wrestling, and now he asked what was going on in the hall. Grettir gave his name.

'But who is asking?' he said.

'My name is Bardi,' said the stranger.

'Are you Bardi Gudmundarson of Asbjarnarness?' said Grettir.

'Yes, the very man,' he said. 'But what are you doing here?'

'Audun and I are having a bit of fun,' said Grettir.

'I'm not so sure about the fun,' said Bardi. 'You two are no match for each other: you are a trouble-maker, Grettir, and full of arrogance, but Audun is gentle and peaceable. So let him get up at once.'

'Some people reach far to get what is close at hand,' said Grettir. 'I think it's more your duty to avenge your brother Hall than to interfere in my dealings with Audun.'

'I'm always being reminded of it,' said Bardi, 'but I'm by no means sure he'll ever be avenged. Just the same, I want you to leave Audun in peace, for he is a quiet man.'

Grettir did as Bardi requested, although it was very much against his will. Bardi asked what the cause of their disagreement was. Grettir replied with this stanza:

Perhaps Audun will throttle you
for your insolence,
and make your throat all swollen,
which would be a pity.
That's what he did
to me as a boy,
a long time ago
when I was still at home.

Bardi said that he had some excuse then for taking revenge. 'And now I'm going to settle the matter between you,' he said. 'I want you to part here and now, and leave things as they are. This must be the end of your quarrel.'

They accepted this, for they were related to each other, but Grettir began then to feel some ill will towards Bardi and his brothers. Grettir joined them as they were leaving, and when they were on their way he said, 'I've been told that you intend to ride south to Borgarfjord this summer, and I want to offer to go with you, Bardi. And I think I'm being more generous than you deserve.'

Bardi was delighted, and accepted the offer quickly and gratefully. Then they parted, but Bardi turned back and said, 'I want to make one condition: you are not to come unless my foster-father Thorarin approves, for he is making the plans for the raid.'

'I thought you would be competent to make your own arrangements,' said Grettir. 'I myself don't have to beg for leave from anyone when I want to go somewhere, and I will be annoyed if you turn down my offer.'

Then each went his own way, and Bardi promised to let Grettir know if Thorarin wanted him to come; otherwise Grettir was not to go. Grettir rode back home to Bjarg, and Bardi over to his own farm.

29

In the summer a great horsefight was held at Langafit below Reykir, and many people came to it. Atli of Bjarg had a fine black-maned grey stallion of Kengala's stock, and he and his father were very fond of this horse. The brothers Kormak and Thorgils of Mel had a black stallion, a fine fighter, and they agreed to pit it against Atli's horse. There were also many other good horses there. Odd the Orphan-Poet, Kormak's kinsman, was to lead their horse in the fight. Odd had grown into a strong man, and had become boastful, quarrelsome, and reckless. Grettir asked his brother Atli who was to lead his horse.

'I'm not sure,' said Atli.

'Do you want me to give you a hand?' said Grettir.

'Then you must control yourself, brother,' said Atli, 'for we are dealing with very arrogant men.'

'Let them pay for their own insolence, if they can't curb it,' said Grettir.

The stalllions were led up, but the mares were all tied together in a group near the edge of the river bank, just above a deep pool. The stallions fought well and provided very good entertainment. Odd kept urging his horse on vigorously, but Grettir gave way. Then Grettir seized the tail of his horse with one hand, while in the other he was holding the staff with which he goaded the stallion. Odd was standing beside his horse, and was not entirely innocent of prodding at Atli's stallion as well as his own, but Grettir pretended not to notice. The stallions were moving towards the river when Odd struck at Grettir with his staff and hit him on the shoulder which was turned towards him. The blow was so heavy that the flesh swelled up, but hardly any blood was drawn. At that moment the stallions had reared themselves up, Grettir ducked under the haunches of his stallion and thrust his staff hard at Odd's chest, so that he broke three ribs and sent Odd tumbling down into the pool below; with him went his stallion and all the mares which had been tied up. Someone dived in and pulled Odd out of the river.

There was a great clamour at this. Kormak and his men seized their weapons, and so did the men of Bjarg. When the men of

Hrutafjord and Vatnsness saw this, they intervened and separated them. Then they all went back home, each side threatening the other; however, all was quiet for a while.

Atli had little to say about the incident, but Grettir was more outspoken, and said that they would meet another time, if he could have his way.

30

There was a man called Thorbjorn who lived at Thoroddstead in Hrutafjord.[1] He was an exceptionally strong man and was nicknamed Oxen-Might. He had a brother Thorodd who was nicknamed Poem-Piece.[2] Thorbjorn was a great fighter and had many men with him, but he was also noted for having more difficulty than any farmer in getting servants, for he hardly paid any wages at all. He was not considered easy to deal with.

There was another man also called Thorbjorn, and nicknamed the Traveller, who was related to Thorbjorn Oxen-Might. The two namesakes were partners, and Thorbjorn the Traveller was a seafaring man; he often stayed at Thoroddsstead, and was thought to do little to improve Thorbjorn Oxen-Might. He was a great mocker, and used to make scurrilous remarks about various people.

A man called Thorir[3] had been living at Melar in Hrutafjord, but after the killings at Fagrabrekka he moved south to Haukadale and lived at Skard. He sold the farm at Melar to Thorhall – the son of Gamli the Vinlander – who was the father of Gamli, who married Grettir's sister Rannveig. So at this time Gamli and Rannveig were living at Melar, and they were well off.

Thorir of Skard had two sons who were called Gunnar and Thorgeir; they were both promising men and had taken charge of

1 Thorbjorn was the son of Arnor Hairy-Nose, the son of Thorodd, who was the original settler of this side of Hrutafjord, as far north as Bakki.
2 Their mother was Gerd, the daughter of Bodvar of Bodvarhills.
3 Thorir was the son of Thorkel of Bordeyr. He had a daughter called Helga who married Helgi Strife. The killings at Fagrabrekka are mentioned in Landnámabók (Sturlubók, chapter 168; Hauksbók, chapter 137).

their father's farm, but they spent most of their time with Thorbjorn Oxen-Might. The brothers were very arrogant men.

In the summer Kormak and Thorgils rode with their kinsman Narfi south to Nordriverdale to deal with some business there. Odd the Orphan-Poet went with them, for he had then recovered from the injuries he had received at the horsefight.

While they were away in the south Grettir set off from Bjarg with two of Atli's servants. They rode to Burfell and then across the ridge to Hrutafjord and arrived at Melar in the evening. They stayed there for three days. Rannveig and Gamli received Grettir warmly and invited him to stay longer, but he wanted to ride back home. Then Grettir heard that Kormak and his men had come back from the south and that they had spent the night at Tongue.

Grettir set off from Melar early in the morning. Gamli asked him to be on his guard and offered to send some men with him. Gamli had a brother called Grim, an outstanding man, and he and another companion rode off with Grettir. They were five in all, and they rode on their way until they came to Hrutafjord Ridge, west of Burfell. There is a huge boulder standing there which is called Grettir's Lift, for he spent most of that day trying to lift it off the ground. He kept hard at it until Kormak came up with his men.

Grettir rode to meet them, and they all dismounted. Grettir said that it was more honourable to strike boldly with weapons than to fight with sticks like common tramps. Kormak told his men to answer bravely and to do their best. Then they went for each other and started fighting. Grettir kept in front of his men and told them to see that no one attacked him from behind. They fought for some time, and men were wounded on both sides.

Thorbjorn Oxen-Might had gone that day with some men over the ridge to Burfell, and as they were riding back home they saw the fighting. The men who were with him on this occasion were Thorbjorn the Traveller, Gunnar Thorisson and his brother Thorgeir, and Thorodd Poem-Piece. When they arrived on the scene, Thorbjorn Oxen-Might urged his men to separate the fighters but they could achieve nothing because the fighters were so furious. Grettir was making great havoc, and when the Thorissons came in his way he pushed them back so hard that they fell flat on the ground. This infuriated them, and Gunnar Thorisson struck one of Atli's servants dead. When Thorbjorn saw this he called on them to stop fighting and said he would support the side that would do as he asked. By this time two of Kormak's servants had been killed, and Grettir realized that it would not end well if Thorbjorn joined forces with the others, so he stopped fighting. All the men who had taken part in the skirmish were wounded. Grettir was not happy that they had been separated.

Then both parties rode home, and no settlement was made over the killings. Thorbjorn the Traveller made many insulting remarks about the affair, which aggravated the ill-feeling between the men of Bjarg and Thorbjorn Oxen-Might, and this grew into serious hostility, as was later revealed. Atli received no offer of compensation for the killing of his servant, and he acted as if he knew nothing about it. Grettir stayed at Bjarg until late summer; it is not mentioned anywhere that he and Kormak ever met again.

31

Bardi Gudmundarson and his brothers rode back home to Asbjarnarness after they parted from Grettir.[1] Bardi was a very noble-minded man. A little later he rode off to see his foster-father, Thorarin the Wise, who welcomed Bardi and asked what progress he had made in gathering his force, for they had previously been making plans for Bardi's expedition. Bardi replied that he had secured the help of someone whose support he thought more valuable than that of any other two men. Thorarin was silent for a moment, and then he said 'That must be Grettir Asmundarson.'

'A wise man's guess is as good as a fact,' said Bardi. 'Yes, he is the man.'

'It is true that Grettir surpasses all the men who are now living in our land,' said Thorarin, 'and it will be difficult to overcome him with weapons, as long as he is in good health. But there is too much violence in his temper, and I doubt if he will have good luck. You can't afford to have many ill-starred men in your following, and there will still be plenty of these even without him. He will certainly not go with you, if I can have my way.'

'I never expected this, foster-father,' said Bardi, 'that you would deny me the support of this man who, at any rate, is a great warrior. But it is not easy for someone who has been pushed as far as I have been to think of everything.'

1 *Bardi and his brothers were the sons of Gudmund, the son of Solmund. Solmund's mother was Thorlaug, the daughter of Sæmund the Hebridean, who was a foster-brother of Ingimund the Old.*

'You will succeed,' said Thorarin, 'as long as you leave the decisions to me.'

The outcome was that Thorarin had his way, and no message was sent to Grettir. Bardi went south to Borgarfjord, and then the Battle of the Moor was fought.[2]

Grettir was at Bjarg when he heard that Bardi had ridden south. He was furious that he had not been sent for, and said that this was not the end of their dealings. He found out when they were expected back from the south, and then he rode down to Thoreyjargnup to lie in wait for Bardi and his men. He went up the hillside behind the farm and waited there.

That day Bardi and his men were riding north from Tvidægra Moor after the battle; there were six of them, all badly wounded. When they came opposite the farm at Thoreyjargnup, Bardi said, 'There is a man up there on the hillside, a tall man carrying weapons. Can you tell who he is?'

They said they couldn't.

'I think this must be Grettir Asmundarson,' said Bardi, 'and if so he will be wanting to see us. I'm afraid that he must have been annoyed at not coming with us. But I don't think we are in very good shape just now, if he is intending to show us hostility. So I propose to send down to Thoreyjargnup for some help, since he is too violent to take chances with.'

They agreed that this was a good idea, and it was done. Bardi and the others rode on their way, and as soon as Grettir saw them he went to meet them. They greeted each other; Grettir asked for the news, and Bardi without any hesitation told him what had happened. Then Grettir asked who these men were who were with him, and Bardi said they were his brothers and his brother-in-law Eyjolf.

'Now that you have cleared your name,' said Grettir, 'the next thing is to find out which of us is stronger.'

'I have more important things to do,' said Bardi, 'than to fight with you for no reason at all. I think I can now be excused from that.'

'It seems to me that you are a coward, Bardi,' said Grettir, 'if you don't dare to fight me.'

'You can call it by any name you choose,' said Bardi, 'but if you want to be insolent, pick on someone else. It seems very likely that you

2 The Battle of the Moor and the events that led to it are described in
   Heiðarvíga Saga. This battle was supposed to have been fought in
   AD 1009, and was regarded as one of the most important events in
   early eleventh-century Iceland. Even the brief *Icelandic Annals* mention
   the battle.

will do just that, too, for you can no longer restrain your arrogance.'

Grettir did not like this prophecy, and he wavered, wondering whether he should attack one of them, but this seemed to him unwise, since there were six of them against him. At that moment several men came from Thoreyjargnup to their rescue, and Grettir moved away from them back to his horse. Bardi and his men went on their way, and there were no farewells between them when they parted. Bardi and Grettir had no further dealings after this, as far as is known.

Grettir once said that he thought he could confidently take on in fight almost any three men at a time, and that he would not flee before four men without trying, but that he would not fight against heavier odds unless he had to in order to defend his life. As he himself says in this stanza:

No matter how fierce the fighting,
I can take on any three
war-hardened warriors
and defeat them all.
But if I can have my way
I wouldn't choose to meet
more than four fighters
in a death-dealing battle.

After his parting from Bardi, Grettir went back to Bjarg. He considered it a great hardship that he could not put his strength to a real test, and so he watched for something difficult to turn up that he might tackle.

32

There was a man called Thorhall who lived at Thorhallsstead in Forsæludale, which runs from Vatnsdale.[1] He was a rich man,

---

1 *Thorhall was the son of Grim, who was the son of Thorhall, the son of*
Fridmund, who was the original settler of Forsæludale. Thorhall Grimsson
had a wife called Gudrun; their son Grim and daughter Thurid were
growing up at this time.

Forsæludale means 'Shadow Valley'; the name is an allusion to the
fact that for several weeks in midwinter the sun does not penetrate into
the bottom of the glen.

particularly in livestock; he had more animals than anyone else. He was not a chieftain, but nevertheless he was a very notable farmer.

Thorhall's farm was haunted, which made it very difficult for him to get a satisfactory shepherd. He consulted many wise men and asked them what he should do about it, but no one could solve the problem.

Thorhall, who had many excellent horses, used to ride to the Althing every summer. One summer, when he was at the Althing, Thorhall went to the booth of Skapti Thoroddsson the Lawspeaker, who was an exceptionally shrewd man and gave good advice whenever he was consulted. (There was this difference between Skapti and his father Thorodd: in spite of the fact that Thorodd was a prescient man he was considered by some to be deceitful, whereas Skapti used to give everyone the advice which he thought would be the most useful, if it were followed; that is why he was called Father-Betterer.) Thorhall went into the booth, and Skapti, who knew what a wealthy man he was, welcomed him and asked him for the news.

'I would like to get some advice from you,' said Thorhall.

'I'm not very good at that,' said Skapti. 'But what is your trouble?'

Thorhall said, 'This is the situation: I'm having much difficulty in keeping shepherds, for some of them have suffered certain injuries, and others have left before their contracts were up, and now no one who knows the circumstances is willing to take on the job.'

'Some evil creature must be at the root of this,' said Skapti, 'and that is why the shepherds are so much more reluctant to work for you than for other farmers. Now that you have sought my advice, I will get you as a shepherd a man called Glam, who is from the Sylgisdales in Sweden; he came to Iceland last summer. Glam is a big and powerful man, but few people find him very likeable.'

Thorhall said he did not mind that as long as the man could take proper care of the sheep. Skapti said that if Glam, with all his strength and courage, failed, other men would not find it an easy job. At that Thorhall left the booth. This was just before the Althing broke up.

Thorhall missed two pale-dun horses and went himself in search of them; because of this people believe that he was not an important man. He went up to Sleda Ridge and south along the mountain known as Armannsfell, and then he saw a man coming down from Goda Wood and leading a horse with a load of faggots. Soon the two men met; Thorhall asked the other his name, and he said he was called Glam. He was a huge man and very strange looking, with glaring grey eyes and a head of wolf-grey hair. Thorhall was some-what taken aback at the sight of Glam, but he realized that this must be the man he had been told about.

'For what kind of work are you best suited?' said Thorhall. Glam said he was well suited for herding sheep in winter.

'Will you herd my sheep, then?' said Thorhall. 'Skapti has entrusted you to me.'

'You'll find me most useful,' said Glam, 'if I'm left free to do things my own way, for I become angry when I'm crossed.'

'That won't do me any harm,' said Thorhall. 'I want you to work for me.'

'I might do that,' said Glam. 'But are there any problems?'

'The place is thought to be haunted,' said Thorhall.

'Spooks will never frighten me,' said Glam. 'They could only make life less dull.'

'You may find that attitude useful,' said Thorhall. 'It's certainly no place for a coward.'

They soon reached an agreement, and Glam was to come at the beginning of winter. Then they parted, and Thorhall found his horses in a place that he had just searched. He rode back and thanked Skapti for the favour he had done him.

The summer passed, and Thorhall heard nothing from the shepherd, nor did anyone seem to know anything about him, but at the arranged time he turned up at Thorhallsstead. Thorhall treated him well, but the rest of the household disliked him, Thorhall's wife in particular.

Glam took charge of the sheep, and it was an easy task for him, since he had a powerful bass voice and the sheep used to gather together whenever he shouted. There was a church at Thorhallsstead, but Glam never went there, for he hated the chants and had absolutely no faith. He was rough and repulsive, and everyone found him thoroughly obnoxious.

Time passed until the day before Christmas. Glam got up early in the morning and demanded his food. The housewife said, 'It's not the custom of Christians to eat today, for tomorrow is the first day of Christmas, and so it's our duty to fast all day.'

He answered, 'You have many superstitions which I consider quite pointless. I can't see that people are any better off nowadays than they were before when they didn't bother with such nonsense. I liked the old customs better when people were still heathens. I want my food now, and I'll have none of this quibbling.'

The housewife said, 'I know for certain that this will be a sorry day for you, since you take this evil course.'

71

Glam told her to bring his food at once, and said that otherwise it would be the worse for her. She didn't dare refuse, and when he had finished his meal he went out in an ugly mood.

It was very dark outside, with fluttering snowflakes and a howling wind. The weather grew worse and worse as the day wore on. During the morning the people could hear the shepherd clearly, but less so in the afternoon. Then the snow began to drift, and in the evening the weather turned into a blizzard.

People went to church for mass, and so time passed until nightfall, but Glam did not come home. There was some discussion of whether or not he should be searched for, but because of the snowstorm and the darkness nothing came of it.

Glam did not come home Christmas Eve. The people waited until mass was over, and when it was broad daylight several men set out in search of him, and found the sheep scattered about in snowdrifts, beaten down by the storm or straying up on the mountain. Then they came upon a large area of trampled snow high up in the valley; it seemed to them as if a violent struggle had taken place there, for in many places stones as well as earth had been torn up. When they searched more carefully they saw Glam lying near by; he was dead, and his body was dark-blue in colour and swollen up to the size of an ox. They were horrified and shrank back from the corpse. However, they tried to carry it down to the church, but they could drag it no farther than down to the edge of a ravine a little distance away.

So they went back home and told Thorhall what had happened. He asked them what could have brought about Glam's death, and they told him they had traced some footprints so huge that they were just as if the bottom of a cask had been thrown down, and that they led right up to the cliffs at the head of the valley – there had been large splashes of blood all along the track. Because of this people thought that the monster which had been there before must have killed Glam, and also that he must have wounded the monster fatally, for there has never been any sign of it since.

On the second day of Christmas another attempt was made to take Glam's body to church. Oxen were used to haul it along, but they could not move it at all when the slope stopped and they came to level ground. And so they had to give up.

On the third day of Christmas a priest came along with them, and they searched for Glam the whole day without finding him. The priest refused to go again, but Glam was found at once when the priest was not among the searchers. Eventually they abandoned the attempt to bring Glam to church, and buried him in a cairn just where he was.

A little later the people found that Glam was not lying quiet. Terrible things happened; many men fell unconscious at the sight of him, and others lost their sanity. Soon after Christmas, people began to see him walking about the farmhouse and were terrified by him; many of them fled away. Then Glam began to sit astride the roof at night and beat it so furiously with his heels that the house came near to breaking. Soon he was walking about day and night, and men hardly found the courage to go up the valley, even on urgent business. All this was a great calamity for the people in the district.

33

In the spring Thorhall engaged new servants and started farming again. The hauntings diminished as the days grew longer, and so time passed until midsummer.

That summer a ship from abroad put in at Hunavatn, and on board was a foreigner called Thorgaut. He was tall and powerful, with the strength of two men. He was on his own, without a job, and he needed to find some employment, since he had no money. Thorhall rode to the ship, saw Thorgaut, and asked if he were willing to work for him. Thorgaut said he was, and added that he was not very particular.

'I must warn you,' said Thorhall, 'that it is no place for weaklings, since the farm has been haunted for some time. I have no wish to deceive you in any way.'

'I can't see myself giving up, even though I should meet some spooks,' said Thorgaut. 'Other men will certainly find it hard to put up with, if it frightens me, and I'm not going to back out on that account.'

They soon came to an agreement, and Thorgaut was to be in charge of the sheep the following winter. The summer passed, and at the beginning of winter Thorgaut began herding the sheep. Everyone liked him.

Glam used to come to the house and sit astride the roof. Thorgaut thought this very amusing, and said the rascal would have to come closer before he was frightened by him. Thorhall warned him to be careful. 'It would be better if you were not to confront him.'

'It is obvious that every trace of courage has been shaken out of all of you,' said Thorgaut, 'but this nonsense is not going to frighten me out of my wits just yet.'

Winter passed until it was Christmas, and on the day before Christmas, when the shepherd was leaving the house to herd the sheep, the housewife said to him, 'I very much hope that the old story will not repeat itself now.'

'Have no fear of that, woman,' said Thorgaut. 'Something worth telling will have to happen before I fail to come back.'

Then he went to his sheep. It was a cold day, and snowing heavily. Thorgaut usually returned home at twilight, but that day he did not come back. People went to church as usual, and it seemed to them that the turn of events was not unfamiliar. Thorhall wanted to organize a search for the shepherd, but the church-goers were unwilling and said they were not going to expose themselves to trolls in the night. The farmer did not have the courage to go by himself, so nothing came of the search.

After breakfast on Christmas Day several men set out in search of the shepherd. First they went to Glam's cairn, for they thought he must have been responsible for the shepherd's disappearance. As they approached the cairn they saw that something remarkable must have happened, and indeed the shepherd was found there with his neck broken and every bone in his body crushed. They brought him back to church, and no one suffered any harm from him afterwards.

Glam began asserting himself even more than ever before, and now he committed so many outrages that the entire household fled away from Thorhallsstead, except for the farmer and his wife. The same cowherd had been there for a long time, and Thorhall did not want him to leave, for the cowherd was a kind man and good at his job. He was getting on in years and very loath to leave; he realized that everything the farmer owned would soon be destroyed if there was no one there to look after the farm.

One morning after midwinter the farmer's wife went to the cowshed to milk the cows at the usual time. It was broad daylight by then, for no one risked going out earlier, except for the cowherd, who used to go out at dawn. The woman heard a crashing noise and a terrible bellowing from the cowshed, so she ran screaming back into the house and said she didn't know what horrible things were happening there.

The farmer went out, and when he came to the cows he found them all goring one another. He didn't like the look of this at all, and went inside. Then he saw where the cowherd was lying on his back with his head in one stall and his feet in another. The farmer went up to him, felt him, and found that he was dead, with his back broken. It had been broken on the edge of the raised slab of stone which separated the two stalls.

The farmer realized that it was impossible for him to stay there any longer, so he fled, taking away with him as many possessions as he could. Every single beast which he left behind was killed by Glam. Then Glam started going through the entire valley, and he laid waste all the farms up from Tongue. Thorhall stayed with friends for the rest of the winter. No one could go to the upper reaches of the valley with a horse or a dog, for it was sure to be killed at once.

In the spring when the days became longer, the hauntings lessened somewhat, and Thorhall wanted to get back to his farm. He had great difficulty in engaging servants, yet he started farming again at Thorhallsstead. Everything happened just as before: when the autumn set in, the hauntings grew worse again. This time it was the farmer's daughter who suffered the most, and eventually she died as the result. Many remedies were tried, but they were all in vain. It seemed obvious to everyone that Vatnsdale would be all laid waste, unless some solution could be found.

34

Now the story goes back to Grettir Asmundarson, who stayed home at Bjarg through the autumn after his encounter with Bardi at Thoreyjargnup. Just before the beginning of winter Grettir set out from home and rode north across the ridges over to Vididale, and stayed at Audunarstead overnight. He and Audun were fully reconciled; Grettir gave him a fine axe as a present, and they agreed to remain friends.[1]

Grettir rode north to Vatnsdale and paid a visit at Tongue, where his uncle Jokul Bardarson was living at the time. Jokul was a tall strong man, and exceptionally arrogant. He was a seafarer, very difficult to deal with, but a man of considerable importance. Jokul

---

1 *Audun lived at Audunarstead for a long time, and had many descendants. His son was Egil, who married Ulfheid, the daughter of Eyjolf Gudmundarson, and their son was Eyjolf, who was killed at the Althing; this Eyjolf was the father of Orm, Bishop Thorlak's chaplain.* Thorlak Thorhallsson (St Thorlak) was bishop of Skalholt from 1176 to 1193.

gave Grettir a good welcome, and he stayed there for three days. By this time Glam's reappearances were so much discussed that people talked about hardly anything else. Grettir enquired closely about all that had happened, and Jokul said that the stories did not exaggerate the facts. 'Do you want to pry into matters there, kinsman?' he asked.

Grettir said he did, but Jokul warned him not to go. 'That would be tempting fate,' he said. 'Your kinsmen have much at stake where you are concerned, for we feel that now there is no young man to compare with you. From evil beings like Glam only evil can be gained, and it is always better to deal with human beings than with monsters of his kind.'

Grettir said he still wanted very much to go to Thorhallsstead and see what had been going on.

Jokul said, 'I see that there is no point in trying to discourage you. The old saying is certainly true that "Good luck and great ability are two different things." '

' "Disaster is close to your own house once it has entered your neighbour's." So you should rather be thinking about what will happen to you in the end,' said Grettir.[2]

Jokul replied, 'It might be that both of us are able to see into the future, and also that neither of us can do anything about it.'

With that they parted, and neither of them liked the other's predictions.

35

Grettir rode over to Thorhallsstead and the farmer welcomed him warmly. He asked Grettir where he was going, and Grettir said he would like to spend the night there, if the farmer didn't mind. Thorhall said he would be very grateful if Grettir stayed. 'But lately few people have found it desirable to spend any time here. You must have heard about our trouble, and I shoudn't like you to come to grief because of me. Even if you manage to get safely away yourself, I know for certain that you will lose your horse, for no one who comes here can keep his horse safe.'

2 Grettir's remark is a prophetic allusion to the fact that King Olaf
   Haraldsson had Jokul put to death several years later, as is related in
   St Olaf's Saga.

Grettir said that horses were easy enough to get, if anything should happen to his. Thorhall was delighted that Grettir was staying and received him with open arms. They stabled Grettir's horse and put a strong lock on the door, and then they went to bed. The night passed and Glam did not come to the house.

Thorhall said, 'Your visit has certainly brought about an improvement here, for Glam has been in the habit of straddling the roof or breaking the doors every night, as indeed you can see clearly for yourself.'

Grettir said, 'This can mean only one of two things: either Glam will resume his old habit very soon, or else he will give it up for more than one night. So I'm going to stay another night and see what happens.'

Then they went to Grettir's horse, and he had not been tampered with. The farmer thought that every sign was pointing the same way. Grettir stayed for the second night, and the thrall did not come to the house. The farmer thought this very promising, and went to look at Grettir's horse, but this time the stable had been broken into, the horse dragged out through the door, and every bone in its body broken apart.

Thorhall told Grettir what had happened, and said that he should save his own life. 'You are sure to die if you wait for Glam,' he said.

Grettir answered, 'The very least I can have in return for my horse is to get a glimpse of the thrall.'

The farmer said that it would do him no good to see Glam. 'For he does not look like any human being,' he said. 'But every hour that you are willing to spend here is a great comfort for me.'

The day passed, and when the people went to bed, Grettir did not take off his clothes, but lay down on the bench opposite the farmer's bedcloset. He covered himself with a shaggy fur cloak, wrapping one end of it around his feet and the other around his head in such a way that he could see out through the neck-hole. The front bench-board was strong, and Grettir put his feet against it. The entire frame of the outer door had been broken away, and a crude hurdle tied carelessly in its place. The wooden partition which before had separated the hall from the entrance passage was also broken away, both below and above the crossbeam. All the beds had been moved out of place, and the house seemed rather uninviting. A light was kept burning in the hall throughout the night.

When about a third of the night had passed, Grettir heard a great noise outside. Someone seemed to be climbing the house and then straddling the roof-top above the hall, and beating his heels against the roof so that every beam in the house was cracking. This went on for a long time, and then it was as if someone was climbing down from the roof, and coming to the door. Then the door was opened, and Grettir saw the thrall stretching his head through it, and the head was hideously huge, with enormous features.

Glam moved slowly, and when he was inside the door he stretched himself up to his full height so that he towered up to the rafters. He turned towards the hall, laid his arms on the crossbeam, and stretched his head into the hall. The farmer did not utter a single sound, for he thought that the noise outside had been quite enough. Grettir lay still and did not move at all.

Glam noticed a heap lying on the bench, so he crossed the hall and pulled hard at the cloak, but Grettir braced his feet against the beam and did not budge. Glam pulled at the cloak a second time, and much harder, but the cloak did not move at all. The third time Glam seized hold of the cloak with both hands and pulled at it so violently that Grettir was forced up from the bench, and then they tore the cloak in two between them.

Glam looked at the torn piece he held in his hand and wondered who could have pulled so hard against him. At that moment Grettir leapt under his arms, grasped him around the waist, and clasped him as hard as he could, hoping to bring him down. But the thrall gripped his arms so tightly that he was forced to break away. Grettir kept retreating from one bench to the other, and they started breaking up the beams and smashing everything that was in their way. Glam wanted to get outside, but Grettir braced his feet against anything he could, and yet Glam succeeded in dragging him out of the hall. Then they had a fierce struggle, for the thrall wanted to force Grettir out of the house, but Grettir realized that, difficult as it was to deal with Glam inside, it would be even worse in the open, and so he struggled with all his might against being dragged outside.

Glam was now using all his power, and when he reached the vestibule he pulled Grettir towards him. Grettir realized that he could resist no longer, and so he flung himself violently into the thrall's arms and at the same time braced his feet against a half-sunken boulder that stood in the entrance. Glam had been striving hard to pull Grettir his way, so he was unprepared for this. He fell backwards and crashed out through the door, his shoulders catching the lintel so that the roof was torn apart, both the rafters and the frozen roof-sods, and as he fell on his back out of the house, Grettir landed on top of him.

Outside the moonlight was bright but intermittent, for there were dark clouds which passed before the moon and then went away. At the very moment when Glam fell, the clouds cleared away, and

Glam glared up at the moon. Grettir himself once said that that was the only sight he ever saw which frightened him. Then, because of exhaustion and the sight of Glam rolling his eyes so fiercely, Grettir was overcome by such a faintness that he could not draw his short sword, and so he remained there lying closer to death than to life.

Glam, who was endowed with more power for evil than any other revenant, then spoke the following words:

'You have been very determined to meet me, Grettir, but it will hardly surprise you if you do not get much luck from me. I will tell you this: you have acquired by now only half of the strength and vigour which you were destined to get if you had not met me. I cannot take away from you what you already have, but I can see to it that you will never be stronger than you are now, and yet you are strong enough, as many will find to their cost. Up until now your deeds have brought you fame, but from now on outlawry and slaughter will come your way, and most of your acts will bring you ill luck and misfortune. You will be made an outlaw and forced to live by yourself. I also lay this curse on you: you will always see before you these eyes of mine, and they will make your solitude unbearable, and this shall drag you to your death.'

As soon as Glam had spoken these words the faintness that had come over Grettir left him. He drew his short sword, cut off Glam's head, and placed it against his buttocks.

Then the farmer came outside. He had put on his clothes while Glam was making his speech, but had not dared to come anywhere near until Glam was laid low. Thorhall praised God and thanked Grettir warmly for vanquishing this unclean spirit. Then they set to work and burned Glam to ashes, gathered them into a skin bag, and buried them at a place far away from all paths of men and pastures of animals. After that they went back home. It was about daybreak, and Grettir lay down to rest, for he was very stiff.

Thorhall sent for men from the neighbouring farms, and showed them and told them what had happened. All who heard about this deed were greatly impressed by it, and said that no man in the entire country was Grettir Asmundarson's equal in strength, in courage, or in accomplishments. Thorhall gave him fine gifts when he left, a good horse, and splendid clothes, for the ones he had been wearing were torn into tatters. They parted the best of friends.

From there Grettir rode over to As in Vatnsdale. Thorvald gave him a good welcome, and questioned him closely about his encounter with Glam. Grettir told him all about their dealings and said that this long struggle had been the greatest test of his strength he had ever experienced. Thorvald warned Grettir to restrain himself. 'If you do that, all will go well with you, but otherwise you will have much bad luck.'

Grettir said that this incident had done little to improve his temper, and that he had now much less control over himself than before, and found it more difficult to put up with any offences. He also said that he could notice one change: he had become so frightened of the dark that he did not dare go anywhere alone after nightfall, because all kinds of phantoms appeared to him then. It has since become a common saying that people who suffer hallucinations have Glam's vision, or that Glam has lent them his eyes.

Afterwards Grettir rode back home to Bjarg, and he stayed there for the rest of the winter.

36

Thorbjorn Oxen-Might held a great autumn feast, and had many guests. It took place while Grettir was north in Vatnsdale. Thorbjorn the Traveller was at the feast, and there was a great deal of gossip. The men of Hrutafjord asked about the encounter on the ridge the summer before; Thorbjorn Oxen-Might gave a good account of Grettir and said that Kormak would have got the worst of it if no one had turned up to separate them. Then Thorbjorn the Traveller said, 'It is certainly true that I didn't see Grettir doing anything to his credit, and I even think he was scared when we arrived on the scene, for he was very eager to leave and he made no attempt to seek vengeance for Atli's servant who was killed there. So in my opinion Grettir has no courage unless he has plenty of men to back him up.'

Thorbjorn the Traveller had a great many other abusive remarks to make about this, but most people disagreed with him and said this was foolish talk, for Grettir would never let the matter rest there if he came to hear of these words. Nothing else happened at the feast, and when it was over the guests went back home.

There was much ill-feeling between the two sides that winter, but neither attacked the other, and nothing more happened then.

37

Early next spring, before the Althing assembled, a ship arrived from Norway. The crew had great news to tell: first, that there had been a change of rulers in Norway, for King Olaf Haraldsson had come to power and Earl Svein had been driven out of the country that spring after the battle of Nesjar.[1] A good many remarkable things were told of King Olaf, and also that he welcomed most those who were in some way outstanding men and made them his retainers. Many of the young men were pleased to hear this and wanted to go abroad. When Grettir was told the news, he was also eager to sail abroad, for like the rest he expected to get some honours from the king. A ship was lying at Gasir in Eyjafjord, and Grettir got a passage on it. He made ready for the voyage, although he still did not have much to take with him.

Asmund was now becoming worn with old age, and hardly ever left his bed. He and Asdis had a young son called Illugi, who was very promising. Atli was in charge of the farm and managed the money affairs; everything seemed to have improved, for he was kind and shrewd.

Grettir travelled to the ship, but Thorbjorn the Traveller had also got a passage on it before it was known that Grettir was sailing. Everyone tried to dissuade Thorbjorn from sailing on the same ship as Grettir, but he said he was going for all that. So he made ready for the voyage, but was rather late, for he did not come north to Gasir until the ship was ready to put out to sea. Just before Thorbjorn left home in the west, Asmund Grey-Locks fell ill, and he was confined to his bed.

It was late in the afternoon when Thorbjorn the Traveller arrived on the beach, and the crew were getting ready for their meal and washing their hands outside the booths.[2] Thorbjorn rode down the

1   The battle of Nesjar in the west of Norway was fought in 1015. It is described in *St Olaf's Saga.*
2   Booths were shelters which had walls of turf and stone, but no permanent roofs.

passage between the booths, and they greeted him and asked the news. He said he had none to tell, 'Except that I think that the great champion Asmund of Bjarg must be dead by now.'

They said that then an important farmer had departed from the world. 'But how did it happen?' they asked.

Thorbjorn said, 'The champion came to a sorry end, for he suffocated like a dog in the smoke of his own fireplace. But he was senile already, so he was no loss.'

They said, 'This is a strange way of talking about a man like him, and Grettir is not going to like this if he should hear of it.'

'I can endure that,' said Thorbjorn. 'Grettir will have to raise his short sword higher than he did last summer on Hrutafjord Ridge before he frightens me.'

Grettir heard every word Thorbjorn said, but he did nothing while Thorbjorn was talking. When he stopped, Grettir said, 'I can tell this of your future, Traveller, that you will never suffocate in the smoke of a room, and yet it may be that you will not die of old age. It is curious why anyone should wish to speak so shamefully about innocent people.'

Thorbjorn said, 'I have nothing to take back, and you did not seem so particularly brave when we saved you from the men of Melar, who were beating you like an ox's head.'

Grettir spoke this stanza:

Some men have tongues
too long and too ready to speak;
that's how they earn
harsh revenge.
But few men have done
more evil than you,
and now your life is forfeit,
your long journey is over.

Thorbjorn answered, 'I think I am no closer to death, for all your babbling.'

Grettir said, 'So far my predictions have never had to outlive their promise, and this one is not likely to, either. Defend yourself, if you want to; you will never have a better opportunity.'

Then Grettir struck at Thorbjorn, who raised his hand with the intention of warding the sword off, but it caught his arm just above the wrist and then swept on at his neck, cutting his head off. The traders said that he was a dealer of heavy blows, as the king's re-tainers were supposed to be, but they thought it no loss that Thor-bjorn had been killed, for he had been quarrelsome and spiteful.

A little afterwards they put out to sea, and late in the summer they reached Hordaland in south Norway. Then they heard that King Olaf was in residence north at Trondheim. Grettir got a passage north on a cargo boat, for he wanted to see the king.

38

There was a man called Thorir who lived at Gard in Adaldale,[1] a notable chieftain and seafarer. He had two sons who were called Thorgeir and Skeggi, both of them young and promising men at this time. Thorir, who had been in Norway in the summer that King Olaf came back east from England, had become a close friend of the king and also of Bishop Sigurd, as can be seen from the fact that Thorir had a large ship built in a forest and asked Bishop Sigurd to consecrate it, which he did. After that Thorir returned to Iceland, and when he tired of seafaring he had the ship broken up. He took the beaks of the prow and stern and fitted them over the main door of his house. They were there for a long time afterwards, and were so weather-wise that one of them used to whistle to foretell a south wind, and the other to foretell a north wind.

When Thorir heard that King Olaf had become the sole ruler of Norway, he thought he had a claim on his friendship, so he sent his sons to Norway to see the king, in the hope that they would become his retainers. They made land in southern Norway late in the autumn, and hired a skiff in which they sailed north along the coast, so that they could meet the king. South of Stad they came to a certain harbour and stayed there for several days. They indulged themselves in food and drink, and only went outside when the weather was good.

Meanwhile, Grettir also was making his way north along the coast. This was at the beginning of winter, and the weather was foul. When they were approaching Stad the weather became particularly bad, with a freezing blizzard, and one evening they just managed to steer the ship up to a grassy bank. Although they were exhausted, they were able to save all their goods and baggage. The

1 *Thorir was the son of Skeggi, who was the son of Bodolf. Skeggi*
  was the first settler of Kelduhverfi, as far up as Keldunness. He married
  Helga, the daughter of Thorgeir of Fiskibrook.

merchants complained bitterly that they had no fire, and thought that because of this their very lives were in danger. When they had been in this distress for most of the evening, they noticed a fire burning on the other side of the channel. When Grettir's shipmates saw it, they said that he would be a lucky man who could bring them fire, but they doubted whether they could sail there, and it seemed too risky. Then they started an argument whether anyone would be capable of fetching the fire. Grettir paid little attention to their argument, yet he said that once there had been men who would not have shrunk from it. The merchants said that it was little help to them what sort of men there once had been, if they were unavailable now. 'Perhaps you think you can do it yourself, Grettir?' they said. 'You are called the most capable man in the whole of Iceland, and you must realize how vital this is for us.'

Grettir said, 'I don't think it is a very difficult job to get the fire, but I'm not so sure that you will pay the reward that will be expected for it.'

They said, 'Why do you think that we are so dishonourable that we will not repay you properly for it?'

'Since you think this is so terribly urgent, I can try to do it,' said Grettir, 'But I have the feeling that this will turn out badly for me.'

They said that this could never happen, and wished him the best of luck for his brave words. Then Grettir made ready for the swim: he stripped, then put on a tunic and trousers of home-spun cloth, tucked up the tunic, and wound a bast rope around his waist. After that he seized a wooden tub and dived overboard. He swam straight across the channel, and when he came ashore on the other side he saw a house there, and from it he could hear loud voices and clamour. He went up to the house.

Inside this house were the sons of Thorir who were mentioned before. They had been there for several days waiting for the weather to improve and for a wind that would carry them north beyond Stad. There were twelve of them there, and they were all drinking. Their ship was in the main harbour, and the house they were in had been built as a shelter for the use of sailors on the coastal run. A great deal of straw had been collected inside, and they had a blazing fire.

Grettir burst suddenly into the house, and he had no idea who the people inside it were. His tunic had frozen hard as soon as he emerged from the water, and he was a terrifying sight, as huge as a troll. The men inside were startled by his appearance, and thought he must be an evil monster. So they started beating him with anything they could lay their hands on, and there was a great commotion, but Grettir kept warding them off strongly with his arms. Some of them were hitting him with burning logs, and the fire was flying all over the house. Then Grettir managed to get out with the fire he wanted, and so he swam back to his companions. They praised him highly for his brave achievement, and said that he could have no equal. They were delighted to have the fire, and so the night passed.

The next morning the weather was fine. The merchants woke up early and made ready to continue their journey, and then they said that they had better see the people who had had the fire, and find out who they were. So they cast off and went across the channel, but there they found no house, only a large heap of ashes with a lot of human bones. It seemed obvious to them that the house must have been burnt down with all the men inside it; they asked Grettir if he was responsible for this disaster, and said it was a terrible crime. Grettir answered that he had been right when he suspected that they would not repay him well for fetching the fire, and he added that it was a foolish thing to give help to worthless men.

This accident caused Grettir much trouble, for wherever the merchants went they said that Grettir had burned these people to death in the house. It soon became known that the victims of the fire were the sons of Thorir of Gard, who were mentioned before, and their companions. The merchants threw Grettir out and refused to have anything to do with him, and he became so despised that hardly anyone was willing to do him a good turn. The outlook seemed very bleak to him, but he wanted above anything else to see the king, so he kept trying to get north to Trondheim, where the king was in residence. The king had heard the whole story before Grettir arrived, and he had been told a good many slanderous things about him. Grettir stayed for several days in town before he could get an audience with the king.

39

One day when the king was in council, Grettir went before him and greeted him respectfully. The king looked at him and said, 'Are you Grettir the Strong?'

'So I have been called,' he replied. 'I have come here in the hope that you would help me to be exonerated from the evil charge which has been levelled against me, for I'm in no way to blame for the accident.'

'You are certainly a brave man,' said King Olaf, 'but I'm not sure that you will have good luck in clearing your name of this charge. However, it seems more likely than not that you didn't burn these men deliberately.'

Grettir said that he was very eager to be cleared of the charge, if the king thought it possible. The king asked him to describe truthfully what had happened, and Grettir gave a full account of everything, just as it occurred. He added that all the men had been alive when he left the house with the fire. 'And now I wish to submit myself to any ordeal that you may think the law may demand,' he said.

'We shall grant you leave to be tried with the ordeal of carrying hot iron, so that you may have a chance to clear yourself,' said King Olaf.

Grettir was pleased at this and began to fast for the ordeal, and so time passed until the appointed day. Then the king and the bishop went to church with a great number of people, for many were curious to see Grettir because of all the stories about him. Grettir himself was led to the church, and when he arrived many people kept looking at him and saying how his strength and stature marked him out from all other men. As he was walking down the aisle, a youth with an unpleasant look on his face suddenly jumped forward and said to Grettir, 'How remarkable it is that in this country, where the people are supposed to be Christians, all sorts of criminals, robbers, and thieves can move about freely and are allowed to undergo ordeals. What is a wicked man more likely to do than to save his own skin as long as he possibly can? Now, there is an evildoer who has been proved guilty of burning innocent people to death, yet he gets the privilege of an ordeal. This is outrageous.'

Then he went up to Grettir, cocked a finger at him, made grimaces, and called him a son of a sea-witch and many other names. Grettir grew angry and lost control of himself. He raised his fist and boxed the boy on the ear, knocking him senseless, and some people said that the boy died on the spot. No one could tell where the boy had come from or what became of him afterwards, but it is thought most likely that he was an unclean spirit which had been sent to bring ill luck to Grettir.

This caused a great tumult in the church, and King Olaf was told that the man who was supposed to undergo the ordeal had started fighting. The king came forward and saw what was going on.

'You are a man of much ill luck, Grettir,' he said. 'In spite of all the preparations for it, the ordeal can't take place now. Your ill luck is not easily turned aside.'

'I had expected, sir, that for my family's sake I would get more honour from you than I seem likely to get now,' said Grettir.

Then he told the king about their relationship, which has been described already.[1] 'I should very much like you to accept me as your retainer,' Grettir continued. 'Many of the men with you will not be thought better warriors than me.'

'I realize that few men alive now equal you in strength and valour,' said the king. 'But your ill luck is so great that you cannot stay with us. You are free to spend the winter wherever you please, but next summer you must go back to Iceland, for that is where you are fated to die.'

Grettir said, 'First I should like to clear my name of the charge of arson, if I'm allowed to, for I did not do it intentionally.'

'That may well be so,' said the king, 'but since your lack of patience ruined the ordeal you cannot now vindicate yourself, and you must let matters rest as they are. Thoughtlessness always leads to trouble. If anyone has ever been accursed, that man must be you.'

Grettir stayed in town for a little while, and this was all the help he got from the king. Then he travelled south with the intention of visiting his brother Thorstein the Galleon at Tonsberg, and there is nothing to tell of his journey until he arrived east in Jæderen.

40

At Christmas Grettir came to a certain farmer called Einar; he was a wealthy man with a wife and a young unmarried daughter called Gyrid, who was very beautiful and was considered a fine match. Einar invited Grettir to stay for Christmas, and he accepted.

At that time it happened in many parts of Norway that outlaws and criminals would come suddenly out of the forests and challenge farmers to duels for their women, or take their possessions by force wherever there were few men to protect them. One day during Christmas a number of troublemakers came down to Einar's farm. Their leader, Snækoll, who was a great berserk, challenged Einar

1 King Olaf and Grettir were third cousins. See the footnote on page 3.

to give him his daughter, or else to defend her if he thought he was man enough. The farmer was past the prime of life and no fighter, so he found himself in a difficult position, and asked Grettir in a low voice what he would suggest – 'Since you are considered a famous man.'

Grettir told him not to agree to anything which he considered disgraceful. The berserk was still on horseback; he was wearing a helmet with the face-guard unclasped and holding an iron-rimmed shield in front of him, so that he appeared very menacing.

He told the farmer, 'You must make your choice at once. What is that big oaf beside you telling you to do? Could it be that he is willing to play games with me?'

'The farmer and I are two of a kind,' said Grettir. 'Neither of us is keen on trouble.'

'You would be really frightened to deal with me,' said Snækoll, 'if I got angry.'

'That remains to be seen,' said Grettir.

When the berserk realized that he was not getting anywhere by talking he began to howl loudly and bite at the rim of his shield. Then he put it into his mouth, kept his mouth wide open over the horn of the shield, and raged furiously. Grettir raced across to him, and when he came beside the berserk's horse he kicked the lower end of the shield so hard that he drove the shield up into the berserk's mouth, splitting it wide open so that his lower jaws were dangling down to his chest. Next Grettir did two things at the same time: he seized the berserk's helmet with his left hand and pulled him off his horse, and with his right hand he drew the short sword which he was wearing and aimed it at the berserk's neck, slicing his head off.

When Snækoll's companions saw this, they scattered in all directions. Grettir did not bother to chase them, because he knew them all to be cowards. The farmer and many others thanked him warmly for what he had done, and this achievement was thought to have been done with great resolution and boldness. Grettir stayed there for the rest of Christmas enjoying much hospitality, and the farmer gave him fine gifts when he left. Grettir travelled east to Tonsberg to see his brother Thorstein, who received him with open arms and asked about his travels and his triumph over the berserk.

Grettir spoke this stanza:

I kicked the berserk's shield
and drove it hard against
his foul feeding-hatch
with my hard-hitting foot.

The iron-clad shield
split his tooth-house right open,
so his jaws came apart
and dangled down his chest.

Thorstein said, 'You would get far in many ways, brother, if bad luck did not dog you.'

Grettir replied, 'Yet what is done will be told of.'

41

Grettir stayed with Thorstein for the rest of the winter and into the following spring. One morning, when they were both lying in the bedroom upstairs, Grettir stretched his arms out from under the bedclothes, and Thorstein, who was already awake, kept looking at them. Grettir woke up a little later.

'I have been watching your arms, brother,' said Thorstein. 'And it doesn't seem strange now that many men have felt your blows to be heavy, because I have never seen such arms on any man.'

'You might have known,' said Grettir, 'that I would not have been able to achieve so much if I had been a weakling.'

'I think it would have been better,' said Thorstein, 'if your arms were thinner and somewhat luckier.'

Grettir said, 'The old saying is true, that no man is his own creator. Let me see your arms.'

Thorstein showed them to him. He was exceptionally tall and slenderly built. Grettir smiled and said, 'There is no need to take a longer look: I can see how your ribs are all hooked together, and I have never seen anything more like a pair of tongs than your arms. I think you're hardly as strong as a woman.'

'That may be so,' said Thorstein. 'But yet you should know that these slender arms of mine will avenge you – or else you will never be avenged at all.'

'How can we know what may happen in the end?' said Grettir. 'But I think this is very unlikely.'

There is nothing more told about their conversation. Later in the spring Grettir got himself a passage on a ship and sailed back to Iceland. The brothers parted in good friendship, and never met again.

42

Now the story continues where it broke off earlier. Thorbjorn Oxen-Might learned that Thorbjorn the Traveller had been killed, as was described before. He was furious when he heard about it, and said he wanted to settle this score.

Asmund Grey-Locks lay ill in bed most of the summer and when he felt his strength was waning he summoned his kinsmen and told them that he wanted Atli to take over the entire estate after his death.

'Yet I am afraid troublemakers will not leave you in peace,' said Asmund. 'So I want my kinsmen to give him all the help they can. I shall not say anything about Grettir, because his luck seems to be on a rolling wheel. Although he is a strong man I'm afraid he will have so much trouble on his hands that he will never be able to give any support to his kinsmen. Illugi is still very young, but he will become a valiant man if he can keep out of harm's way.'

When Asmund had made all the arrangements he wanted for his sons, his illness took a turn for the worse. He died a little later and was buried at Bjarg where he had already built a church. The people in the district thought him a great loss.

Atli soon became a prosperous farmer and had many men with him. He was a good provider, and late in the summer he went west to Snæfellsness to buy dried fish. He set off with a number of pack-horses and rode over to Melar in Hrutafjord to his brother-in-law Gamli. Gamli's brother, Grim Thorhallsson, and another man joined him there. They rode west through Haukadale Pass and followed the usual route west to Snæfellsness. There they bought a lot of dried fish, which they loaded on seven pack-horses, and when they were ready they set off for home.

43

Thorbjorn Oxen-Might heard that Atli and Grim had set off from home. At this time Gunnar and Thorgeir, the sons of Thorir of Skard, were staying with him. Thorbjorn was envious of Atli's popularity, and so he urged the Thorrissons to ambush Atli on his way back home from Snæfellsness. The Thorissons rode home to Skard and waited there for Atli and his men to pass by with their pack-horses. When Atli passed the farm at Skard the people there saw them, and the brothers wasted no time but took their servants and rode off after them. Atli saw them coming and told his men to unload the horses.

'The Thorissons must be intending to offer me compensation for my servant whom Gunnar killed last summer,' said Atli. 'We mustn't be the first to attack, but we will defend ourselves if they begin the fight.'

The pursuers now came up and jumped off their horses. Atli greeted them and asked them the news. 'Gunnar, are you going to pay me some compensation for my servant?' he added.

Gunnar said, 'You men of Bjarg deserve something else rather than compensation for that. The death of Thorbjorn the Traveller, whom Grettir killed, needs to be paid for much more urgently.'

'That has nothing to do with me,' said Atli, 'and you are not the plaintiff in that lawsuit, either.'

Gunnar said that this made no difference. 'Now let's attack them and make some use of Grettir's absence.'

There were eight of them together, and they set on Atli, who had five men with him. Atli moved ahead of his men, and drew the sword which Jokul had once owned and which Grettir had given to Atli.

Then Thorgeir said, 'All these bold men have a great deal in common: Grettir carried his short sword high last summer at Hrutafjord Ridge.'

Atli said, 'But he must be more used to this kind of work than I am.'

Then they started fighting. Gunnar was in a furious mood and kept attacking Atli fiercely. When they had been fighting for a while,

Atli said, 'It's no credit for us to be killing each other's servants, and it would be more fitting if we were to settle the issue between ourselves – though I have never fought with weapons before.'

Gunnar would not agree, but Atli told his servants to look after the horses. 'I'm going to find out what these men can do.'

Then he started fighting so hard that Gunnar and his men had to fall back, and Atli killed two of them. After that he turned against Gunnar and aimed a blow at him which sliced across his shield just below the handle and went right into his leg below the knee. He followed this up at once with a second blow which gave Gunnar his death wound.

Meanwhile, Grim Thorhallsson attacked Thorgeir and they fought for a long time, because both were powerful men. When Thorgeir saw that his brother Gunnar had fallen, he tried to get away. Grim ran after him and chased him until Thorgeir stumbled and fell flat on the ground. Then Grim struck his axe between his shoulders, and it went deep into his body. They spared the lives of the three others. Then they bound up their wounds, loaded the packs on the horses, and rode home, where they gave notice of these killings.

Atli stayed at home throughout the autumn, and had many men with him. Thorbjorn Oxen-Might was enraged but could do nothing because Atli had so many friends. Grim and Gamli – Atli's brother-in-law – stayed the winter with him, and so did his other brother-in-law Glum Ospaksson, who was then farming at Eyr in Bitra. There was a large band of men at Bjarg that winter, and a great deal of merry-making.

44

Thorbjorn Oxen-Might started proceedings against Grim and Atli for the killings of the Thorissons, but they prepared their defence on the ground that the Thorissons had forfeited their impunity by making an unlawful assault on them. The case was heard at the Hunavatn Assembly, and both parties were there with a large following. Atli had plenty of supporters, for he had many powerful kinsmen. Then friends of both sides intervened and tried to bring about a settlement; they all agreed that Atli was a good man, peaceable and yet stalwart when he was attacked. Thorbjorn realized that the most honourable thing for him to do was to accept a settlement. Atli stipulated that he would agree neither to banishment from the district nor to exile abroad.

The arbitrators were then chosen: Thorvald Asgeirsson on behalf of Atli, and Solvi the Proud[1] for Thorbjorn. Solvi was a vain man, but also shrewd, which is why Thorbjorn chose him to arbitrate on his behalf. Afterwards the arbitrators announced their verdict: for the killing of the Thorissons a half compensation was to be paid, and the other half was remitted because of the assault and attempt on Atli's life. The killing of Atli's servant on Hrutafjord Ridge was balanced off against the death of the two servants who were killed along with the Thorissons, and Grim Thorhallsson was to leave the district. Atli insisted on paying all the fines himself.

Atli was pleased with the verdict, but Thorbjorn was disappointed. However, when they parted they appeared to be reconciled, although Thorbjorn blurted out that this would not be the end of their dealings, if he could have his way.

Atli rode home from the assembly and thanked Thorvald warmly for his support. Grim Thorhallsson moved south to Gilsbakki in Borgarfjord and became a successful farmer.

45

Thorbjorn Oxen-Might had a servant called Ali who was both stubborn and lazy. Thorbjorn told him to work harder, or else he would beat him, but Ali replied abusively and said that he had no intention of working harder. Thorbjorn told him not to dare do otherwise, but Ali kept on refusing until Thorbjorn could stand it no longer, but flung him down and treated him roughly. Then Ali ran away north across the ridge over to Midfjord, and did not stop until he came to Bjarg. Atli was at home and asked him where he was going. Ali said he was looking for a new job.

'Aren't you Thorbjorn's servant?' said Atli.

1 *He was the son of Asbrand, the son of Thorbrand, the son of Harald
   Ring, who was the original settler of Vatnsness – from Ambattar River
   in the west and to Thver River in the east, including the region from
   Bjarg down to the sea at Bjarg Estuary.*

'We didn't get on at all,' said Ali. 'I didn't stay there long,. but it was longer than I liked. And before we parted Thorbjorn played so roughly on my throat that I shall never again go back there to work, whatever may become of me. It's certainly true that you and he treat your servants in completely different ways. I would very much like to work for you, if there is any chance of that.'

'I have plenty of hands without looking for them in Thorbjorn's household and robbing him of the servants he has already hired,' said Atli. 'I think that you are a weakling, and that you had better go back to him.'

Ali said, 'I will never go there again of my own free will,' and he stayed at Bjarg for some time.

One morning he joined Atli's servants and started working as if he were all hands. He kept this up for a good part of the summer. Atli ignored him, but let him have his food, for he was pleased with the work he was doing.

When Thorbjorn heard that Ali was staying with Atli, he rode over to Bjarg with two companions and asked Atli to come and talk with him. Atli came outside and greeted them.

Thorbjorn said, 'So you still keep on defying and annoying me, Atli. Why did you play this dirty trick of hiring my servant?'

'It is by no means clear to me that he is your servant,' said Atli. 'If you can produce any proof that he is a member of your household, I will certainly not hold him here. Otherwise I cannot throw him out of my house.'

'You must have your way then, for the time being,' said Thorbjorn. 'But I claim him as my servant and I forbid you to let him work for you. I shall come here another time, and it is by no means certain that we will part then on more friendly terms than now.'

Atli said, 'I shall stay at home and wait for whatever happens.'

With that Thorbjorn rode back home.

In the evening when the servants came home, Atli told them of his talk with Thorbjorn and asked Ali to leave, because he did not want to keep him there any longer.

Ali said, 'The old saying is certainly true: "An overpraised man will always let you down." I never believed that you would throw me out after I worked myself to death this summer, thinking that you would take care of me. But this is just how your sort of people turn out, although you have the pretence of goodness about you. And now I shall be whipped before your eyes, if you refuse to help me.'

Atli was moved by what he said, and gave up the idea of throwing him out. And so time passed until the haymaking season started.

One day just before midsummer Thorbjorn Oxen-Might rode over to Bjarg. He was wearing a helmet and girded with a sword, and in his hand he carried a barbed spear with a very broad blade. It was a rainy day.

Atli had sent some of his servants to mow the meadow, and some of them were fishing north at Horn. Atli himself and several others were still at home.

Thorbjorn arrived just before noon. He was alone and rode right up to the door; it was shut and there was no one to be seen outside. He knocked on the door, and then he went to the back of the house so that he could not be seen from the door. The people inside heard the knock, and one of the women went outside. Thorbjorn caught a glimpse of her, but took care not to let her see him, for he had another idea in mind. The woman went back into the hall, and Atli asked her who had arrived. She replied that she hadn't seen anyone outside, and just as they were discussing this, Thorbjorn gave a loud knock on the door.

Atli said, 'This must be someone wanting to see me, and he will have some business with me, though I do not know how useful it will be.'

He went out to the door, but did not see anyone there. It was raining hard, so he did not go outside but put his hands on the door-frame and looked around. Suddenly Thorbjorn came rushing up to the door, and with both hands he drove the spear into Atli's waist, forcing it right through his body.

Atli said, as he received the thrust, 'Broad spears are becoming fashionable nowadays.'

With that he fell forward onto the threshold. The women now came out from the hall and saw that Atli was dead. Thorbjorn, who had already mounted, declared that he was the killer, and then he rode back home.

Asdis of Bjarg sent for the neighbours, and Atli's body was prepared for burial; he was laid to rest beside his father. His death was widely mourned, for he had been intelligent and well-liked. No compensation was paid for his killing, nor was any claim made, because it was Grettir's duty to take up the prosecution whenever he came back to Iceland. So nothing was done about the matter that summer. Thorbjorn earned much ill-will by his deed, but he was allowed to stay at home in peace.

46

That same summer, just before the Althing, a ship put in at Gasir, and with it came news of Grettir's travels, including the house-burning. Thorir of Gard was furious over this story and intended to avenge his sons on Grettir. Thorir rode to the Althing with a large following, and started court proceedings over the burning, but other men refused to take part in this, since there was no one present to answer the charge. Thorir demanded that Grettir should be made an outlaw throughout the land for this terrible crime.

Then Skapti the Lawspeaker said, 'It was certainly an evil act, if it has been truly reported. But usually a story is only half told when it is told by a single person. Most people prefer the more sinister explanation, whenever there are two possibilities. So for the time being I'm not going to give a verdict which makes Grettir an outlaw.'

Thorir was a great chieftain, powerful in his own district, and well liked by many other important men. He followed up his case with resolution, and there was no chance of Grettir's acquittal. Thorir had Grettir made an outlaw throughout the land, and from then on he was Grettir's fiercest enemy, as was borne out by later events. He put a price on Grettir's head, as was the custom with outlaws, and then rode back home. Many people said that this had been done more by force than by law. However, the matter rested there, and all was quiet until after midsummer.

47

Late in the summer Grettir Asmundarson landed at Hvit River in Borgarfjord. The men of the district came down to the ship, and Grettir learned all the news at the same time: first, that his father was dead; second, that his brother had been killed; and third, that he himself had been made an outlaw throughout the land.

Then Grettir spoke this stanza:

Three blows have hit me now:
I've been made an outlaw,
and silently I mourn
my brother's and my father's deaths.
Yet other warriors would show
their grief more openly
than I did at the news
I heard this morning.

It is said that this news did not affect Grettir's mood in the least, and that he was just as cheerful as he had been before. He stayed at the ship for some time, since he could not get a horse to his liking.

There was a man called Svein who lived at Bakki, north of Thingness. He was a good farmer and a very cheerful sort of man, and he used to compose humorous verses. He owned an exceptionally swift mare, black in colour, which he called Saddlehead.

Grettir set out from Vellir one night, for he did not want the merchants to know about his departure. He got himself a black cloak with a hood which he wore on top of his clothes, so as to be less conspicuous. He went up by Thingness, and so north to Bakki; by then it was daylight. He saw a black horse near the home meadow, caught it, bridled it, mounted, and rode up along the Hvit River below Bæ, north to Flokadale River, and so up to the path above Kalfaness. The servants at Bakki were just getting up about the time when Grettir was there, and they told the farmer that a stranger had mounted his horse. Svein got up, laughed, and said:

That warrior rode away
who stole my Saddlehead;
the thief took the mare
from her home pasture.
No doubt he'll show
his wicked strength
in other deeds.
He played me a dirty trick.

Then he took a horse and gave chase. Grettir rode on until he came near the farm at Kropp, and there he saw a man called Halli who said he was going down to the ship at Vellir. Grettir said:

Tell the people
wherever you go
that you've seen Saddlehead
far away at Kropp.
A fellow with a black hood
and a bag full of tricks
was riding the mare.
Hasten away, Halli!

With that they parted. Halli rode down the path and met Svein just before he reached Kalfaness. They gave each other a hurried greeting, and Svein said:

Did you see that loafer,
with his quarrelsome cunning,
riding my mount,
to my great annoyance?
All the farmers here
should punish such thieves,
and if I catch him,
I'll give him a hiding.

'You should be able to do that,' said Halli. 'I met a man who told me he was riding Saddlehead and asked me to tell this to the people lower down in the district. He is a tall man, wearing a black cloak.'

'He must think very highly of himself,' said Svein, 'and I am going to find out who he is.' Then he rode on in pursuit.

Grettir came to Deildartongue and saw a woman standing outside the farmhouse. Grettir went to talk with her, and said:

Give my light-hearted verse
to that generous fellow.
It was Grettir who borrowed
his precious mare.
The outspoken poet
intends to ride her
so hard that he'll spend
the night at Gilsbakki.

The woman memorized the verse, and Grettir rode on his way. Svein arrived there a little later, before the woman had gone back inside. When he came up, Svein said:

Who was that fellow
who rode off just now
on a black mare
in this foul weather?
He'll be fleeing all day,
with his eyes wet like a dog's.
That brave man chooses
to run away fast.

She told him what she had been taught. He pondered over the verse and said, 'It's not unlikely that I'm no match for this man, but I'm going to meet him, nonetheless.'

He rode on north through the district, and he and Grettir were now within sight of each other. The weather was wet and stormy. Grettir reached Gilsbakki that day, and when Grim Thorhallsson knew he had come he gave him a warm welcome and invited him to stay. Grettir accepted, and set Saddlehead free. As he was telling Grim how he had taken her, Svein came riding up and dismounted. When he saw his horse he said:

Who rode my mare?
What will my payment be?
Who has seen a bigger thief?
What's the skulker plotting?

Grettir had taken off his wet clothes by then. He heard the verse, and answered:

I rode the mare
to Grim's large farm.
I've no payment to offer,
but let us be friends.

'And so it shall be,' said Svein, 'for I have been fully compensated for your ride on my mare.'

Afterwards each of them recited the verses which he had composed, and Grettir said he couldn't blame Svein for looking after his property. He and Svein stayed there overnight and had a lot of fun out of the whole episode. They called these stanzas the Saddlehead Verses. In the morning Svein rode back home, and he and Grettir parted the best of friends.

Grim told Grettir what had happened north in Midfjord during his absence abroad. He also told Grettir that Atli was still unatoned for, and that Thorbjorn Oxen-Might had now become so over-bearing that it seemed uncertain whether Asdis would be able to stay on at Bjarg under these circumstances.

Grettir remained with Grim for only a few days, because he didn't want the news of his arrival to reach Midfjord before he got there himself. Grim told him to come again whenever he needed any help. 'But I would like,' he said, 'to avoid the penalty of outlawry, which would legally fall on me if I harboured you.'

Grettir said that Grim was a generous man. 'And it seems likely that I will be in greater need of your help later,' he added.

Grettir rode north across Tvidægra Moor and then all the way to Bjarg. It was the middle of the night when he arrived, and everyone there was asleep, except for his mother. Grettir went to the back of the house and came in through the door there, for he knew the passage that led from it. He came into the hall, and went up to his mother's bed, feeling his way in the dark. His mother asked who was there, and he told her. She sat up in the bed and embraced him, and then she sighed heavily. 'Welcome home, son,' she said. 'How my sons keep failing me! The one who was most useful has now been killed; you have been declared an outlaw and a criminal; and the third one is still too young to accomplish anything.'

'There is an old saying,' said Grettir, 'that the best way of enduring one sorrow is to suffer a greater one. There are other things beside a payment of money which would console us, and I think that Atli will be avenged. As far as I am concerned, some people at least will be glad when Thorbjorn and I fight it out.'

She said that he was probably right. Grettir stayed there for a while, though only a few people knew about it, and he started enquiring what was going on in the district. The news of his arrival in Midfjord had not spread. Grettir heard that Thorbjorn Oxen-Might was at home and had only a few men with him. This was late in the hay-making season.

48

One fine day Grettir set off and rode west across the ridge over to Thoroddsstead. He arrived there just before noon and knocked on the door. Some women came outside and greeted him; they had no idea who he was. He asked for Thorbjorn, and they said he had gone to the meadow to bundle the hay, and had taken with him his sixteen-year-old son, Arnor. Thorbjorn was a very hardworking man, never idle for a moment. When Grettir had been told this, he took leave of the women, set off, and rode on the path towards Reykir. Stretching down from the ridge above that farm is a bog with good grass, and that is where Thorbjorn had cut a great deal of hay, which had now dried. He intended to bring it home, and his son was helping him bundle it, while there was also a woman raking.

Grettir rode up to the meadow. Thorbjorn and his son were farther up; they had just finished making the first bundle, and were now working on the second. Thorbjorn had left his shield and sword beside the finished bundle, but the boy had a small axe with him. Thorbjorn saw the rider, and said to the boy, 'There is someone coming towards us, so we must stop bundling the hay and see what he wants.' They did so, and Grettir dismounted. He was wearing a helmet, while he had his short sword at his waist, and was carrying a long barbless spear with a silver-inlaid socket. He sat down on the ground and pulled out the shaft pin, for he did not want Thorbjorn to be able to hurl the spear back at him.

Thorbjorn said, 'This is a big man, and I am not good at re-cognizing people if it is not Grettir Asmundarson, who must be thinking that he has grievances against us. So we will have to be brave and not let him see any fright in us. We must make a plan here: I shall confront him and see what happens between us, for I think I can confidently pit myself against any one man. But you are to go behind his back, take your axe in both hands, and strike him between the shoulders. You need not worry that he will do you any harm, since his back will be turned to you.'

Neither Thorbjorn nor his son was wearing a helmet. Grettir came up the meadow, and as soon as he was within range he hurled the spear at Thorbjorn, but its head was looser than he thought, so the spear swerved in the flight, the shaft fell off, and the head plunged into the ground. Thorbjorn seized his shield, put it in front of him, drew his sword, and turned to meet Grettir, for now he was certain who he was. Grettir drew his short sword and when he swung it back he noticed the boy behind him. Grettir kept moving around and, when he saw that the boy was within striking range, Grettir swung the short sword so that the back of it crashed into Arnor's head, breaking the skull and killing him instantly. Then Thorbjorn rushed at Grettir and aimed a blow at him which he warded off with a small shield he was carrying in his left hand. Grettir swung his short sword forward so that it split Thorbjorn's shield; the weapon caught Thorbjorn in the head and went right into the brain. He fell down dead, and Grettir did not inflict any other wounds on him. Then he started looking for his spear, but he could not find it, so he went back to his horse and rode down to Reykir, where he reported the killings.

The woman who was raking in the meadow witnessed the killings. She was frightened, ran home, and said that Thorbjorn and his son had been killed. The people there were startled by this, for no one had heard about Grettir's travels. They sent for men from neighbouring farms, and soon a large force had gathered. Then the bodies were brought to church. Thorodd Poem-Piece started proceedings in the action over the killings, and he had with him a number of men.

Grettir rode back home to Bjarg and told his mother what had happened. She was pleased and said he had now shown he was descended from the Vatnsdalers. 'But this will be the beginning and root of your outlawry,' she said, 'and I know for certain that Thorbjorn's kinsmen will not let you stay here for long. They must have realized by now that you can be stirred into action.'

Then Grettir said:

Thorbjorn's been killed
in a fight at Hrutafjord.
The 'Oxen-Might' showed
his last insolence.
The debt has been paid
for the death of Atli.
Thorbjorn got his reward
when he embraced the fair earth.

Asdis said this was true. 'But I don't know what you are intending to do now,' she added.

Grettir said he would seek out his kinsmen and friends in the west. 'I'm not going to cause you any trouble,' he said.

Then he made ready to leave, and he and his mother parted with great affection. First he went over to Melar in Hrutafjord and told his brother-in-law Gamli in detail how Thorbjorn had been killed. Gamli asked him to hasten away from Hrutafjord, since Thorbjorn's kinsmen had assembled many men. 'But we will support you the best we can in the action over Atli's killing.'

With that Grettir set off and rode west across Laxriverdale Moor. He did not halt until he came to Thorstein Kuggason, at Ljarwoods, and he stayed there for most of the autumn.

49

Thorodd Poem-Piece made enquiries about who had killed Thorbjorn and his son, and when he came with his men to Reykir they were told that Grettir had called there to declare that he was the killer. Thorodd realized what must have happened, so he rode over to Bjarg and asked if Grettir was there. A large force of men had already gathered at Bjarg, and Asdis said that Grettir had ridden away. 'And I wouldn't hide him from you if he were here. You should be quite content to leave things as they are, for what has happened now is certainly not too great a revenge for Atli. You never bothered to ask me how his killing grieved me, and it is good that this has come about.'

Thorodd and his men rode back home, for there was nothing they could do there.

The spear which Grettir lost was not found until within the memory of men still alive; in the last years of Sturla Thordarson the Lawman it was discovered in the very bog where Thorbjorn was killed.[1] This bog is now called Spjotsmyr,[2] and that is why Thorbjorn is thought to have been killed there. But in some sources he is said to have been killed at Midfitjar.

Thorbjorn's kinsmen heard that Grettir was staying at Ljarwoods, so they gathered a force with the intention of going there. Gamli of Melar heard about this, and he warned Thorstein and Grettir of their plan. When Thorstein received the message he sent Grettir over to Tongue to Snorri the Priest, for he and Snorri were on friendly terms at the time.[3] Thorstein told Grettir to ask Snorri for help, but

1 Sturla Thordarson (1214-84) was one of the greatest authors in
   thirteenth-century Iceland. His works include *Hákonar Saga Gamla*
   (the life of King Hakon the Old, who ruled Norway from 1216 to 1263),
   Magnús Saga Lagabœtis (the life of King Magnus the Law-Amender,
   Hakon's son and successor, 1263-80; this biography is not now extant
   apart from small fragments), *Íslendinga Saga* (which describes
   life and politics in Iceland during the turbulent period from 1200 to
   1263), and *Sturlubók* (a version of *Landnámabók*).
2 Literally, 'Spear-bog'
3 Snorri the Priest (967-1031) was one of the most remarkable men in
   Iceland during this period. Reliable sources suggest that he was

if Snorri refused, Grettir was to go west to Thorgils Arason at Reykjahills. 'He will certainly take you in over the winter. You must stay there in the Westfjords until the matter is settled.'

Grettir said he would follow his advice, and he rode over to Tongue, saw Snorri the Priest, and asked him to take him in.

Snorri said, 'I'm getting old now, and I can't be bothered to take care of outlaws unless it happens to be my duty. And for what reason did the great warrior turn you out?'

Grettir replied that Thorstein had often been generous with his help. 'But now it has come to the point where I need the help of more than one man.'

Snorri said, 'I will be free with my advice, if that can help you, but you will have to look somewhere else for a place to stay.'

With that they parted, and Grettir rode west to Reykjaness. The men of Hrutafjord had reached Samsstead when they were told that Grettir had left Ljarwoods, so they went back home.

50

Grettir arrived at Reykjahills about the end of autumn, and asked Thorgils to give him shelter over the winter. Thorgils told him that he was welcome to his food there, just like any other free man. 'But the fare here is not very luxurious,' he added.

Grettir said he did not mind about that.

'There is also another drawback,' said Thorgils. 'I have two men staying here who are a bit troublesome, the sworn-brothers Thorgeir and Thormod,[1] and I am not sure how well you will get on together, but they are certainly free to stay here whenever they want. You can also stay here if you like, but you will not be allowed to harass one another.'

Grettir said he would not be the one to start any trouble, especially since the master of the house did not want it.

---

historically very influential, but apart from that he plays an important part in many of the sagas, particularly *Eyrbyggja Saga*, *Laxdœla Saga*, and *Heiðarvíga Saga*, but also *Njal's Saga*, *Gisli's Saga*, and several others.

1 See note on page 57.

A little later the sworn-brothers came home. Thorgeir and Grettir were not friendly towards each other, but Thormod was easier to get on with. Thorgils gave the sworn-brothers the same warning that he had given Grettir, and all three respected Thorgils so much that none of them said a harsh word to the other, although they did not always think alike. And so the first part of winter passed.

It is said that Thorgils owned some islands which are called Olaf's Isles and lie out in the bay about six miles from Reykjaness. On these islands Thorgils was fattening a big ox which had been left there the previous autumn. Thorgils kept saying that he wanted to have the ox fetched before Christmas, and one day the sworn-brothers offered to get the beast if they could find a third man to help them. Grettir said he would go, and they were pleased with that, so all three put out in a ten-oared boat. It was a cold day with a wind blowing from the north. The boat had been laid up at Hvalshausholm. They sailed down the bay before an increasing wind, made the islands, and found the ox. Grettir asked the sworn-brothers whether they would prefer to get the ox aboard or to hold the boat in position, since there was a heavy surf. They asked him to hold the boat, and he took a stand beside the boat midships on the seaward side. The water reached up to his shoulders, but he held the boat so firmly that it did not move. Thorgeir took hold of the ox's hocks and Thormod of its front, and between them they lifted the ox up into the boat. Then they sat down and started rowing, with Thormod in the bow, Thorgeir midships, and Grettir in the stern. They rowed up the bay and when they passed Hafraklett the gale had become very strong.

Thorgeir said, 'The stern is not keeping up with us.'

Grettir replied, 'The stern will never be far behind if there is good rowing midships.'

At that Thorgeir pulled the oars so hard that both the oar-pins came off. Then he said, 'Grettir, you must work a bit harder while I fix the oar-pins.'

Grettir rowed very hard while Thorgeir was fixing the pins, and when Thorgeir started rowing again Grettir's oars had become so worn that they snapped as he hit them against the gunwales. Thormod said it would be better to row less hard and break nothing. Grettir seized two heavy planks which were lying in the boat, cut big holes in the gunwales, and started rowing so furiously that every beam in the boat was creaking. But it was a sturdy boat, with sturdy men on board, and so they managed to make Hvalshausholm.

Grettir asked them which they would prefer: to take the ox home, or to haul the boat ashore. They chose to beach the boat, and they pulled it up with all the water that was inside it, as well as the ice, for it was heavily frozen. Grettir started leading the ox, which was very fat and too stiff for walking. The ox soon became exhausted, and when they got as far as Titlingsstead it could walk no farther. The sworn-brothers went home, for neither side was willing to give the other any help. Thorgils asked about Grettir, and they told him where they had left him. Thorgils sent some men to meet him; when they came down to Hellishills they saw someone coming up towards them carrying an ox on his back, and it was Grettir. Everyone was amazed at how much he could manage.

Thorgeir was particularly jealous of Grettir's strength. One day shortly after Christmas, Grettir went alone to the bath.[2] Thorgeir knew about this and said to Thormod, 'Let's go there and see how Grettir takes it if I go for him when he comes from the bath.'

'I don't like the idea at all,' said Thormod. 'You will never get anywhere with him.'

'I'm going to try, just the same.' said Thorgeir, and turned down the slope, holding his axe high. Grettir was coming back from his bath and when they met, Thorgeir said, 'Is it true, Grettir, that you have said you would never flee before a single man?'

'I'm not so sure about that,' said Grettir, 'but I have never fled before you.'

Thorgeir raised the axe, and at that moment Grettir plunged himself against Thorgeir's waist, knocking him down hard. Thorgeir said to Thormod, 'Are you going to stand by idly while this monster is crushing me?'

Thormod seized hold of Grettir's feet and tried to pull him off Thorgeir, but could not budge him an inch. Thormod was girded with a short sword, and he was about to draw it when Thorgils came up to them and told them to control themselves and not to annoy Grettir. They did as he asked, and said this was all in fun. It is not mentioned that they had any other dealings, and Thorgils was thought to have shown his great luck by being able to restrain such arrogant men.

In the spring they all went away. Grettir went north to Thorska-fjord, and when he was asked how he liked the food and lodgings at

2 At Reykjahills (*Reykhólar*, 'Steam-hills') there are a number of geysers and hot springs, as the name of the farm suggests. In earlier times, as indeed now, the hot springs were used for bathing as well as for washing clothes. The 'bath' referred to here seems to have been an open-air one. The most famous of these Icelandic 'baths' is Snorralaug at Reykholt which still stands, and was at one time used by the famous historian Snorri Sturluson, who lived at Reykholt from about 1206 to 1241.

Reykjahills the winter before, he said, 'I have never been anywhere else where I was so glad to get my food as I was at Reykjahills – that's to say when I managed to get it at all.'

Then he travelled on west across the moor.

51

Thorgils Arason rode with a large following to the Althing, which was attended by all the most important men in the land. He soon met Skapti the Lawspeaker, and they went aside to talk.

Skapti said, 'Is it true, Thorgils, that you have kept over the winter the three outlaws who are considered to be the most arrogant of men, and that you have managed to keep them from causing any harm to one another?'

Thorgils said this was true.

'This shows what an exceptional chieftain you are,' said Skapti. 'But what can you tell me about their tempers? How brave is each of them?'

Thorgils said, 'I think they are all exceptionally brave, yet I think that two of them know what fear is. But differently so, for Thormod fears God and is a very religious man, whereas Grettir is so frightened of the dark that if he could help it he would never go anywhere after nightfall. But in my opinion, my kinsman Thorgeir does not know what fear is.'

'Their tempers must be just as you have described them,' said Skapti, and that was the end of their talk.

At this Althing Thorodd Poem-Piece raised a court action against Grettir for the killing of Thorbjorn Oxen-Might, because Atli's kinsmen had prevented him from bringing the lawsuit at the Hunavatn Assembly, and Thorodd thought that his suit would be less likely to be quashed at the Althing. Atli's kinsmen consulted Skapti about the case, and he told them that he could see a valid point of law which should secure for them a full compensation for Atli's killing.

The cases were referred to judgment, and most people thought that the two killings, of Atli and Thorbjorn, would balance each other off. But when Skapti heard this, he went to the judges and asked what gave them that idea. They replied that both victims had been farmers of equal standing.

Skapti asked, 'Which happened first, Grettir's sentence of out-lawry, or the killing of Atli?'

When this had been worked out it became evident that a week had passed between the two events, for Grettir had been sentenced to outlawry during the Althing, and Atli was killed after its dissolution.

Skapti said, 'As I expected, you were making an error in your appraisal of the case. You have judged a man to be a litigant, even though he has already been made an outlaw, and for that reason can neither plead nor defend a case in a court of law. Now I declare that Grettir is not a litigant in this case, so that the man who is the next of kin according to law must take the action over Atli's killing.'

Thorodd Poem-Piece said, 'Who, then, is to answer for the killing of my brother Thorbjorn?'

'You can decide that for yourself,' said Skapti, 'but Grettir's kinsmen are not going to squander their money for Grettir or his actions, unless he is given peace.'

When Thorvald Asgeirsson realized that Grettir had been dis-qualified as a litigant, he and others enquired about the men who were most closely related to Atli, and it was clear that these were Skeggi (the son of Gamli of Melar) and Ospak (the son of Glum of Eyr in Bitra). Both these men were valiant and zealous. The outcome was that Thorodd was ordered to pay two hundred ounces of silver in compensation for Atli.

Then Snorri the Priest said, 'Do you, men of Hrutafjord, agree to drop this fine, if Grettir is acquitted? He will prove a formidable enemy as long as he remains an outlaw.'

Grettir's kinsmen supported this strongly, and said they were not in the least concerned about the money if he could get back his rights and freedom. Thorodd said he realized that he was in a difficult position, and that as far as he was concerned he would accept the proposal. Snorri asked them first to find out whether Thorir of Gard would approve of Grettir's acquittal. But when Thorir heard this, he was furious and said that Grettir must never be released from his outlawry.

'And not only shall he never be acquitted,' said Thorir, 'but a higher price shall be offered for his head than for any other outlaw.'

Since Thorir was so adamant about this, nothing could be done about the acquittal. Gamli and his friends took the money for safekeeping, but Thorodd Poem-Piece received no compensation for his brother Thorbjorn. He and Thorir each offered twenty-four ounces of silver as a reward for Grettir's head. This was considered most unusual, for never before had more been offered than a total of twenty-four ounces. Snorri the Priest said that it was very foolish to strive to keep in outlawry someone who was capable of working so much damage, and that many would suffer for it. Then the Althing broke up and everyone rode home.

52

When Grettir had crossed Thorskafjord Moor west into Langadale, he let his hands sweep over the property of the small farmers there, and took from each whatever he wanted. From some he obtained weapons, from others clothing. The victims took this in different ways, but they all agreed, after Grettir had left, that they had parted most unwillingly with their property.

At that time Vermund the Slender, the brother of Killer-Styr, was living at Vatnsfjord; he was married to Thorbjorg, called Thorbjorg the Stout, the daughter of Olaf Hoskuldsson the Peacock.[1] Vermund was away at the Althing at the time when Grettir was in Langadale.

Grettir went north across the ridge over to Laugabol, where a man called Helgi was living; he was the leading farmer there at the time. Grettir took from him a fine horse. Next he went east to Gervidale where a man called Thorkel was living; he was wealthy but small-minded. Grettir took from him all the things he wanted, and Thorkel dared neither protest nor defend his property. From there Grettir went to Eyrar and then north along the fjord on that side, taking from every farm food and clothing, and giving some of the farmers rough treatment; most of them found this very hard to put up with. Then Grettir became bolder and ceased to be on guard. He travelled all the way to Vatnsfjord, went to a shieling in the valley, and stayed there for several days. He used to sleep in the woods, and did not suspect any danger.

As soon as the shepherds became aware of this, they went down to the farms and told the farmers that an enemy had arrived who would be difficult to deal with. The farmers gathered forces and thirty of them went secretly into the woods so that Grettir did not

1 These people are known from other sagas: Vermund the Slender and his brother Killer-Styr from *Eyrbyggja Saga* and *Heiðarvíga Saga*, and Olaf the Peacock and his daughter Thorbjorg from *Laxdœla Saga*. The characterization of Vermund and his wife is in full harmony with the accounts in other sagas.

know about them. They told a shepherd to keep watch for the best chance to capture Grettir; however, they were still not sure who the stranger was.

One day, when Grettir was lying asleep, the farmers crept up on him. When they saw him, they started arguing how they should go about capturing him without risking their lives. They decided that ten men should rush him while others were to tie his legs securely. So they attacked him, but Grettir gave a violent start, threw them off him, and managed to get on his hands and knees. Then they put a rope around his legs, but Grettir kicked two of them so hard on the ears that they were knocked senseless. After that they all crowded on him, one after another; he struggled hard for a long time, but in the end they overcame him.

When they had tied him up, they started arguing about what should be done with him, and they asked Helgi of Laugabol to take him into custody until Vermund came back from the Althing.

Helgi said, 'I can think of plenty other more useful jobs for my servants than to watch Grettir. My farm is difficult enough to run as it is, and I refuse to have anything to do with him.'

Then they asked Thorkel of Gervidale to take in Grettir, since Thorkel was such a wealthy farmer. He refused and said that this was out of the question. 'There are only the two of us on the farm, my wife and myself, and we live far away from other people. You shall never saddle me with such a burden.'

Then they said, 'You, Thorolf of Eyr, could take Grettir and keep him until the Althing is over, or else you could escort him to the next farm and then be responsible for seeing that he does not break free. You must leave him as securely tied up as he is now when you receive him.'

Thorolf said, 'I will not take in Grettir, because I have neither the money nor the means to keep him. Moreover, he was not captured on my land. It seems more of a liability than an honour to take Grettir or to have anything to do with him, and he shall never set foot in my house.'

Then each farmer in turn was asked, but all refused. It is about this argument that wits composed the poem *Grettir's Move*, which is adorned with a good many humorous words to make it funnier.[2]

2 This poem is no longer extant in its entirety, but it was preserved in one of the MSS of *Grettir's Saga* until some prudish owner erased it so thoroughly that it was only with the help of ultra-violet light and other modern techniques that parts of it were deciphered. It seems to have been a crude and somewhat licentious composition. See Ólafur Halldórsson's article 'Grettisfærsla,' in *Opuscula* I, *Bibliotheca Arnamagnæana*, XX (Copenhagen 1960), 49-77.

When they had discussed the problem for a long time, they finally agreed not to turn their good luck into bad, and so they set to work and erected a gallows then and there in the woods, with the intention of hanging Grettir on the spot. The preparations were made with a great deal of uproar.

Then they saw three riders coming towards them from the valley below. One of them was wearing coloured clothing; they guessed this must be Thorbjorg the Stout of Vatnsfjord, and so it was. She was on her way up to the shieling. Thorbjorg was a very forceful and shrewd woman; whenever Vermund was away from home, she used to take charge in the district and make all the decisions. She turned off her path and went up to the gathering; someone helped her to dismount, and the farmers gave her a good welcome.

Thorbjorg said, 'What sort of a meeting is this? Who is the thick-necked fellow that sits here in bonds?'

Grettir told her who he was, and greeted her.

She said, 'Grettir, what made you want to cause trouble in my district?'

'There are things beyond my control,' said Grettir. 'And I have to be somewhere.'

'What terrible ill luck,' she said, 'that these miserable men should take you captive without your being able to do anything about it. And you men, what are you intending to do with Grettir?'

The farmers said they were going to hang him on the gallows to punish him for his crimes.

She said, 'It's probably true that Grettir deserves this, but it would be too great an undertaking for you men of Isafjord to put Grettir to death, because he is a man of noble kin and great renown, though he has run out of luck. Now, Grettir, what do you want to do to save your life, if I should give you the chance?'

He said, 'What do you ask of me?'

'You must swear an oath,' she said, 'never again to raid around Isafjord, and you are not to take vengeance on any of these men who attacked you.'

Grettir said she could have it her way, and then he was set free. He once said himself that it had never taken him a greater effort to control his temper than on this occasion, when he stopped himself from striking the boastful farmers. Thorbjorg invited Grettir to come home with her, and gave him a horse to ride. So he went down to Vatnsfjord and stayed there until Vermund came home, and Thorbjorg treated him very hospitably. She won much fame throughout the region from this encounter.

Vermund was furious when he got home. He asked what Grettir

was doing there, and Thorbjorg told him everything that had happened between Grettir and the men of Isafjord.

'What has he got in his favour,' said Vermund, 'to make you want to save his life?'

'There were a good many reasons for this,' said Thorbjorg. 'First, you will be considered a greater chieftain than ever before because you have a wife who had the courage to do this. Second, Grettir's kinswoman, Hrefna,[3] would certainly expect me to save him from being killed. And third, Grettir himself is an outstanding man in many respects.'

'You are a shrewd woman, in most ways,' said Vermund. 'And I thank you for what you have done.'

Then he said to Grettir, 'It must have been humiliating for a great warrior like you, Grettir, to have been seized by such wretches. But this is precisely what happens to troublemakers.'

Then Grettir said:

My luck grew worse
near the icy fjord,
when the old hogs held
my life in their hands.

'What were they going to do to you after they captured you?' asked Vermund.

They were all saying
I deserved to be hanged,
until they saw Thorbjorg,
that great much-praised lady.

Vermund said, 'Would they have hanged you, if they had been left to themselves?'

Grettir said:

My head would soon
have been put in a noose,
if that wise lady Thorbjorg
had not saved my life.

Vermund said, 'Did she invite you home with her?'
Grettir answered:

3 Hrefna was also Thorbjorg's sister-in-law, since she was the wife of Kjartan Olafsson, Thorbjorg's brother and the hero of *Laxdœla Saga*.

Yes, Thorbjorg invited me .
to come home with her.
She gave me my life,
and a fine horse to ride on.

'You will have a momentous and troublesome life,' said Vermund,
'and this should teach you to be on your guard against your enemies.
I cannot be bothered to keep you here and thus earn the ill will of
many powerful men. It would be best for you once again to seek
your kinsmen, since few men will be willing to take you in unless
they have to. And you are not a very willing follower of other
men.'

Grettir stayed on at Vatnsfjord for some time, and from there he
travelled to the Westfjords, where he sought out several important
men, but every time something came up to prevent them from taking
him in.

53

Late in the autumn Grettir went back south again, and he made no
halt until he arrived at Ljarwoods and saw his kinsman Thorstein
Kuggason. Thorstein gave him a good welcome and invited him to
stay over the winter, which Grettir accepted. Thorstein was clever
with his hands and very hard-working, and he kept his men hard
at work too. But Grettir had little inclination for work, and for that
reason they did not get on so well together. Thorstein had built a
church on his farm; he also built a bridge some distance away from
the house, and it was made with much ingenuity. Under the beams
which supported the bridge there were rings and bells fixed on the
outside in such a way that when someone walked across the bridge
the rings shook and the clang could be heard all the way over to
Skarfsstead, some two miles away. Thorstein took much trouble
over this bridge, for he was a very skilful blacksmith. Grettir was
good at hammering the iron, but most of the time he was too lazy.
However, he was quiet throughout the winter, and nothing happened
there worth telling about.

The men of Hrutafjord heard that Grettir was staying with
Thorstein, and early in the spring they gathered a force. When

Thorstein knew about this, he told Grettir to look for shelter elsewhere. 'I can see that you don't want to do any work, and I can't be bothered with loafers.'

'Where do you want me to go, then?' asked Grettir

Thorstein told him to go south to see his kinsmen there. 'You can come back to me if they should fail you.'

Grettir did as he suggested; he went south to Borgarfjord to see Grim Thorhallsson, and stayed with him until after the Althing. Then Grim told him to go to Skapti the Lawspeaker at Hjalli. Grettir travelled right across the moors, skirting the farms, and made no halt until he arrived at Tongue and met Thorhall, the son of Asgrim and grandson of Ellida-Grim. Thorhall knew about Grettir because of his ancestry,[1] and also because Grettir was now famous throughout the land for his prowess. Thorhall was a shrewd man and treated Grettir generously, but he did not want him to stay there long.

54

Grettir set out from Tongue and travelled up to Haukadale and so north to Kjol, where he stayed for most of the summer. It was by no means a rare event for Grettir to relieve travellers of their baggage on their way north or south across Kjol, since otherwise there were no supplies available to him.

One day when Grettir was north at Dufunefsskeid, he saw a man riding south across Kjol. He was a big man on a fine horse, with a nail-studded bridle, and he was leading a pack-horse which was loaded with bags. The man was wearing a big hat which concealed his face. Grettir liked the horse and the baggage, so he went to meet the stranger, greeted him, and asked him his name. He said he was called Lopt.

'But I know your name,' he said. 'You must be Grettir Asmundarson the Strong. Where are you going?'

'I haven't decided yet,' said Grettir. 'At the moment I'm only concerned with finding out if you are willing to hand over some of your belongings.'

1 Grettir's great-grandfather, Onund Treefoot, came to Iceland with Asmund, the brother of Thorhall's great-grandfather. See chapters 7 and 8.

Lopt said, 'Why should I give you what is mine? And what are you willing to give in return?'

'Haven't you heard that I never pay for anything I take?' said Grettir. 'Yet most people will admit that I usually get what I ask for.'

Lopt said, 'You can offer your kind of deal to those who like it, but I'm not going to part with my property in this manner. So it's better for each of us to go his own way.'

And with that he whipped on his horse and rode past Grettir.

Grettir said, 'We musn't part so hastily,' and then he seized hold of the reins, pulled them out of Lopt's grip, and held on to them with both hands.

Lopt said, 'Go on your way, for you will never take anything from me as long as I can help it.'

'We'll soon see about that,' said Grettir.

Lopt reached down to the bridle, got hold of the reins between the bit and Grettir's grip, and pulled so hard that Grettir's hands slid along the reins until he had to let go. Grettir looked at his palms and realized what powerful hands Lopt must have. He watched Lopt go away, and called after him, 'Where are you going now?'

Lopt replied with this verse:

Where the blizzards rage
Like a boiling cauldron
Behind the icy peaks:
There you can find me.

'It's not possible to find your place unless you give me clearer directions,' said Grettir.

The other replied with this verse:

I mustn't keep you in the dark
if you want to visit me.
My home's above Borgarfjord
at a place called Ball Glacier.

With that they parted. Grettir realized that he was no match for Lopt in strength, and he made this verse:

Illugi the Brave
and Atli the Quiet
were too far away

115

when the wicked Lopt
pulled the reins
through my hands.
My mother would weep
if she thought I was frightened.

Then Grettir travelled south from Kjol and rode over to Hjalli, where he met Skapti. He asked him for help, and Skapti said, 'I have been told that you have been making a lot of trouble and robbing people of their property. That ill befits a man of such noble kin as you. It would be much better for you if you did not steal, and since I bear the title of lawspeaker in this land it would not do for me to break the law by sheltering outlaws. So I want you to find a place to live where you don't have to steal from people.'

Grettir said he would gladly do that, but added that he could hardly bear the thought of being alone because of his fear of the dark. Skapti said he could not expect to have everything just as he wanted it. 'You must never trust anyone, or else the same thing will happen to you that happened in the Westfjords,' he added. 'Many a man has lost his life through overconfidence.'

Grettir thanked him for his good advice, and in the autumn he travelled west to Borgarfjord to see his friend Grim Thorhallsson. Grettir had told him what Skapti had advised, and Grim said that Grettir should go north to the Fiskiwaters on Arnarwater Moor, which he did.

55

Grettir travelled north to Arnarwater Moor, and built himself a hut there, the ruins of which can still be seen. He settled down there, and since he was determined that whatever happened he would not steal, he got some nets and a boat and lived by fishing. He found life on the moor very miserable, because of his great fear of the dark. When other outlaws heard where Grettir had settled down, they were eager to join him, for they realized how much protection he could give them.

There was a man in the north called Grim; he was an outlaw, and the men of Hrutafjord bribed him to kill Grettir, promising him both freedom and money if he should succeed. So he went to Grettir and asked him for shelter.

'I can't see how you would possibly be better off with me,' said Grettir. 'You outlaws are an untrustworthy lot, but on the other hand I hate being alone if there is an alternative. Anyone who wants to stay with me, however, must do all the necessary work around here.'

Grim said that he would do this, and urged Grettir strongly to take him in, so eventually Grettir was talked into it. Grim stayed there for a part of the winter, waiting for an opportunity to kill Grettir, but the odds seemed very much against him. Grettir was suspicious of him, and kept his weapons handy day and night; Grim never had the courage to attack when Grettir was awake.

One morning, when Grim came back from fishing, he walked into the hut and stamped his feet down to see if Grettir was asleep. Grettir lay quietly and did not stir. His short sword was hanging on the wall above him. Grim thought that he would never get a better chance, so he made a lot of noise to see if Grettir would say anything, but nothing happened. Then Grim realized that Grettir must be fast asleep, so he crept quietly up to the bed, snatched the short sword from the wall, and raised it. At that moment Grettir jumped onto the floor and grabbed the short sword as Grim was about to strike him with it. With his other hand Grettir took hold of Grim's shoulder and threw him down so hard that he was almost knocked senseless.

'And so you have turned out, despite all your good promises,' said Grettir.

When he had forced Grim to tell him the whole story, Grettir killed him. And now he realized what it could mean to take in outlaws. The winter passed, and Grettir suffered more from his fear of the dark than from anything else.

56

Thorir of Gard was told where Grettir was now living, and he tried to think of a way to kill him. There was a man called Thorir Red-Beard, an exceptionally strong man and a killer, so that he had been made an outlaw throughout the land. Thorir of Gard sent word to him, and when they met he asked Red-Beard to go and kill Grettir the Strong. Red-Beard said that it was no easy job, for Grettir was an intelligent man, and always on guard.

Thorir asked him to try. 'It would be a deed fit for such a brave man as you, and in return I will have you freed from outlawry, and will give you a great deal of money besides.'

Red-Beard accepted the proposal, and Thorir told him how he should go about killing Grettir. Red-Beard travelled first to the east in order to make his journey seem less suspicious. Then he went to Arnarwater Moor, after Grettir had been there for a year, and when the two men met, Red-Beard asked Grettir to let him stay there over the winter.

Grettir said, 'I don't like to have more men amuse themselves with me the way that other man did who came here last autumn. He seemed very plausible, but he had been here only a little while when he tried to kill me. So I'm not going to risk taking on any more outlaws.'

Thorir replied, 'No one can blame you a bit for not trusting outlaws. But you will have heard of me because of all my killings and other crimes, and not at all because I was guilty of anything as shameful as having betrayed my master. It's hard to be wicked, for one wicked man is supposed to be just like any other. I wouldn't have come here if I had had the choice of anything better, but I don't think we shall be defeated by most men, if we can stand together. You could risk finding out how much you like me, and then let me go if you see any deceit in me.'

Grettir said, 'I will take that risk, but you can know for certain that it will be your death if I suspect any treachery.'

Thorir agreed to this, and then Grettir took him on. He soon found out that Red-Beard had the strength of two men whenever strength was needed. He was willing to do anything that Grettir asked. Grettir did not have to do any work at all, and never before in all his outlawry had he had so easy a time. However, Grettir was so vigilant that Red-Beard never found a chance to get at him.

Thorir Red-Beard stayed two years with Grettir on the moor, and then he began to tire of it, so he started thinking up a plan which would take Grettir unawares. One night in the spring, after they had gone to sleep, a very strong gale blew up. Grettir awoke and asked where their boat was. Thorir jumped up, ran to the boat, broke it into pieces, and scattered the fragments all over the place as if the storm had broken it. Then he went back into the hut and said in a loud voice: 'Trouble has come, my friend. Our boat is broken into pieces, and the nets are way out in the lake.'

'You must get them, then,' said Grettir, 'for I think you are to blame for the ruined boat.'

Thorir answered, 'It so happens that I am not as good a swimmer as I might be, although in other skills I can pit myself against any man. I should remind you that since I joined you I haven't let you do any work, and I would not be asking this of you if I could manage it myself.'

Grettir got up, took his weapons, and went down to the lake. A tongue of land jutted out into the lake there, with a big creek on one side. The lake was very deep near the land, and the water had eaten into the high banks so that they were overhanging.

Grettir said, 'Swim out for the nets and show me what you can do.'

'I already told you,' said Thorir, 'that I am no swimmer. I don't know what has become of all your strength and courage.'

'I can certainly get the nets,' said Grettir. 'But don't betray me now, when I am relying on you.'

Thorir said, 'Don't expect me to do anything so shameful.'

Grettir said, 'You yourself will show what kind of man you are.'

Then he threw off his clothes and weapons and swam out for the nets. He bundled them together, swam back, and threw them up on the bank. When he started to come ashore, Thorir seized the short sword, drew it, turned swiftly against Grettir as he was climbing up the bank, and struck at him. Grettir threw himself backwards into the water and sank like a stone. Thorir kept watching the lake, intending to keep him from landing if he should come up again. But Grettir swam underwater, close to the bank, so that Thorir could not see him. When he reached the creek behind Thorir, he went ashore there. Thorir had not expected this, and before he knew what had happened, Grettir seized hold of him, lifted him above his head, and flung him down so hard that the short sword was thrown out of his hand. Grettir seized it and without a word to Thorir struck his head off. That was the end of Thorir; after this Grettir refused to take in outlaws, although he could hardly bear being alone.

57

At the Althing Thorir of Gard heard that Thorir Red-Beard had been killed, and then he realized that he had no easy matter on his hands. He decided to ride west from the Althing over the lower moors, taking nearly eighty men with him, in order that he might kill Grettir. But Grim Thorhallsson heard of this and sent Grettir word to be on his guard. Grettir, who was always on the outlook for travellers, one day saw a number of riders coming towards his hut. He climbed up to a certain pass between two cliffs, and did not want to flee farther, for he had seen only part of the group. Soon Thorir came up there with his men; he urged them to dispatch Grettir at once and said that his wickedness would soon come to an end.

Grettir said, ' "There's many a slip between the cup and the lip." You have come a long way, and some of you should have something to show for our meeting before it is over.'

Thorir kept urging his men to attack. The pass was very narrow, so Grettir could easily defend it in front, but he was surprised that he was never attacked or injured from behind. Soon some of Thorir's men were killed and others were badly wounded, but they still could make no headway.

Then Thorir said, 'I have heard that Grettir was a man outstanding in strength and courage, but I had not known before that he was also a sorcerer – as I can now see that he must be, since twice as many men get killed behind his back as in front of him. I know now that we are dealing with a troll and no human being.'

He told his men to ride away, and so they did. Grettir, who was exhausted, was surprised at what had happened. Thorir and his men rode on their way north through the districts; people thought their excursion had been shameful. He had lost eighteen men, and many others were wounded.

Grettir walked farther up the pass, and saw, sitting against a crag, a big man who was badly wounded. Grettir asked him his name, and he said it was Hallmund.

'It may help you to remember me if I tell you that when we met last summer at Kjol you thought my grip on the reins was rather too firm. But now I think I have made amends.'

'One thing is certain,' said Grettir, 'that you have shown me what a noble-minded man you are. When I shall be able to repay you is another matter.'

Hallmund said, 'I want you to come home with me, because you must be lonely here on the moor.'

Grettir accepted willingly, so they set off and went south near Ball Glacier, where Hallmund had a large cave, and a brawny and impressive-looking daughter. They treated Grettir very hospitably, and she tended their wounds. Grettir stayed there for a long time that summer. He composed a poem on Hallmund, which includes this couplet:

Hallmund takes long strides
In his mountain hall.

And also this stanza:

The murderous sword
wended its bloody way
in the raging battle
at Hrutafjord.
Warriors will hold
a funeral feast
for the men of the north,
but Hallmund saved me.

It has been said that Grettir killed six men in the fight, and Hallmund twelve.

Late in the summer Grettir began to long to get away from the wilderness and see his friends and kinsmen. Hallmund asked him to visit him whenever he came south again, and Grettir promised to do this. He went first to Borgarfjord, and then over to the Breidafjord Dales, where he asked Thorstein Kuggason for advice about what he should try next. Thorstein said that the number of Grettir's enemies kept increasing, and that few men would now be willing to take him in. 'But you might go south to Myrar, and see what is available there.' So in the autumn Grettir went south to Myrar.

58

At this time Bjorn the Hitardale Champion was living at Holm.[1] He was a great chieftain, very resolute, and often took in outlaws. Grettir came to Holm, and Bjorn gave him a good welcome, for there had been friendship between their ancestors. Grettir asked him if he would give him any help, and Bjorn said that since Grettir

---

1 *Bjorn was the son of Arngeir, the son of Bersi the Godless, the son of Balki, who was the original settler of Hrutafjord, as was mentioned earlier.* See chapter 5.

The life story of Bjorn is told in *Bjarnar Saga Hitdælakappa*, one of the sagas known to the author of *Grettir's Saga*.

now had enemies all over the country, men would have to be careful not to risk outlawry by helping him. 'However, I shall do my best to help you, if you promise to leave in peace all those who are in my protection, whatever you choose to do with other men in the district.' Grettir agreed to that.

Bjorn said, 'I have been thinking that with the proper arrangements there would be a safe hiding-place, and one easily defended, in the mountain west of Hitar River. There is a hole right through the mountain, and it can be seen from the main path which runs below. Between the path and this cave there is a scree slope so steep that no one is likely to climb it if the cave is defended by a good fighter. It seems to me the best and the only solution for you is to stay in the cave, because from there it is easy to get supplies from Myrar and from the coast.'

Grettir said he would follow his advice, and do whatever he suggested. Then he went to Fagraskogafell and settled down in the cave. He covered the entrance with grey homespun cloth, so that from the path it seemed as if one were looking right through the mountain. Then Grettir started searching for supplies in the district, and the men of Myrar thought him a most unwelcome guest.

Thord Kolbeinsson was then living at Hitarness; he was a good poet. At that time there was much enmity between Bjorn and Thord, so that the trouble Grettir was causing for Thord's men and cattle did not disturb Bjorn in the least.

Grettir often stayed with Bjorn, and they competed in many sports. In the saga about Bjorn they are said to have been equally good, but most people think that Grettir was the strongest man who has been in Iceland since the time that Orm Storolfsson and Thorolf Skolmsson gave up their trials of strength.[1] Grettir and Bjorn swam together down Hitar River, all the way from the lake down to the sea. They laid the stepping stones in the river, which have never moved since, in spite of all the floods and ice.

For a whole winter Grettir stayed at Fagraskogafell without being attacked, in spite of the great losses that many men suffered because of him. They could do nothing about it, since his place was so easily defended, and also because he was on good terms with his nearest neighbours.

1 These two strong men are known from other sources. There is a story
   about Orm which probably dates from the thirteenth century, and Thorolf
   is mentioned in *Heimskringla* and elsewhere.

59

There was a man called Gisli, the son of that Thorstein whose death Snorri the Priest had contrived.[1] Gisli was a tall strong man, well equipped with weapons and clothes. He had a high opinion of himself, and used to boast a lot. He was a seafaring trader, and in the summer, after Grettir had spent one winter at the mountains, Gisli came to Hvitriver from abroad. Thord Kolbeinsson rode to his ship and Gisli gave him a good welcome and asked him to take any of his goods that he wanted. Thord accepted this, and they started talking.

Gisli said, 'Is it true what I have been told, that you don't know how to get rid of this outlaw who has been giving you all this trouble?'

Thord said, 'We have not tried yet, but most people think that he will be very difficult to attack, as indeed many men have already discovered to their grief.'

'I can understand why you have been finding it so difficult to deal with Bjorn, since you aren't able to get rid of Grettir. It is too bad that I shall be so far away next winter, when I might be able to solve this problem for you.'

'You will find Grettir easier to talk about than to deal with,' said Thord.

'You don't need to tell me about Grettir,' said Gisli. 'I have experienced greater hazards when I was raiding with Canute the Great in the British Isles. Everyone thought I deserved my place then. If I get the chance to meet Grettir I will certainly trust myself and my weapons.'

Thord said that Gisli could expect to be well rewarded if he killed Grettir. 'He has a higher price on his head than any other outlaw. First there were forty-eight ounces of silver, and this summer Thorir of Gard added twenty-four more. Yet everyone agrees that whoever gets the reward will have earned it.'

'Money will do anything,' said Gisli, 'and this applies not least to us merchants. We must keep this talk a secret, for it may be that

1 This killing and Snorri's part in it are described in *Heiðarvíga Saga* and *Eyrbyggja Saga*.

Grettir will be more on his guard when he knows that you have been consulting me. I'm going to stay for the winter out in Olduhrygg, and isn't his den right on my way? He will not suspect anything, and I'm not going to take many men with me to attack him.'

Thord was pleased with this plan; he rode home and said nothing about it. But as the saying goes, 'Woods have ears,' and some of Bjorn's friends had been present at the meeting, and told him everything. When Bjorn saw Grettir, he brought this up, and said they would soon see how Grettir would do against Gisli. 'It might be amusing,' said Bjorn, 'if you were to push him around a little, but not kill him, if you can help it.'

Grettir grinned, and made no reply.

In the autumn when the sheep were being rounded up Grettir went down to Flysjuhverfi to get hold of some, and he managed to catch four wethers. The farmers found out what he was doing, and went after him. Just when Grettir reached the slope below his cave, the farmers came up and tried to drive the wethers away. There were six of them; they did not attack him with weapons, but tried to bar his way. Struggling with the wethers had made Grettir lose his temper, so he seized two of the farmers and flung them down the slope, knocking them out. When the others saw this they became less keen. Grettir took the wethers, hooked them together by their horns, and slung them over his shoulders, a pair on each side. Then he climbed to his hiding place, and the farmers went back. They were thought to have had the worst of it, and were even unhappier with their lot than they had been before.

Gisli stayed at his ship during the autumn until it had been laid up for the winter. There were many things to delay him, so he was late in leaving and rode off just before the beginning of winter. He went north and stayed overnight at Hraun, south of Hitar River.

In the morning, before he set off, Gisli said to his companions: 'We'll ride in our coloured clothing today, and let that outlaw see that we are not the common tramps you meet every day.'

There were three of them together, and they all did as Gisli suggested. When they had crossed the river, he spoke to them again: 'I'm told the outlaw is hiding somewhere up in these mountains, and it's not easy to get about there. Don't you think he will be keen to come to meet us and look at our belongings?' They said that Grettir usually behaved like that.

That morning Grettir had go. up early in his lair. It was a cold frosty day with a little fresh snow on the ground. He saw three men riding north across Hitar River, and their elegant clothing and enamelled shields glittered in the sun. It occurred to him who they might be, and he thought he needed some of their clothes. He was also curious to meet the boaster, so he took his weapons and ran down the scree.

When Gisli heard the stones rattling he said, 'A man is coming down the slope over there – he is a big man, and he must be wanting to meet us. Let's act boldly, for now our quarry is within reach.'

Gisli's companions said that the man wouldn't be running towards them unless he was very sure of himself. 'And if he's asking for trouble, we'd better give him some.'

They all dismounted, and just then Grettir came up and seized hold of a bag of clothes which Gisli had tied to the saddle behind him.

'I'll take this; I often stoop for trifles,' said Grettir.

Gisli said, 'No you won't; don't you realize whom you're dealing with?'

Grettir said, 'I'm not quite sure. Anyway, it doesn't matter much who you are, since I'm asking for so little.'

'It may be that you think this a trifle,' said Gisli, 'but I would rather lose three thousand ells of homespun. What barefaced impudence – so let's attack him, boys, and see what he can do.'

They attacked; Grettir retreated before them and moved over to a boulder which stands near the path and is now called Grettir's Lift. There he defended himself. Gisli kept urging on his companions, but Grettir saw that he was not as brave as he pretended, for he always stayed behind his men. Grettir became tired of the scuffle, and swiped at one of Gisli's companions with his short sword, killing him. Then he came forward from the boulder so fiercely that Gisli started running west along the mountain. At that point his other companion was killed.

Grettir said, 'No one could guess that you had fought so bravely in many different places. You took scant leave of your men.'

Gisli answered, '"The fire feels the hottest to the man who is burned." It is hard to fight a man from Hell.'

They only exchanged a few blows before Gisli dropped his weapons and again started running away along the mountain. Grettir gave him time to throw off anything he wanted to, and whenever Gisli got the chance he took off some garment. Grettir held back and always kept some distance between them. Gisli ran west all the way across the mountain, then over Kaldriverdale, through Aslaugarhlid, and passed above Kolbeinsstead, so that he came out onto Borgar Lava. By that time Gisli was wearing only his underclothes and was completely exhausted. Grettir kept pressing him; by then he was within striking distance, so he pulled off a big branch. But Gisli kept running and did not stop until he reached Haffjord River, which was in flood and almost unfordable. He intended to rush into the river, but Grettir caught up with him and seized him. He soon showed Gisli how much stronger he was, and forced him to the ground.

'Are you that man Gisli who wanted to meet Grettir Asmundarson?' he asked.

Gisli answered, 'Now I have met him, but I don't yet know how we shall part. You can keep all the things you have taken, only let me go.'

Grettir said, 'You may find it hard to understand what I'm trying to teach you, so I must let you have a reminder.' Then he pulled Gisli's shirt up over his head and gave him a good hiding with the branch on his back and on both sides. Gisli kept turning away from him, but Grettir whipped him all over, and then he let him go. Gisli thought that he would prefer not to take another lesson from Grettir or to suffer such a lashing again, and indeed he never again put himself in a position to deserve a similar beating.

Once Gisli was back on his feet, he jumped into a deep pool in the river and swam across. In the night he reached a farm called Hrossholt. He was completely exhausted, and lay there in bed for a week, with his whole body badly swollen. Then he went on to his lodgings.

Grettir turned back, picked up all the things which Gisli had discarded, and took them to his cave. Gisli never recovered them, and most people thought he had received what he deserved for his showing off and bragging.

Grettir composed this about their dealings:

A horse that can't use his teeth
never lingers in a fight,
but runs away
as fast as he can.
And so eager Gisli
ran farting from me,
shedding as he went
all his honour.

In the following spring Gisli made ready to go to his ship. He gave strict orders that none of his belongings should be transported by the route south along the mountain, for he said that the devil himself lived there. Gisli rode along by the sea all the way south to the ship. He never met Grettir again, and he was thought very little of for the rest of his life. He is now out of the story.

Afterwards the enmity between Thord Kolbeinsson and Grettir grew even worse, and Thord made many plans to drive Grettir away or to have him killed.

60

When Grettir had stayed for two winters at Fagraskogafell and the third had begun, he went south to Myrar, to a farm called Lækjarbend, and took from there six wethers against the owner's will. Then he went down to Akrar and from there took two bulls and many wethers, and drove them north up along Hitar River.

The farmers learned of his travels, and they sent word to Thord at Hitarness, asking him to take care of putting Grettir to death. He declined, but when they insisted, he told his son Arnor – who was later known as the Earl's Poet[1] – to go along with them. Thord urged them not to let Grettir get away. They sent for men throughout the district; a man called Bjarni, who lived at Jorvi in Flysjuhverfi, gathered forces west of Hitar River. The plan was that the two bands should join at the river.

Grettir had two men with him; one of them was a farmer's son from Fagraskogar called Eyjolf, who was an able man.

Thorarin of Akrar and Thorfinn of Lækjarbend were the first to arrive on the scene, and they had almost twenty men in all. Grettir was then trying to get west across the river. Then Thorgeir, Arnor, and Bjarni came up with their men from the west side. There was a narrow spit of land jutting out into the river on Grettir's side, and he drove the beasts out to the tip of it as soon as he saw the men coming, for he never liked to give up anything that he had once laid his hands on. The farmers of Myrar attacked at once with a will. Grettir told his companions to see that no one attacked him from behind. It was not possible for many men to approach him at the same time, but the fight was a fierce one. Grettir kept striking right and left with his short sword, and the attackers found it hard to get near him. Some of them were killed and others wounded. The men who were to come from the west were slow in getting across the river

---

1 Arnor Thordarson was one of the outstanding court poets of the eleventh century. He lived for years with the earls of Orkney, from whom he acquired his nickname.

because the ford was some distance away. The attackers fought only for a short time and then they fell back. Thorarin of Akrar was a very old man, so that he was not in the attack.

When the fight stopped, Thrand and Thorgils Ingjaldsson, Thorarin's son and nephew, came up, together with Finnbogi, the son of Thorgeir Thorhaddsson of Hitardale, and Steinolf Thorleifsson of Hraundale, and they urged the men strongly to keep on fighting. So they made a fresh attack, and Grettir realized that he would either have to flee or do his very best. He fought so furiously that no one could stand up to him, but there were so many against him that he thought he would not get out alive, and he wanted only to accomplish as much as he could before he was killed. He wanted especially to take with him the life of a worthy opponent, so he rushed at Steinolf of Hraundale and struck him on the head, splitting it right down to the shoulders. He followed this up immediately with a blow at Thorgils Ingjaldsson, striking him in the waist and almost severing his body. Then Thrand, who wanted to avenge his cousin, came forward, but Grettir struck him on his right thigh and sliced off the muscles, so that he was out of the fight. Next Grettir gave Finnbogi a serious wound.

Then Thorarin called out and told them to retreat. 'The longer you go on fighting him, the greater damage he will inflict on you. He is now singling out his victims.'

They did as he suggested and turned away. Ten men were killed, five others were fatally wounded or maimed for life, and most of the men who had been in the battle had some wounds. Grettir was exhausted but only slightly hurt. The men of Myrar went away; they had suffered a great loss because many of their best men had fallen. Those who came from the west were slow in travelling and only reached the scene after the fight had ended. When they saw how badly the others had done, Arnor refused to expose himself to any danger. For that he was severely criticized by his father and many others; people think that he was no hero. The place where they fought is now called Grettir's Spit.

Grettir and his companions got some horses and rode up to the mountain. Each of them had some wounds; when they came up to Fagraskogar, Eyjolf stayed behind. The farmer's daughter was outside the house, and asked them for news. Grettir told her what had happened, and spoke this verse:

It will be no easy matter,
my gracious lady,
to heal the gaping gash

on Steinolf's head,
and others fell beside him.
There's little hope for Thorgils,
since all his bones are broken.
Eight men lie dead there.

Afterwards Grettir went up to his cave and spent the winter there.

61

When Bjorn met Grettir, he told him that the situation had become serious. 'You will not be allowed to stay here much longer. You have killed my friends and kinsmen, yet I shall not break my promise to you as long as you remain here.'

Grettir said he had been forced to defend his life and limbs. 'It's unfortunate that you are offended,' he said.

Bjorn said nothing could be done about it.

A little later the relatives of the men Grettir had killed came to Bjorn and asked him not to let that great trouble-maker stay there any longer to grieve them. Bjorn agreed to see to it as soon as winter was over.

Thrand Thorarinsson of Akrar was healed;[1] he later became a notable man. There is nothing more to be told of Grettir's dealings with the men of Myrar during his stay on the mountain. Bjorn preserved his friendship with him, although he lost some of his other friends by letting Grettir stay there, since they did not like having their kinsmen unatoned for.

At the time of the Althing Grettir left Myrar and went once more over to Borgarfjord, where he saw Grim Thorhallsson and asked his advice about what he should do. Grim said that he was not in a position to give him shelter, so Grettir went to see his friend Hallmund and stayed with him until the end of the summer.

In the autumn Grettir went up to Geitland and waited there until the weather cleared. Then he climbed up Geitland Glacier and went

---

1 *Thrand married Steinunn, the daughter of Hrut of Kambsness. Thorleif of Hraundale, Steinolf's father, was an important man, and from him are descended the Hraundalers.* Hrut of Kambsness figures prominently in the first chapters of *Njal's Saga* and in *Laxdæla Saga*.

southeast across the ice, carrying a kettle and a flint for making fire. It is thought that he followed directions given to him by Hallmund, who had extensive knowledge of these parts. He travelled on until he came upon a long and narrow valley in the middle of the glacier which was surrounded on all sides by overhanging ice. He managed to scramble down into it at one place, and then he saw beautiful slopes covered with grass and brushwood. There were hot springs in the valley, and Grettir thought that this must be the reason that the glacier had not covered the valley. A stream flowed along the valley with level meadows on either side. The sun shone in the valley only for a brief time each day. Grettir was impressed by the number of sheep there, and they were much fatter and in better condition than any he had ever seen.

Grettir prepared to stay there, and built a hut with what wood he could find. He caught sheep for his food, and each of them yielded more meat than two elsewhere. There was a certain hornless dun-coloured ewe, with a lamb; this ewe seemed to him the biggest and finest of all the sheep. Grettir was anxious to catch her lamb, and when he succeeded he slaughtered it and saw that there were forty pounds of suet in it, and that the rest of the carcass was even better. When the ewe had lost her lamb she used to climb on to the roof of Grettir's hut every night and bleat so much that he was unable to sleep. She disturbed him so much that he was sorry that he had killed the lamb.

Every evening at dusk he heard someone up the valley calling the sheep, and then they all flocked together to their fold. Grettir has said that a certain half-troll named Thorir, a giant, ruled over the valley, and that he himself stayed there under his protection. Grettir named the valley after him, calling it Thorisdale. He said that he had had a good deal of fun with Thorir's daughters, and that they liked it too, for there were not many visitors around. Grettir observed the fast of Lent by eating only suet and liver.

Nothing happened there over the winter, and finally Grettir found the place so dull that he could not stay there any longer. So he left the valley, walked south across the ice, and came down just north of the centre of Skjaldbreid. There he put up a slab of stone, chiselled a hole in it, and said that if a man put his eye close to the hole in the slab he could see the ravine which runs down from Thorisdale. Afterwards he travelled to the southern districts, and then to the Eastfjords. This journey took him all summer and winter, and he went to see all of the leading men, but he had become so hard-pressed that nowhere could he get food and lodging. So he went back into the north, and stayed there at various places.

62

Shortly after Grettir left Arnarwater Moor, a man called Grim came to live there. He was the son of the widow at Kropp, and he had been outlawed for killing the son of Eid Skeggjason of As. He settled down at the place where Grettir had stayed, and caught a lot of fish in the lake.

Hallmund was resentful that Grim had taken Grettir's place, and decided to see to it that he would not benefit from all his fishing. It happened one day that Grim caught over a hundred fish, carried them back to his hut, and stored them outside. When he came out the next morning every fish had vanished, and he thought this very strange. He went again to the lake, and this time caught over two hundred fish. He brought them home and stored them as before, but the same thing happened again, and they had all vanished in the morning. He realized there must be something wrong. The third day he caught over three hundred fish, carried them home, and kept watch in his hut all night. He kept looking out through the hole in the door to see if anyone came. The night went on, and when about a third of it had passed, he heard someone walking outside with heavy steps. When he heard this he seized his axe, which was very sharp, and determined to see what was going on. The stranger had a huge basket on his back; he put it down and looked around, but saw no one outside. Then, feeling very pleased with himself, he set to work, and swept all the fish into the basket. The fish filled the basket, and they were so heavy that Grim thought no horse could carry a heavier load. The stranger seized the basket and lifted it, and as he was getting up Grim rushed out of the hut and swung the axe with both hands at his neck, sinking the blade right up to the helve. The stranger turned quickly and raced south to the mountain, with the basket on his back. Grim ran after him, for he wanted to know what he had done to him. They went south to Ball Glacier, and there the stranger went into a cave. A bright fire was burning inside, and by it sat a tall handsome woman. Grim heard her greet him as father, and call him Hallmund. He dropped his burden heavily, and heaved a great sigh. She asked him why he was covered with blood.

He answered with this verse:

I see now that no man can trust
in his own strength, for his courage will fail
on his dying day,
as his life is ebbing out.

She asked him exactly what had happened, and he told her all about their dealings. 'You must now listen to me,' he said, 'and I will tell you my achievements. I will put them into a poem, and you must carve it later in runes on a staff.'

She agreed, and then he recited *Hallmund's Poem*, which includes these stanzas:

Grettir thought me strong
when I pulled the reins
out of his grip; I saw him
gaze at his empty hands.

When Thorir came
to Arnarwater Moor,
Grettir and I played the battle-game
against eighty men.

Grettir thought his blows
were hitting their shields,
but it was my sword
that impressed them much more.

I sent heads and hands flying
from Grettir's opponents,
so that eighteen champions
were left lying dead.

I dealt harshly with giants
and all their kindred;
I played rough with rock-dwellers,
and beat half-trolls and monsters.

I was the scourge of ogres,
and I punished the elves.

Hallmund mentioned many exploits in the poem, for he had been in every part of the country.

Then his daughter said, 'This man didn't let you slip through his fingers – and you might have expected such an outcome after what you had done to provoke him. Who will avenge you now?'

Hallmund said, 'It is not certain that I will ever be avenged. I know that Grettir would do it if he could get the opportunity, but it will not be easy to fight the good luck of this man, because he has a great destiny.'

Hallmund's strength had been ebbing away as he spoke the poem, and he died just when he finished it.

The daughter was overcome with grief and wept bitterly. Then Grim came forward and told her to take heart. 'Everyone must die when his time is up. And what happened was mostly his own doing; I could hardly stand idly by while he robbed me.'

She admitted that there had been much in what he said. 'Injustice always leads to trouble.'

Then she became a bit more cheerful to talk to. Grim stayed many nights in the cave and learnt the poem; they got on handsomely together. He spent the winter after Hallmund's death on Arnarwater Moor. Afterwards Thorkel Eyjolfsson came to meet him on the moor, and they fought there. The outcome was that Grim had Thorkel's life in his hands, but would not kill him. Thorkel invited him home, got him a passage abroad, and gave him much money. Each of them was considered to have acted well towards the other.[1] Afterwards Grim became a seafaring trader, and great stories are told about him.

63

Meanwhile, Grettir had gone west from the fjords. He travelled in secrecy and was lying low because he did not want to meet Thorir. During the summer he lived out in the open at various places on Modrudale Moor, and at times on Reykja Moor. Thorir learned that he was on Reykja Moor, and so he gathered a force and rode to the moor, determined not to let him get away. Grettir did not know about this until they had come very close to him. He was then staying at a certain shieling close to the path, and had one companion with him. When they saw the men approaching there was not a

---

1 This incident is described in greater detail in *Laxdœla Saga*, which evidently was the author's source of information.

moment to spare. Grettir said they must stun their horses and drag them into the shieling, and this they did.

Thorir rode north across the moor, but he and his men did not find Grettir, and so they went back home. When they had gone off towards the west, Grettir said, 'They will not be pleased with their trip unless they find us. Now you go look after our horses, and I'll go see them. It would be a good joke on them if they didn't recognize me.'

His companions tried to dissuade him, but nevertheless Grettir put on other clothes, with a big hood that covered his face, and, with a staff in his hand, walked down to the path in front of them. They greeted him and asked him if he had seen any men riding on the moor.

'I must have seen the men you are looking for. You have almost found them, since they were just south of those bogs over to the left there.'

When they heard that, they galloped out into the bogs. There was such a swamp there that they could not get through. They struggled there for most of the day, and cursed the tramp for making such fools of them. Grettir had gone back immediately to his companion, and when they met, he spoke these verses:

I did not ride to meet these warriors,
for the test would have been too hard.
I made my escape alone,
and I have no wish to see them.
You may think me mad,
but I wait for a better chance.

I keep out of harm's way,
far from Thorir's forces.

They then rode as fast as they could west across the moor and past the farm at Gard, before Thorir came down from the moor with his men. When they were near the farm, a man joined them, but did not recognize them. They saw a woman outside who was young and splendidly dressed; Grettir asked who she might be. The newcomer said that she was Thorir's daughter. Then Grettir said:

This wise and gold-decked lady
can take my words to her father,
not that they matter much,
but I've ridden past his mansion.

I only had two companions
as I passed this splendid farm:
with this small retinue
I rode through his meadow.

From this the newcomer guessed who these men must be, and he rode down to the house and reported that Grettir had ridden by. When Thorir came home, many people thought that Grettir had made a fool of him. Then Thorir set spies to watch out for Grettir, wherever he might go. But Grettir decided to send his companion west with their horses, and he himself went up into the mountains in disguise. At the beginning of winter he came back north without having been recognized. Everyone thought that Thorir had come off just as badly, or even worse, in their dealings this time.

64

There was a priest called Stein who lived at Eyjardaleriver in Bardardale; he was a good farmer and owned a lot of livestock. He had a son, Kjartan, who was a vigorous young man. A man called Thorstein the White was living at Sandhaugar, south of Eyjardaleriver. He had a wife called Steinvor, who was young and cheerful; their children were still small. The farm at Sandhaugar was said to be haunted by trolls. Two years before Grettir came to the north it happened that Steinvor had gone to the Christmas mass at Eyjardaleriver, as was her custom, but her husband stayed home. In the evening the household went to bed, and during the night they heard a great noise in the hall, as something moved towards the farmer's bed. No one had the courage to get up and see what was happening, for there were only a few people on the farm. When the housewife came home in the morning her husband had vanished, and no one knew what had become of him.

Twelve months passed, and the next Christmas the housewife again wished to go to mass. She asked her servant to stay home; he was unwilling, but told her she could have her own way. Everything happened just as before, and the servant disappeared. This was thought a great marvel. When some spatterings of blood were discovered in the outer doorway, people realized monsters must have taken both men.

The news of this spread far and wide. Grettir got to hear of it, and since he was so good at putting an end to hauntings and ghosts, he set off for Bardardale and arrived at Sandhaugar on the day before Christmas. He concealed his identity and called himself Gest. The housewife thought that he was an exceptionally big man, but the rest of the household were frightened by him. He asked if he could stay for the night, and the housewife said he was welcome. 'But you must look after your own safety.'

He said that so it should be. 'I will stay here,' he said, 'but you go to mass, if you want.'

She said, 'I think you must be a very brave man, if you dare to stay here at home.'

'I'm always willing to try something new,' he said.

'I don't want to stay at home,' she said, 'but I can't get across the river.'

'I will help you across,' he said.

Then she made herself ready to go to church, and took along her small daughter. There had been a great thaw, and the river was in flood, and filled with broken ice.

The housewife said, 'Neither men nor horses can cross the river now.'

'There must be fords in it,' said Grettir, 'and don't be frightened.'

'Take the girl first,' said the housewife. 'She is lighter.'

'I can't be bothered to make two trips for this,' said Grettir. 'I will carry you on my arm.'

She crossed herself and said, 'This is impossible. And what are you going to do with the girl?'

'I'll think of something,' he said.

He picked them both up and put the girl on her mother's knee, and carried them on his left arm; he had his right arm free, and in this way he waded into the water. The women were so frightened they did not dare to scream. The river immediately crashed against his chest, and a huge ice-floe was driven at him, but he pushed his free hand against it, and fended it off. Then the water became so deep that the river was surging on his shoulder, but he waded through it strongly until he reached the bank on the other side, and tossed the women onto dry land.

Then he turned back, and it was already dusk when he reached Sandhaugar. He asked for food, and when he had eaten he told the household to go to the back of the hall. Then he took the table and other available timber and built a bulwark across the hall; it was so high that none of the household could get over it. No one dared to contradict him or to murmur in any way. The door in the hall was on the sidewall, close to the gable, and by the door there was a raised wooden floor. He lay down on it, but did not take off his clothes. There was a light burning in the hall near the door.

The housewife arrived at Eyjardaleriver for mass, and everyone wondered how she could have crossed the river. She said she did not know whether it was a man or a troll who had carried her across. The priest said that it certainly must have been a man. 'But there will be few men who are his equal,' he said, 'and we should keep silent about it, for it may be that this man is meant to put an end to your troubles.' She spent the night there.

65

Now to tell of Grettir: as midnight was approaching he heard a loud noise outside, and then a great she-troll came into the hall. She carried a trough in one hand and a big cleaver in the other. She looked around when she came inside, saw where Grettir was lying, and rushed at him. He got up to meet her; they started grappling fiercely with each other, and fought for a long time in the hall. She was the stronger, but he eluded her skilfully, and everything that came in their way was smashed, even the partition. She dragged him out through the door and into the entryway, but there he stood firm. She wanted to drag him out of the house, but could not do it until they had broken away the whole frame of the outer door and carried it out on their shoulders. The ogress shoved him down to the river and all the way to the edge of the gorge. Although he was exceedingly weary, he had to fight even harder than before, or else let her throw him down into the gorge. They kept fighting all night, and he thought he had never come up against so powerful a monster before. She held him so tightly to herself that he could not use either of his hands, and was forced to clasp his arms around the woman's waist. When they reached the gorge, he gave the ogress a swing, so that his right hand was freed. At once he seized the short sword at his waist, drew it, and struck at her shoulder, slicing off her right arm. With that he was freed, and she dived down into the gorge and vanished under the waterfall.

Grettir was stiff and worn out, and he lay for a long time at the top of the cliff. When the dawn broke he went back to the house and lay down on his bed, all bruised and swollen. When the housewife came home from church, she thought her house had been terribly disarranged. She went up to Grettir and asked him what had happened and why everything was broken and smashed. He told her the whole story; she was greatly impressed, and asked who he was. He gave her his true name, and asked her to send for a priest, because he wanted to see one. She did this, and when the priest Stein came over to Sandhaugar he soon found out that it was Grettir Asmundarson who had been calling himself Gest. The priest asked him what he thought had happened to the men who had disappeared. Grettir said he thought they must have disappeared into the gorge, but the priest answered that he could not believe that story without some evidence. Grettir said they would soon find out, and with that the priest went back home. Grettir lay in bed for many days, and the housewife took good care of him. And so the Christmas season passed.

Grettir said that the she-troll dived down into the gorge when she received the wound, but the men of Bardardale claim that the day dawned upon her as they were wrestling, and that she died when he cut off her arm – and she still stands there on the cliff, turned into stone.

The people in the valley sheltered Grettir secretly for the rest of the winter.

It happened one day after the Christmas season that Grettir went to Eyjardaleriver, and when he met the priest there he said, 'I know, priest, that you put little belief in what I say. I want you to come with me to the river and see for yourself whether there is any evidence.'

The priest agreed, and when they came to the waterfall they saw there was a cave down under the cliff. The cliff was so sheer that it could not be climbed, and it was almost ten fathoms down to the water. They had brought a rope with them.

The priest said, 'It is utterly impossible for you to get down there.'

Grettir replied, 'It is certainly possible, and especially for those who are men of courage. I am going to find out what there is in the waterfall, and you must look after the rope.'

The priest told him to have it his own way, and he drove a peg into the top of the cliff, piled stones around it, and sat down.

66

Now to tell of Grettir: he tied a stone to a loop at the end of the rope, and dropped it down to the water.

'How do you intend to get down?' asked the priest.

'I have a feeling that I don't want to be tied up when I reach the waterfall,' said Grettir.

After that he got ready for the descent: he wore few clothes, and girded himself with a short sword, but had no other weapon. Then he plunged down from the cliff and into the waterfall. The priest glimpsed the soles of his feet, but had no idea what happened to him after that. Grettir dived under the waterfall; this was a difficult thing to do, because the eddy was so strong that he had to dive down to the riverbed before he could get behind the waterfall. Inside, there was a ledge, and he climbed up on it. Above it, and behind the waterfall, there was a huge cave under the cliff edge where the river came crashing down. He went into the cave, where a great log-fire was burning. Grettir saw sitting there an immensely huge giant of terrifying appearance. When Grettir approached him the giant jumped up, seized a pike, and struck with it at his visitor. This pike, which had a wooden shaft, could be used both for striking and thrusting; such a weapon was called a *hepti-sax*.[1] Grettir parried the blow with his short sword, and hit the shaft, cutting it in two. Then the giant tried to reach back to get a sword which hung there in the cave, but at that moment Grettir struck him in the chest and sliced away his front ribs and belly, so that his entrails gushed out of him and into the river, which swept them downstream. The priest, who was sitting by the rope, noticed some bloodstained shreds of flesh being swept down the river. He assumed that Grettir must be dead, and thought there was no reason to stay, so he ran home, leaving the rope unattended. It was evening by then, and the priest reported that Grettir was certainly dead. He added that such a man was a great loss.

But meanwhile, Grettir kept striking the giant furiously until he

---

1 This word is unique to *Grettir's Saga*, and it is interesting to note that a similar compound, *hæft-mēce*, occurs in *Beowulf* (line 1457) as a term for the sword Hrunting which Unferth loans to Beowulf.

was dead. Then he went farther back in the cave, lit a light, and made a search. It is not known how much treasure he found in the cave, but people think it was a fair amount. He stayed there into the night, and found the bones of two men, which he put into a bag. Then he made his way out of the cave and swam to the rope, thinking to find the priest there. When he realized that the priest had gone home, he had to climb up the rope, hand over hand, but he managed to get to the top of the cliff. Then he went back to Eyjardaleriver and left the bag containing the bones on the church-porch. Beside it he left a staff on which these verses were beautifully carved in runes:

Alone I made my way
into the gloomy gorge.
The rock-spitting cascade
gave me a cold wet greeting.
The crushing waterfall
embraced me forcibly.
In this ogre-infested place,
the eddy slapped my shoulder.

The ugly giant came out
to welcome me;
he grappled with me
in a long hard struggle.
I cut the shaft of his hepti-sax,
and then my gleaming sword
ripped the breast and belly open
of this black monster.

In the runes Grettir also said that these bones had been taken by him from the cave. Next morning when the priest came to church he found the staff and the bones, and he read the runes. Grettir had gone back to Sandhaugar.

67

When the priest next saw Grettir, he questioned him closely about what had happened and Grettir gave him all the details of his excursion, and told him that he had not stood faithfully by the rope.

The priest admitted it. People realized that these monsters must have been responsible for the disappearance of men from the valley, and indeed there was never again any trouble there from ghosts or monsters. So Grettir was thought to have rid the countryside of a great curse. The priest buried the bones in the churchyard.

Grettir stayed the winter at Sandhaugar, but only a few people knew he was there. However, Thorir of Gard heard a rumour that Grettir was in Bardardale, and he sent men to kill him. Grettir was advised to leave, and so he went off towards the west. When he came to Modruvellir he went to Gudmund the Powerful, and asked him for help. Gudmund said it would not be easy for him to take in Grettir. 'Your best course,' he said, 'is to find a place to stay where you need not be in fear of your life.'

Grettir said he did not know of any such place.

Gudmund said, 'There is an island in Skagafjord called Drang Isle; it would be a safe stronghold because you can only get up on it by using ladders. If you could once get there, I don't think that anyone could attack you with weapons or by any other means, as long as you looked after the ladder.'

'I will try this,' said Grettir. 'But I have become so afraid of the dark that I could not stay there all by myself, even to save my life.'

Gudmund said, 'That may be, but be sure you trust no one so well that you do not trust yourself still better; most men are hard to judge.'

Grettir thanked him for the good advice, and set off from Modruvellir. He did not stop until he came home to Bjarg, where his mother and Illugi gave him a good welcome. He stayed there for several days, and then he heard that Thorstein Kuggason had been killed. The killing had taken place in the autumn, before Grettir had gone to Bardardale, and Grettir thought it a serious blow.

Afterwards Grettir rode south across Holtavordu Moor with the intention of avenging Hallmund, if he could find Grim. But when he reached Nordriverdale he learned that Grim had left two or three years earlier, as has been related already. Grettir had been slow in hearing about this, because first he had been in hiding for two years, and then he had spent the third winter at Thorisdale, so he had not met anyone who could tell him the news.

Next Grettir went over to the Breidafjord Dales and ambushed travellers who passed through Brattabrekka. He also robbed the smallholders of their possessions. By this time it was about midsummer.

Late that summer Steinvor of Sandhaugar gave birth to a son, and he was named Skeggi. At first he was thought to be the son of

Kjartan, the son of the priest Stein at Eyjardaleriver. Skeggi was unlike his brothers and sisters because of his size and strength. When he was fifteen years old, he was the strongest man there in the north, and so it was concluded that he was Grettir's son. Everyone expected him to become an outstanding man, but he died when he was seventeen, and there is no saga about him.

68

After the killing of Thorstein Kuggason, Snorri the Priest became very unfriendly towards his own son Thorodd, and towards Sam, the son of Bork the Stout, but it is not clear what they had done to deserve this, except that they had refused to carry out some important deed which Snorri had requested of them. For this reason, Snorri the Priest threw Thorodd out and told him not to come back until he had killed some outlaw – and so it had to be.

Thorodd went over to the Dales. At Breidabolstead in Sokkolfsdale there lived a widow called Geirlaug whose shepherd had been sentenced to outlawry for assault; he was only a youth. Thorodd heard about this, and rode over to Breidabolstead. He asked where the shepherd was, and the housewife said he was with the sheep. 'And what do you want with him?'

'I want his life,' said Thorodd, 'for he is a condemned outlaw.'

She replied, 'It is no great achievement for you to kill him, that poor wretch, considering what a hero you think you are. I can tell you about a much greater deed, if you really want to test yourself.'

'What is that?' he said.

She replied, 'Up in the mountain over there Grettir Asmundarson is hiding. Go and fight with him; that would be more fitting for you.'

Thorodd was pleased with this. 'That's what I shall do,' he said.

He spurred his horse and rode up the valley, and when he came to the high ground north of Austurriver, he saw a pale-dun horse with a saddle. He also saw there a big man carrying weapons, and he turned to meet him.

Grettir greeted him, and asked who he was. Thorodd gave his name and said, 'Why don't you ask me my errand, rather than my name?'

'The reason,' said Grettir, 'is that your errand will be trivial. But aren't you the son of Snorri the Priest?'

'I certainly am,' said Thorodd. 'And now I'm going to find out which of us is the better.'

'The answer to that is obvious,' said Grettir. 'Or have you never heard that I have brought little luck to those who have touched me?'

'I know that,' said Thorodd, 'but still I will take the risk.'

Then he drew his sword and attacked furiously, but Grettir defended himself with a shield and did not use a weapon against him. This went on for a while, and Grettir was still unwounded.

'Let's stop playing this game,' he said, 'because you will never get the better of me.'

Thorodd kept striking at him frantically, and Grettir got tired of it, grabbed hold of him, and set him down.

'I can do anything I want with you,' said Grettir, 'and I have no reason to fear that you will kill me, but I do fear old Snorri the Priest, your father, and his plottings, which have brought many a man to his knees. You should only undertake what is within your strength; fighting with me is not child's play.'

When Thorodd saw he could achieve nothing, he calmed down a little, and so they parted. Thorodd rode back home to Tongue and told his father about his dealings with Grettir.

Snorri the Priest smiled and said, 'Many a man is full of conceit, but there was a great difference between you two. You struck at him, but he could do anything he wanted with you, and yet he acted wisely in not killing you, for I couldn't have put up with the thought of leaving you unavenged. So if I am ever in a position to help him, I will.'

Snorri made it clear that he thought Grettir had treated Thorodd well, and after that his counsels were always friendly to Grettir.

69

Grettir rode north to Bjarg a little after he and Thorodd had parted, and he stayed there in secret for some time. By now his fear of the dark had grown so intense that he did not dare go anywhere after it became dusk. His mother invited him to stay on, but she added that she knew this would not do him much good, since he had enemies in every part of the country.

Grettir replied that he was not going to put her in any trouble on his account. 'But I cannot stay alone by myself any longer,' he said, 'even to save my life.'

Illugi, his brother, who was then fifteen years old and an exceptionally promising man, was present at their talk. Grettir told his mother what Gudmund the Powerful had advised him, and said that he would try, if possible, to get to Drang Isle. But he added that he could not stay there unless he could find someone to be with him whom he could trust.

Then Illugi spoke, 'I will go with you, brother, although I don't know how much good my company will do you, except that I will be faithful, and never desert you while you live. Also I will know better what is happening to you if I go with you.'

Grettir said, 'Of all the men in the world you are the one who would give me most comfort, and if my mother will not oppose it, I would like you to come with me.'

Asdis said, 'So it has come to this. I am now trapped between two griefs: I cannot bear to lose Illugi, but I know Grettir's plight has become so serious that something must be done for him. Although I find it hard to see both my sons go away from me, I will agree, if it means that Grettir will suffer less than before.'

Illugi was delighted, for he was looking forward to going with Grettir. Asdis gave them a good deal of money, and they made ready to leave. She walked out with them to see them off, and before they parted, she spoke thus: 'Now you are going, my two sons, and you are fated to die together, and no one can escape the destiny that is shaped for him. I shall never again see either of you, and you must share between you what comes. I do not know what luck you will find there on Drang Isle, but you will never leave it alive, and many men will grudge your stay there. Be on your guard against treachery, but you will be slain by weapons. I have had some very strange dreams. Keep clear of sorcerers, for there are few things stronger than witchcraft.'

When she had said this, she wept bitterly.

Grettir said, 'Don't weep, mother, for it will be said that you bore sons and not daughters, if we are attacked with weapons. Farewell.'

Then they parted, and the brothers travelled north through the district to see their kinsmen. They stayed with them over the autumn until the beginning of winter. Then they went to Skagafjord, north over Vatns Pass and Reykja Pass, across Sæmundarhlid, and so to Langholt. Late one day they arrived at Glaumbæ; Grettir had his cloak-hood back over his shoulders, as was his custom in good weather or bad. After they had walked on a short distance from Glaumbæ, a man came to meet them; he was tall and thin, with a large head, and poorly dressed. He greeted them, and they asked each other's names. The brothers told him who they were, and he said his name was Thorbjorn. He was a vagrant, too lazy to work, and always boasting; some people found him amusing or made sport of him. He started to be very familiar with them, and kept telling them stories about people in the district. Grettir thought him very amusing. Thorbjorn asked if they did not need a man to work for them. 'I would be glad to go with you,' he said.

He told such a good story that they let him come along. It was cold, and there was a drifting snowstorm. Since Thorbjorn was such a blusterer and joker, he had been nicknamed Glaum.[1] 'The men at Glaumbæ were very impressed to see you going hoodless in this bad weather,' said Glaum. 'They wondered whether you were any the braver for being indifferent to the cold. There were two farmer's sons there, very strong men, and the shepherd asked them to come with him to the sheep, but they could hardly put on enough clothes against the cold.' Grettir said, 'I noticed a young man in the doorway pulling on his mittens, and another one going from the cowshed to the dungheap, and neither of them would frighten me.'

Then they travelled down to Reyniness, and spent the night there. From there they went down to the coast, to a farm called Reykir, where a man named Thorvald, a good farmer, was living. Grettir told him that he wanted to get out to Drang Isle, and asked him for help. The farmer stalled, and said that the men of Skagafjord would not think Grettir a welcome guest. Grettir took out the purse that his mother had given him, and handed it to the farmer. His eyes lit up at the sight of the money, and he told his servants to ferry them across the same night, in the moonlight. Reykir is the farm closest to the island, and is about four miles from it.

When they arrived on the island, Grettir liked what he saw there, for it was grassy, and on all sides were steep cliffs which could not be scaled without the help of ladders. If the upper ladder was pulled up, it was impossible to get to the top. The cliffs were teeming with seafowl in the summer. On the island there were eighty sheep owned by various farmers, mostly rams and ewes which were being fattened there for slaughtering.

Grettir settled down on the island. By this time he had been an outlaw for fifteen or sixteen years, according to Sturla Thordarson.

---

1 The nickname *Glaum* means 'noise,' 'noisy merrymaking,' and the like.

70

When Grettir came to Drang Isle, these were the leading men in Skagafjord: Hjalti Thordarson[1] was living at Hof in Hjaltadale; he was a noble chieftain and very well liked. Hjalti had a brother called Thorbjorn Ongul, a tall strong man, harsh and ruthless. Their father Thord had married in his old age, and this wife was not the mother of these brothers. She had been rough with her stepchildren, and especially with Thorbjorn, who was a mischievous troublemaker. On one occasion when Thorbjorn was playing draughts his stepmother came near and saw that the game was *hnettafl*; the pieces were large, with big tails.[2] She thought he was lazy and shouted at him, and he answered back angrily. Then she seized a piece and stabbed its tail into his cheek, but it slipped into his eye, so that the eyeball came out of its socket and was hanging on his cheek. He jumped up and knocked her about mercilessly, so that she took to her bed and later died. People said that she had been pregnant at the time. After that Thorbjorn became the most difficult of men. Later he took over his share of the inheritance, and lived first at Vidvik.

There was a man called Halldor[3] who lived at Hof in Hofdastrand and was married to Thordis, the sister of Hjalti and Thorbjorn Ongul. Halldor was a successful farmer and had a lot of livestock. He had a friend called Bjorn, who lived at Haganess in Fljot. All these men supported one another in every dispute.

There was a famous man called Tungu-Stein[4] who lived at Steinsstead. There was also a man called Eirik,[5] who lived at Hof

1 *Hjalti was the son of Thord, who was the son of Hjalti, the son of Thord Skalp.*
2 *Hnettafl* (or *hneftafl*) was a kind of board game. It is mentioned several times in early Icelandic literature, but little is known of how it was played. In order to keep the pieces in position, each square of the board would sometimes have a hole into which the tail-end of the pieces could fit.
3 *Halldor was the son of Thorgeir, who was the son of Thord of Hofdi.*
4 *Tungu-Stein was the son of Bjorn, who was the son of Ofeig Thin-Beard, the son of Hreidar Crow, to whom Eirik of Goddale gave the tongue of land below Skalamyri.*
5 *Eirik was the son of Dueller-Starri, who was the son of Eirik of Goddale, the son of Hroald, the son of Geirmund Straight-Beard.*

in Goddales. All these were important men. Two brothers, both called Thord, were living at Breidriver in Slettahlid. They were brawny men, and yet peaceable.

All those who have been mentioned owned a share in Drang Isle, and it is said that no less than twenty farmers had a share in the island. No one of them was willing to sell his part to the other owners. Hjalti and Thorbjorn had the greatest shares, for they were richer than the rest.

71

Time went on until the winter solstice. Then the farmers made ready to fetch their sheep from the island for slaughtering. They manned a large boat; most of the farmers sent one man, but some two. When they came near the island they saw people on it, and thought this strange, but they assumed that a ship must have been wrecked there, and that the crew had managed to get ashore. They rowed up to the place where the ladders were, but the men on the top hauled the ladders up. This startled the farmers, and they called up and asked the men who they were. Grettir named himself and his companions. The farmers asked who had ferried him out to the island. Grettir replied, 'I was ferried by someone who owned the boat and a pair of hands, and who was a better friend of mine than of yours.'

The farmers said, 'Allow us to get our sheep, and then come back to the mainland with us. We won't make you pay for the sheep you have already slaughtered.'

Grettir said, 'That is a handsome offer, but either side will have to be content with what they already have. To be short, I will tell you that I will never go away from here, unless I am dragged off dead. I will not surrender what I have gained already.'

The farmers were silent, and thought they had a dangerous guest on the island. They made him many generous offers, both in money and in fair promises, but Grettir refused them all. So the farmers went away, ill-pleased with their luck, and told the men of the district that a wolf had come to the island. This came as a great surprise, and there seemed to be no easy remedy for it. They had meetings about it during the winter, but they could not think of a way to get him off the island.

72

So time passed until the Hegraness Assembly convened in the spring.
A great many men came from all the districts in the jurisdiction of
the assembly. They stayed there for a long time during the spring,
both for business and for pleasure, since there were then many merry-
makers in the district.

When Grettir heard that most of the men had gone to the assembly,
he made an arrangement with his friends – for he was always on
good terms with those who were nearest to him, and never kept back
from them anything he could provide. He said he wanted to go to
the mainland for provisions, and that Illugi and Glaum should
remain behind. Illugi did not think this was a good idea, but still he
let Grettir do as he wished. Grettir told them to look after the ladder,
for everything depended on it. After that he went over to the mainland and got whatever he needed. He went secretly, and no one, in
any of the places where he went, realized that Grettir had come
ashore.

Grettir heard that there was a lot of merriment at the assembly.
He was curious to go there, so he put on some old and disreputable
clothing, and arrived at the assembly when the men were going from
the court back to their booths. Some of the young men were saying
that.in such fine weather it would be good to have some wrestling
and other sports. There was loud approval of this, and men started
gathering and sitting down below the booths. Hjalti and his brother
Thorbjorn Ongul were the leaders in the games; Thorbjorn was a
boisterous man, and organized the games with great vigour. Everyone had to do what Thorbjorn wanted; he grabbed each man by
the shoulder and pushed him on to the field. First the weakest men
wrestled together, then the less weak, and so on. It was all great
entertainment. When all except the strongest had wrestled, the
farmers were talking about who could be found to take on one or
the other of the two Thords who were mentioned earlier. But no one
was willing to; the Thords went up to various men and challenged
them, but the more these men were urged, the more unwilling they
became. Then Thorbjorn Ongul looked around and saw a big man
sitting down, with his face half-covered. Thorbjorn grabbed at him,

and gave him a strong pull, but the man remained seated and did not budge an inch.

Then Thorbjorn said, 'No one else has sat so firmly today when I pulled him. Who is this man?'

He answered, 'I'm called Gest.'

Thorbjorn said, 'You must be willing to entertain us a bit, and you are a most welcome guest.'

He answered, 'Many things can change very suddenly, and I will not jump into this play of yours, since I'm so unfamiliar with everything here.'

Many people said that he would deserve a good turn from them if he would entertain them in some way, a total stranger as he was. He asked what they wanted him to do, and they told him that he should wrestle with someone. He said he had given up scuffling. 'But there was a time when I thought it great fun.'

Since he did not give them a blunt refusal, they became more and more insistent.

He said, 'If it seems so important to have me drawn into your sport, you can have your way, provided you promise me safe conduct here at the assembly, and until I get back to my home.'

They all jumped up and said that they were most willing. The man who was most eager that the stranger be given safe conduct was called Hafr.[1] He lived at Knappstead, and was a very eloquent man. He announced the terms of the truce in a most authoritative manner; this is how he began:

'Now I proclaim a truce between all men, particularly a truce for this man called Gest who sits here beside me, and including every chieftain and important farmer, every man able to bear weapons and to fight, and all others in the jurisdiction of this assembly of Hegraness, wheresoever they are from, whether they be named or un-named – on behalf of all these we promise peace and safe conduct to this stranger called Gest, for games, wrestling, and all other sports, for his stay here and for his journey back home, whether he travel by land or by sea, whether he go by ship or by conveyance.

'He shall have peace at every place, specified or unspecified, as long as he has need of it for a safe journey home, while this truce is in force.

'I proclaim this truce on behalf of all of us and our kinsmen, our friends and relatives, both men and women, slaves and bondmaids, farmhands and free men.

1 Hafr was the son of Thorarin, the son of Hafr, who was the son of Thord Knapp, the original settler of the region between Stifla in Fljot and Tongueriver.

'He shall be branded a truce-breaker who violates this pledge or destroys this peace – to be banished and driven away from God and good men, from heaven and all holy men; he shall be deemed unfit to live among men, and, like a wolf, shall be an outlaw everywhere – wherever Christians go to church or heathens hold sacrifices, where-ever fire burns, the earth grows, a speaking child calls his mother and a mother bears a son, wherever people kindle fires, where a ship sails, shields glitter, the sun shines, snow drifts, a Lapp goes on skis, a fir tree grows, where a falcon flies on a long summer's day with a fair breeze blowing under both wings, where the heavens turn, where lands are lived in, where the wind washes water down to the sea, where men sow seed – in all those places the trucebreaker shall be barred from churches and Christians, from heathens, from houses and holes, from every place except Hell alone.

'Now we shall all agree and be at peace with one another, and be of good will, whether we meet on a mountain or on a beach, whether on a ship or on skis, on earth or on ice, at sea or on horseback – just as when one meets his friend at the ford or his brother on the road; we shall be in concord as a son should be with his father and a father with his son, in all their exchanges.

'Now let us clasp hands, and we must all observe the truce properly and every single word in this pledge. To this may God and all good men be my witnesses, and also those who hear my words and are now present.'[2]

Many people remarked that much had been promised.

Gest said, 'You have spoken well about this, if your words remain good. I shan't make you wait long for what I have to offer.'

He threw off his cloak and then his clothes. The men were dumb-founded, and they kept looking at one another, for they realized that this must be Grettir Asmundarson, since he surpassed other men in size and strength. They all fell silent, and Hafr saw he had made a fool of himself. The farmers broke up into groups of two, and each man blamed the man he was with, but they blamed most of all the man who had proclaimed the truce.

Then Grettir said, 'You must tell me precisely what is in your minds, because I'm not going to sit here without clothes for very long. You have much more to lose by breaking the truce than I have.'

They had little to say, and sat down. Hjalti Thordarson and Thorbjorn Ongul, together with their brother-in-law Halldor, went

2 This truce formula, composed in rhythmic alliterative prose, is the only archaic passage in the saga. Similar formulæ are to be found in the early law texts, but the author's immediate source was probably *Heiðarvíga Saga*.

aside to talk. Some of the farmers wanted to keep the truce, but others did not, and they kept nodding their heads portentously at one another.

Grettir spoke this verse:

No one guessed who I was
when I came here this morning,
even the people
who had met me before.
But now they all falter
and even words fail them.
Poor Hafr's drivel
had a sorry ending.

Then Tungu-Stein said, 'So that is what you think, Grettir. But what decision will the chieftains make? It is true that you are a man of outstanding courage, but don't you see how the men are putting their heads together?'

Then Grettir spoke this verse:

Warriors who always sheltered
behind their shields
are now busy whispering
and mumbling into their beards.
They flock together in groups,
now that they know who I am,
and everyone regrets
the offer of safe-conduct.

Then Hjalti Thordarson said, 'That must not be; we shall honour our pledge, even though we have been made such fools of. I don't want others to have, as precedent, the fact that we broke a truce which we ourselves had made and given. Grettir shall be free to go wherever he wants, and he can have a safe conduct until he finishes his journey. After that this truce will no longer be valid, whatever happens between us.'

Everyone thanked him for this, and thought that he had acted as a chieftain should, under these circumstances. But Thorbjorn Ongul was silent.

It was then suggested that one of the two Thords should take on Grettir, who said he wouldn't mind. So one of the two brothers came forward; Grettir stood waiting, and Thord attacked forcefully, but Grettir did not budge an inch. Then Grettir reached over Thord's back, seized his breeches, snatched him up, and threw him back over his head so that Thord landed very heavily on his shoulders.

Then it was suggested that both brothers should go for him at the same time, and this they did. It was a fierce struggle; now one and now the other side was winning, but still Grettir always managed to keep one of them down, though all of them got thrown to their knees or flat on the ground from time to time. They seized each other so strongly that they were bruised and scratched all over. Everyone thought this excellent entertainment, and when the bout was over they all thanked the wrestlers. Those who were there agreed that Grettir was stronger than the other two together, even though each of the brothers had the strength of two sturdy men. The brothers were so equally matched that neither could throw the other, when they wrestled together.

Grettir did not stay long at the assembly. The farmers asked him to give up the island, but he refused, and there was nothing they could do about it. Grettir went back to the island, and Illugi was glad to see him. They lived there quietly for some time, and Grettir told them about his journey. So the summer passed.

Everyone thought that the men of Skagafjord had acted with great honour in upholding their pledges. When one considers what Grettir had done against them, it can be seen how noble-minded men were in those days.

The lesser farmers agreed among themselves that it was no use to own a small share in Drang Isle. They offered to sell their shares to the Thordarsons, but Hjalti refused to buy. The farmers had stipulated that anyone who bought their shares should either kill Grettir or drive him away. Thorbjorn Ongul said he would not hesitate to undertake an attack on Grettir, provided that he was paid for it. His brother Hjalti handed over to him his share in the island, because Thorbjorn was the more ruthless and unpopular of the two. Other farmers did the same, and so Thorbjorn Ongul acquired most of the island at a low price. He promised to drive Grettir away from it.

73

Late in the summer Thorbjorn Ongul took a fully manned large boat over to Drang Isle. Grettir came to the edge of the cliff, and they talked together. Thorbjorn asked Grettir, as a favour, to leave the island. Grettir said there was no hope of that.

Thorbjorn said, 'It might be that if you did this I could do you a good turn too. Most of the farmers have now handed over to me their shares in the island.'

Grettir said, 'Now that you have told me that you own most of the island, my mind is made up never to leave. It is very proper that we should be sharing this soup between us. Although it is true that I found it hard to have all the men of Skagafjord against me, now neither of us need show the other any mercy, since we shall not be smothered by our popularity. You might as well give up your visits here, for my mind is completely made up.'

'Everything awaits its own hour,' said Thorbjorn, 'and you are awaiting an evil end.'

'That's a risk I must take,' said Grettir.

With that they parted, and Thorbjorn went back home.

74

It is said that when Grettir had been on Drang Isle for two years, he and his companions had slaughtered most of the sheep which had been there. But it is also said that they spared one ram which had a grey belly and huge horns. They had a lot of fun with the ram, for he was so tame that he used to wait outside and follow them wherever they went. In the evenings he used to come up to their hut and rub his horns against the door.

They liked it on the island; there was plenty to eat because of all the seafowl and eggs. But firewood was very scarce, and Grettir was always telling Glaum to look for driftwood; pieces of wood were often driven ashore, and Glaum used to carry them home for the fire. The brothers did not have to do anything, except to go fowling in the cliffs whenever they liked. Glaum was getting lazy, and started complaining and neglecting his duties even more than before. He was supposed to watch the fire every night, and Grettir warned him strictly about doing this, for they had no boat. Then it happened one night that the fire went out. Grettir was furious and said that Glaum deserved to be flogged. Glaum said he had a miserable life, staying there as an outlaw, and being beaten and abused whenever anything went wrong. Grettir asked Illugi what they should do, and he said there was nothing now but to wait for a boat to come. Grettir said it was too uncertain to wait for that. 'Instead, I will take the risk, and see if I can make it to the mainland.'

'That's taking a big chance,' said Illugi, 'and we will all be lost if anything happens to you.'

'I shall not be drowned,' said Grettir. 'But this has taught me to trust the scoundrel less from now on, since there was so much at stake here.'

The closest point on the mainland is four miles from the island.

75

Grettir got ready for swimming: he put on a tunic of homespun cloth which he tucked into his trousers; then the others made his fingers webbed. The weather was fine. He set off from the island late in the afternoon; Illugi was greatly concerned about his trip. Grettir started swimming up the fjord with the current behind him, and the sea calm. He swam strongly, and made Reykjaness by sunset. He walked up to the farm at Reykir and took a bath, for he was feeling very cold. He basked in the warm pool[1] for a good part of the night, and then he went into the hall. It was very hot there, for a fire had been burning earlier, and the room had not cooled off. Grettir was exhausted and fell fast asleep; he lay there until the following day.

Late in the morning the household got up, and the first people to go into the room were two women, a maidservant and the farmer's daughter. Grettir was asleep, and his cover had rolled off down to the floor. The women saw and recognized who he was.

The maidservant said, 'What do you know, dear, here is Grettir Asmundarson, and lying there stark naked. He is certainly big enough in the chest, but it seems to me very odd how small he is farther down. That part of him isn't up to the rest of him.'

The farmer's daughter said, 'Why do you keep running off at the mouth like that, you silly little fool? Keep quiet!'

'I can't keep quiet about this, dear,' said the maid, 'since I never would have believed it, even if someone had told me.'

She kept going over and peeping at him, and then running back to the farmer's daughter and bursting out laughing. Grettir heard what

1 As the name *Reykir*, 'steams,' indicates, there are hot springs there. See note on page 106.

she was saying, and when she ran across the room again he seized her and spoke a stanza:

The hussy is taking a risk.
It's seldom one can get
so close a look
at a hair-girt sword.
I bet that other men's testicles
won't be bigger than mine,
though their penises may be
larger than this one.

After this he pulled her up on the bench, and the farmer's daughter ran out of the room. Then he spoke this stanza:

The wench has complained
that my penis is small,
and the boastful slut
may well be right.
But a small one can grow,
and I'm still a young man,
so wait until I get
into action, my lass.

The maid kept crying out, but in the end, before they parted, she had stopped taunting him.

A little later he got dressed, went to Thorvald, the farmer, and told him about his difficulties. Grettir asked him to ferry him back to the island, and Thorvald did this. He got a boat and took him over, and Grettir thanked him for this noble gesture.

When it became known that Grettir had swum four miles, everyone thought that his valour was outstanding both on land and on sea. The men of Skagafjord criticized Thorbjorn Ongul severely for not getting Grettir out of Drang Isle, and they threatened to take back their former shares. It seemed to Thorbjorn that he was in a difficult position, but he asked them to be patient.

76

That summer a ship from abroad put in at the mouth of Gonguskards River. There was a man on board called Hæring; he was young and so agile that he could climb any cliff. He lodged with Thorbjorn Ongul, and stayed there until late in the autumn.

Hæring kept urging Thorbjorn to go to Drang Isle; he said he wanted to see for himself whether the cliffs were so formidable that they could nowhere be climbed. Thorbjorn said that Hæring would certainly not be working without pay if he could manage to get on the island and wound Grettir or kill him. He made this sound very attractive for Hæring. So after that they went to Drang Isle and smuggled him ashore at a certain place. He was supposed to steal up on Grettir and his companions if he could get on top of the island; meanwhile, Thorbjorn and the crew moved over to the ladder and started talking with Grettir. Thorbjorn asked Grettir whether he was thinking of leaving the island. He answered that he was resolved to stay.

'You have made great fools of us,' said Thorbjorn. 'I don't know when we can take our revenge, but you are obviously not afraid of anything.'

They kept on arguing, and came to no agreement.

Meanwhile, Hæring was climbing back and forth up the face of the cliff, and finally managed to get to the top at a certain place where no one has ever climbed it, before or since. When he reached the top, he saw the brothers standing with their backs to him, so he thought that in a moment he would have won both fame and riches. The brothers were completely unsuspecting, for they thought that no one could get up the cliff except where the ladders were. Grettir was still bickering with Thorbjorn, and there were plenty of cutting words flung about by both of them. Then Illugi happened to glance in another direction, and he saw the man closing in on them.

Illugi said, 'Someone is coming up at us with a raised axe, and he seems to me rather unfriendly.'

'Why don't you turn and deal with him, then,' said Grettir, 'while I look after the ladder?'

Illugi rushed at Hæring, and the Easterner turned and ran away from him all round the island. Illugi chased him to the edge, and there Hæring threw himself down over it, breaking every bone in his body, and killing himself. The place where he perished is still called Hæring's Leap.

Illugi came back, and Grettir asked him how he had parted with the man he had been supposed to deal with.

'He didn't trust me to look after him,' said Illugi, 'and he broke his neck at the foot of the cliff. The farmers can say prayers for him, since he must be dead.'

When Ongul heard that, he told his men to put off. 'I have now made two trips to see Grettir, and I'll not make a third one unless I know more than I do now. It seems likely that they can keep sitting on Drang Isle, for all I can do about it. Yet I suspect that Grettir is more than halfway through his stay there.'

With that they went back home, and this trip was considered even sorrier than the first one. Grettir stayed on the island that winter without seeing Thorbjorn at all.

This same winter Skapti Thoroddson, the Lawspeaker, died. This was a great loss for Grettir, since Skapti had promised to press for his acquittal when he had been an outlaw for twenty years, and this winter was in the nineteenth year of his outlawry. In the spring Snorri the Priest died, and many other events occurred that year, although they do not concern this story.[1]

77

That summer at the Althing Grettir's kinsmen had many discussions about his outlawry. Some of them thought he had already served his full sentence, since he had been an outlaw for more than nineteen years. But the men who had charges against him would not agree, and said that during this time Grettir had committed many offences punishable by outlawry, and that his sentence should therefore be extended.

At this Althing a new Lawspeaker was elected. Stein Thorgestsson,[1]

1 Skapti Thoroddsson died in 1030, and Snorri the Priest in 1031.
1 *Stein was the son of Thorgest, the son of Stein the Fast-Sailing, the son of Thorir Autumn-Dusk. The mother of Stein the Lawspeaker was Arnora, the daughter of Thord Gellir.*

a wise man. He was asked to give a ruling and he told them to find out whether this was the twentieth summer since Grettir was sentenced to outlawry. So it proved to be. Then Thorir of Gard came forward and raised every objection that he could think of. He dug up the fact that Grettir had been in Iceland for a year before the sentence was passed on him, which meant that he had only been an outlaw for nineteen years. The lawspeaker ruled that no one should be an outlaw for more than twenty years in all, even though he committed acts punishable by outlawry during that period. 'But before that time is up, I will not rule that anyone is released from outlawry.'

For this reason the attempt at acquittal came to nothing this time, but it was thought certain that Grettir would be freed the following summer. The men of Skagafjord were displeased that Grettir might be freed from outlawry, and they told Thorbjorn Ongul either to give the island back to them or to kill Grettir. He found himself in a predicament, for he could not see how to kill Grettir, and yet he wanted to keep the island. He looked for any way by which he could vanquish Grettir, whether by strength or by craft, or by any other means.

78

Thorbjorn Ongul had a foster-mother called Thurid; she was very old, and people thought her of little use. She had known a great deal about magic and had been a sorceress when she was young and people were still pagan. By this time she was thought to have forgotten everything about it. But though the country had been Christianized, there were still many sparks of heathenism around. It was the law of the land that it was not forbidden to hold sacrifices and other pagan rites in secret, but such practices were punishable by the lesser outlawry,[1] if they were done publicly. In many cases it happened that 'you can't teach an old dog new tricks,' and 'what's learned in childhood becomes second nature.' And so, when Thorbjorn had run out of ideas, he sought help from the least likely quarter. He went to his foster-mother and asked what advice she could give him.

1 See appendix, page 191.

She replied, 'This seems to bear out the old saying that "many people go to the goat-shed in search of wool." What is less likely than that I should be more clever than all the farmers in the district, or that I should be of any use when there is something important at stake? However, I can't see how I could do worse than you have, even though I can hardly get out of my bed. If you agree to follow my advice, I will tell you how to go about it.'

He agreed to this, and said she had always given him good advice.

Nothing further happened, and time passed until late in the summer. Then, one fine day, the old woman said to Ongul, 'Now the weather is bright and clear. I want you to go over to Drang Isle and throw insults at Grettir. I will go with you to see how well he can control his tongue. If I see them I can be sure about how much good luck they will have, and then I will pronounce on them such words as I see fit.'

Ongul answered, 'I am getting tired of these trips to Drang Isle, for I am always in a worse mood when I come back than when I go.'

The old woman said, 'I will do nothing to help you unless you let me have my way.'

'You certainly may, foster-mother,' he said. 'But I have said that when I went there for a third time something would get settled between us.'

'You will have to take the risk,' said the old woman, 'and you will have many difficulties before Grettir is laid to the ground. You will often think that your lot is in doubt before the end comes, and you will have to suffer for it. But you are so firmly committed that something must be done.'

Then Thorbjorn Ongul had a ten-oared boat launched and took a crew of eleven men. The old woman went with them. They rowed out to Drang Isle, and when the brothers saw them, they went over to the ladder. They started discussing the matter again, and Thorbjorn said he had come once more to find out if Grettir was willing to leave. He added that he would consider his losses and Grettir's stay on the island up to this time to be unimportant, provided they could now come to an agreement.

Grettir said he would not leave, and had no compromise to accept or to offer. 'I have told you this often enough and there is no use discussing it with me. You can do what you want, but I am staying here whatever happens.'

Thorbjorn realized what results he was likely to get this time, and he said, 'I knew already what hellhounds I have to deal with here. It seems likely that some days will pass before I come again.'

159

'I wouldn't count it among my sorrows if you never came again,' said Grettir.

The old woman was lying in the stern, covered up with blankets. She stirred a bit and said, 'These are strong men but luckless, and there is a great difference betweeen you and them. You make them many good offers, and they refuse them all. There are few things which lead more certainly to disaster than not to want what is good. Now I make this pronouncement on you, Grettir, that you be deprived of your good luck and all good fortune, deprived of all help and all wisdom – and ever the more, the longer you live. I think that you will have fewer days of happiness in the future than you have had in the past.'

When Grettir heard this he was very startled, and he said, 'What fiend is in the boat with them?'

Illugi answered, 'I think it must be the old woman, Thorbjorn's foster-mother.'

'Curses on that witch,' said Grettir. 'We could not have expected anything worse than her. No other words have ever affected me as much as hers, and I know for certain that through her and her sorcery I shall suffer greatly. But she shall have something to remember her visit by.'

He picked up a piece of rock and hurled it down at the boat, hitting the heap of clothes. It was a longer throw than Thorbjorn thought any man capable of. Then there came up a loud shriek, for the stone had hit the old woman in the thigh and broken the bone.

Illugi said, 'I wish you hadn't done that.'

'Don't blame me for it,' said Grettir. 'I'm afraid that I have not done enough, for it would not be too great a revenge for both of us if one old woman should lose her life.'

'How could she be balanced against us?' asked Illugi. 'That would be a sorry price for the two of us.'

Thorbjorn turned back home, and no farewells were said on either side. Then he said to the old woman, 'This has turned out as I expected, and you have gained little glory by your trip to the island. You have been maimed, and we are no closer than before to gaining honour. We have to suffer one disgrace after another without taking any revenge.'

She replied, 'This is the beginning of their bad luck, and I think that from now on they will be going downwards. I have no fear that I won't be able to repay them for this gift they have given me, if I live.'

'I think you are a brave woman, foster-mother,' said Thorbjorn.

They went home, and the old woman took to her bed. She lay

there for nearly a month, and then the bone set so that she could get up.

Everyone laughed about the excursion Thorbjorn and the old woman had made. It seemed as if Thorbjorn had suffered a series of setbacks in his dealings with Grettir: first at the assembly when the truce was given; then when Hæring lost his life; and now a third time when the old woman's thigh-bone was broken; while Thorbjorn had done nothing to settle the score. He was greatly upset by such talk.

79

Late in the autumn, three weeks before the beginning of winter, the old woman asked to be taken in a cart down to the shore. Thorbjorn asked what she wanted to do.

'Nothing very much,' she said, 'yet it may be the portent of greater events to come.'

What she asked was done, and when she came to the shore she limped along beside the sea as if something was guiding her. Lying before her there was a tree-trunk with its roots, as heavy as a man could carry. She looked at the tree and asked them to turn it over for her; it seemed to have been burned and scraped on the other side. She told them to carve a small smooth surface on it, where it had been scraped. Then she took her knife, cut some runes on the tree, smeared them with her blood, and chanted some spells over them. She walked backwards around the trunk going against the course of the sun, and pronounced many powerful charms. Afterwards she told them to push the trunk into the sea, and she laid a spell on it, that it should drift out to Drang Isle and cause Grettir every grief. Then she went back home to Vidvik. Thorbjorn said he did not know what good this would do, and the old woman said he would find out later. The wind was blowing landwards, yet the old woman's tree drifted against the wind, and at a remarkable speed.

As was mentioned earlier, Grettir and his companions were very content with their situation on Drang Isle. The day after the old woman had put the spell on the tree, Grettir and Illugi went down the cliff to look for firewood. When they came to the west side of

161

the island, they found a large trunk with roots that had drifted ashore.

Illugi said, 'Here is a lot of firewood, brother. Let's take it home.'

Grettir kicked it and said, 'An evil tree, sent to us by evil. We must get other wood for the fire.'

With that he threw it out to sea, and warned Illugi not to take it home. 'It has been sent to destroy us.'

They went back to their hut and did not mention this to Glaum. The next day they found the tree again, at a place closer to the ladder than the day before. Grettir pushed it into the sea and said they must never take it home.

The night passed, and then a gale started blowing with a lot of rain. The brothers couldn't be bothered to go outside, and they told Glaum to look for firewood. He started chafing and said that they were tormenting him by making him suffer outside in every storm. He went down the ladder and saw the old woman's tree, which he thought a good find. He picked it up and struggled back with it to the hut. When he threw it down there was a loud crash. Grettir heard this and said, 'Glaum must have brought us something. I'll go out and see what it is.' He picked up an axe and went outside.

Glaum said, 'Just do as good a job in chopping as I did in providing.'

Grettir got angry at the slave, and without thinking what tree it was he swung the axe at it with both hands. When the axe hit the wood it turned flat and glanced off into Grettir's right leg above the knee, going right into the bone. It was a serious wound.

Grettir looked at the tree and said, 'The evil-wisher has won the day, and this is not the end of it. This is the same tree that I threw away on two occasions. You have now committed two blunders, Glaum. The first was that you let our fire go out, and the second, that you brought home this tree of ill-luck. If you commit a third blunder it will be the death of you and the death of us all.'

Illugi came and dressed Grettir's wound. It bled little, and Grettir slept well that night. Three nights passed, and there was still no pain in the wound. When they took the dressing off the wound had closed and seemed to be nearly healed.

Illugi said, 'I think this wound won't give you much trouble.'

'That would be good,' said Grettir, 'but this has been a strange experience, whatever comes of it, and I have a foreboding that you will be wrong.'

80

That evening they lay down to sleep, but about midnight Grettir began to move about violently. Illugi asked why he was so restless, and Grettir replied that his leg hurt. 'It seems to me likely that it has a different colour now.'

They got a light, and when the wound had been unbandaged the leg was swollen and coal-black, while the wound had opened wide and looked much uglier than before. It gave Grettir much pain, so that he could not lie quiet or get a wink of sleep.

Then Grettir said, 'We must face the truth: this illness of mine is not a mere accident, for it is caused by sorcery. The old woman is trying to avenge the blow she received from my stone.'

Illugi said, 'I told you that no good would come from the old woman.'

'It will all come to the same in the end,' said Grettir.[1] 'But now we must be on our guard, because Thorbjorn Ongul and the old woman won't be intending to stop here. I want you, Glaum, to watch the ladder every day from now on, and to pull it up in the evening. Do this faithfully, for much is at stake. If you betray us, you will soon suffer.'

Glaum promised solemnly to do this. Soon the weather began to worsen, with a cold northeasterly wind setting in. Every evening Grettir asked if the ladder had been hauled up.

Glaum said, 'This is certainly a good time to expect visitors! Do you think anyone is so anxious to take your life that he will sacrifice his own for it? This weather is far worse than just impossible to travel in. It seems to me that your courage has vanished, if you think that everything might be the death of you two.'

'You will certainly cringe more than either of us, whatever the circumstances,' said Grettir. 'And you must look after the ladder, whether you want to or not.'

They drove him out of the hut every morning, and he did not like it at all. The pain in Grettir's leg grew worse, and the whole leg

---

1 One of the four principal manuscripts gives here five stanzas, which we omit.

became swollen. The upper and lower parts of his thigh began to fester all around the wound, and he seemed close to death.

Illugi sat by his side day and night, and thought of nothing else. Over a week had now passed since Grettir's injury.

81

Thorbjorn stayed home in Vidvik, and was unhappy about his failure to deal with Grettir. Just over a week after the old woman put the spell on the tree, she came to talk to Thorbjorn. She asked him if he did not intend to visit Grettir, and he replied that this was the one thing he had made up his mind about. 'But perhaps you would like to see him, foster-mother?' he asked.

'I'm not going to see him,' she said, 'but I have sent him my greetings, and I expect they have reached him by now. I think you would be well advised to set off at once and go quickly to see him, or else you will never be able to overcome him.'

Thorbjorn replied, 'I have had so many humiliating trips there already that I am not going to make another one. And in any case the weather is sufficient reason, since this raging gale makes it impossible to go anywhere, however urgent the need.'

She said, 'How utterly helpless you are! You don't see how to go about it, so I must tell you further what to do. First, you must go and gather men, and then ride over to your brother-in-law Halldor at Hof, and get his advice.

'If I have some power over Grettir's health, is it so absurd that I should be responsible for this breeze which now has been blowing for a while.'

It seemed possible to Thorbjorn that the old woman could see further than he had thought, and so he at once sent around the district for men. But he was answered very quickly; none of the men who had given up their shares in the island was willing to help in any way. They said that Thorbjorn was welcome to both the island and the attack on Grettir. But Tungu-Stein lent him two of his men; Thorbjorn's brother Hjalti sent three men; Erik of Goddales sent one man; and Thorbjorn himself took six men from home.

Thorbjorn and these twelve men rode over to Hof. Halldor invited them to stay and asked why they had come. Thorbjorn told him the whole story, and Halldor asked whose idea this was. Thorbjorn said that his foster-mother was urging him to do it.

'Then this will lead to no good,' said Halldor, 'for she is a sorceress, and sorcery is now forbidden.'

'I cannot worry about everything,' said Thorbjorn. 'And now the issue shall be settled once and for all, if I can have my way. But how can I get to the island?'

'I see that you have placed your trust in something,' said Halldor, 'though I don't know how good that something is. But if you must go ahead with this, then go out to Haganess in Fljot and see my friend Bjorn. He has a good large boat, and ask him, in my name, to lend it to you. From there you can sail to Drang Isle, but I don't like the prospect of your trip, if Grettir is in good health. You can be sure of this, that if you overcome him by dishonourable means there will be plenty of men to seek redress. Don't kill Illugi, if you can help it. But I realize that this scheme is not altogether of a Christian nature.'

Halldor sent six men with him; one was called Kar, another Thorleif, and the third Brand – the names of the others are not known. From there these eighteen men travelled out to Fljot until they came to Haganess, and gave Bjorn the message from Halldor. He said he would do it for Halldor's sake, although he did not owe Thorbjorn anything. He thought it was madness to go, and tried to dissuade them, but they refused to turn back, went to the beach, and launched the boat. All the rigging was nearby in the boat-house, and they made ready to put out. Everyone ashore thought the crossing impossible.

Thorbjorn and his men hoisted sail, and at once the boat gathered speed and swept along down the fjord. When they reached the deep water out in the fjord, the wind abated, so that they thought it not too strong. They reached Drang Isle in the evening, after dark.

82

By this time Grettir was so ill that he could no longer stand on his feet. Illugi stayed with him, and Glaum was supposed to be on guard, but he kept protesting, and said that they seemed to think that their lives might simply vanish, even if nothing happened. He left the hut very much against his will, and when he came to the ladder he started talking to himself, saying that he wasn't going to pull up the ladder. Then he became very drowsy, lay down, and slept all day, until Thorbjorn arrived at the island.

When they saw that the ladder had not been pulled up, Thorbjorn said, 'This is a change, for there is no one about, and the ladder is still in place. It may be that more will happen on our trip than we thought at first. Now we must go to the hut and set boldly to work. We can be certain that if they are in good health, every one of us will need to do his best.'

They climbed up onto the island, looked around, and saw where a man lay close to the ladder, snoring loudly. Thorbjorn recognized Glaum, went up to him, struck him on the ear with the hilt of his sword, and told the rascal to wake up. 'He's a sorry man whose life depends on your loyalty,' he said.

Glaum looked up and said, 'Now they will act the way they always do. Do you think I have too much freedom, though I lie out here in the cold?'

Ongul said, 'Are you out of your mind? Don't you realize that your enemies are here and that they are going to kill you all?'

Glaum did not say a word, but started screaming at the top of his lungs, now that he recognized them.

'Shut up and tell us at once about the arrangements in your hut,' said Ongul, 'or else I will kill you.'

Glaum was as silent as if he had been submerged under water.

Ongul said, 'Are the brothers in the hut? Why aren't they up and outside?'

'It's not easy for them,' said Glaum, 'for Grettir is ill and dying, and Illugi is sitting by him.'

Ongul asked about Grettir's health, and what had happened, so Glaum told him all about Grettir's injury.

Then Ongul laughed and said, 'The old saying is certainly true: "Old friends are always best," and also in your case, "It's a bad thing to have a slave for a friend." Your master may not be a good man, but you have betrayed him in the most shameful way.'

The others abused him for his faithlessness; then they beat him almost beyond recovery and left him lying there. After that they went up to the hut and hammered on the door.

Then Illugi said, 'The grey-bellied ram is knocking at the door, brother.'

'He is knocking hard,' said Grettir, 'and mercilessly.'

At that moment the door broke. Illugi seized his weapons and guarded the door, so that they couldn't get inside. They kept up

166

the attack for a long time, but could only reach at him with their spears, and Illugi severed every spearshaft. When they realized they were not getting anywhere, they jumped up onto the roof and broke in there. Then Grettir got to his feet, seized a spear, and thrust it between the rafters, running it right through Kar, a servant of Hall-dor of Hof. Ongul told his men to be wary and to guard themselves, 'Because we can certainly overcome them, if we go about it wisely.'

Then they exposed the ends of the ridge-beam and forced it until it broke. Grettir, who could not rise from his knees, seized the short sword he had taken from Kar's mound. At that moment they jumped down into the hut, and there was a fierce fight. Grettir struck with his sword at Vikar, Hjalti Thordarson's servant, and caught him on the left shoulder as he was jumping down into the hut. The sword went all the way through his shoulder and out at the right side, slicing him in two, so that the two parts of his trunk tumbled down on top of Grettir, preventing him from getting his sword up again as quickly as he would have liked. At that moment Thorbjorn Ongul thrust at him between his shoulders, and wounded him seriously.

Then Grettir said, ' "Bare is his back, who has no brother." '

Illugi threw a shield over him and defended him so bravely that everyone praised him.

Grettir said to Ongul, 'Who guided you to the island?'

Ongul said, 'It was Christ who guided us here.'

'But I think,' said Grettir, 'that that evil old woman, your nurse, must have guided you, for you are sure to have followed her advice.'

'It will make no difference to you,' said Ongul, 'who our guide has been.'

The attackers fought hard, but Illugi put up a brave defence. Grettir was unable to fight because of his wounds and his illness. Then Ongul told his men to close in on Illugi with their shields. 'I have never found anyone like him, and yet he is so young.'

They did as he told them, and pressed at Illugi with rafters and weapons, so that he could not defend himself. Then they captured him and held him. He had wounded most of the attackers and killed three of Ongul's companions.

Then they approached Grettir, who had slumped forward. He could make no resistance, for he was already at the point of death because of his wounded leg; his thigh had festered all the way up to his intestines. They gave him many wounds, but there was little or no bleeding. When they thought that he must be dead, Ongul grabbed at Grettir's short sword, and said that he had carried it long enough, but Grettir had locked his fingers so tightly around the hilt that Ongul could not free it. Others went and tried; before they stopped, eight of them had tried to free it, but with no success.

Then Ongul said, 'Why should we spare the outlaw? Put his hand on that beam.'

They did this, and Ongul cut his hand off at the wrist; then the fingers straightened and let go of the hilt. Ongul seized the short sword with both hands and struck at Grettir's head. It was a heavy blow, more than the weapon could take, and a piece was broken off its edge. When the men saw this, they asked Ongul why he was spoiling so fine a weapon.

He answered, 'This will be a good proof, should people ask about it.'

They said that this was unneccessary, since the man was already dead.

'I shall do even more,' said Ongul.

Then he struck at Grettir's neck two or three times before the head came off. 'Now I know for certain that Grettir is dead,' said Ongul. 'We have felled a great fighter. And we must take the head with us back to the mainland, for I don't want to lose the money which has been put upon it. Now they can't deny that I have killed Grettir.'

They told him he could have his own way, although they disapproved, for everyone thought that what he had done was shameful.

Then Ongul said to Illugi, 'It is a great pity that a man of your courage was foolish enough to join this outlaw in his crimes, for now you can be killed with impunity.'

Illugi replied, 'You will find out before the Althing is over next summer who will be the outlaws; neither you nor your old nurse will judge this case. Grettir was killed by your sorcery and witchcraft, although you assaulted him with weapons when he was dying, and so added brutal cowardice to your sorcery.'

Ongul said, 'You speak bravely, but it will not turn out this way. I will show that I think you would be a great loss, for I will give you your life, if you will swear to us an oath never to take vengeance on those who took part in this.'

Illugi said, 'That might have been worth talking about if Grettir had been able to defend himself, and you had overcome him bravely and openly. It is out of the question that I might save my life by becoming a coward like you. I will say only that no one will be a greater enemy of yours than I, if I live, for I will be slow to forget what you have done to Grettir. I would prefer to die.'

Then Ongul talked with his companions, and asked whether they should let Illugi live, or not. They said he must make the decision, because he was the leader of the expedition. Ongul said he did not want this man around threatening his life, since he had refused to promise or pledge any truce.

When Illugi knew that they were going to kill him, he laughed and said, 'Now you have chosen what is more to my liking.'

They led him then, at dawn, to the east of the island, and killed him. They all praised his courage, and it seemed to all of them that he was unlike any other man of his years.

They buried both the brothers there on the island, but took with them Grettir's head and also all they could use of their weapons and clothing. Ongul kept the good short sword for himself, although they shared the other possessions between them, and he carried it for a long time afterwards. They took Glaum with them, and he complained bitterly.

That night the weather became calm, and in the morning they rowed back to the mainland. Ongul went ashore at the nearest point to his home, and sent the ship north to Bjorn. When they came near Osland, Glaum started complaining so much that they refused to take him with them any further, and killed him there. He wept terribly before he was killed. Ongul went home to Vidvik, very pleased with what he had accomplished on this trip. Grettir's head was put in salt in a certain storehouse at Vidvik which was afterwards called Grettir's Shed. It lay there for the rest of the winter.

Ongul was despised for what he had done, once it became known that Grettir had been overcome by means of witchcraft. He stayed at home in quiet until after Christmas, and then went to see Thorir of Gard; he told him about the killings and said he had a right to the money which had been put on Grettir's head.

Thorir said he would not deny that he was responsible for Grettir's outlawry. 'I have suffered many things at his hands, but I would never have taken his life by making myself a criminal or a sorcerer, as you have done. I will never give you any money, and in my opinion you should be put to death for your sorcery and witchcraft.'

Ongul answered, 'I think you are acting more out of stinginess and meanness than out of any concern about the way in which Grettir was killed.'

Thorir said it was a simple matter for them to wait until the Althing and accept there the ruling of the Lawspeaker. With that they parted and there was nothing but ill will between Thorir and Thorbjorn Ongul.

83

The kinsmen of Grettir and Illugi were furious when they heard of
the killings, and they felt that Ongul had committed a cowardly
crime in killing a dying man, and also in resorting to witchcraft.
They consulted all the wisest men, and everyone spoke badly of
Ongul's case.

Ongul rode west to Midfjord after four weeks of summer had
passed. When Asdis heard of his journey, she sent for men. Many of
her friends came: her sons-in-law Gamli and Glum, and their sons
Skeggi (who was nick-named Short-Hand) and Ospak, who was
mentioned already. Asdis was so well liked that all the men of
Midfjord came to her aid, even those who had previously been
Grettir's enemies. The first of these was Thorodd Poem-Piece, together with most of the men of Hrutafjord.

Ongul came to Bjorg with twenty men, and they carried with
them Grettir's head. The men who had promised Asdis help had
not yet all arrived. Ongul and his men walked into the hall with the
head and put it down on the floor. Asdis herself was there, and
many others. No greetings were given.

Ongul spoke this stanza:

From Drang Isle I've carried
Grettir's greedy head.
The lady, against her will,
Must mourn for his red hair.
You can see the traitor's face
on the floor before you.
It will rot away,
unless you preserve it in salt.

Asdis sat quietly while he was speaking, and then she spoke this
verse:

You'd have fled into the sea,
like sheep before a wolf,
if Grettir had been well
when you met on the island.

I never speak harm of people,
but I can tell you this:
once more you've made yourself
the laughingstock of the north.

Then many people said it was not strange that she had borne brave sons, since she was so brave in such trying circumstances.

Ospak was outside talking to some of Ongul's men who had not gone into the house. He asked them about the killings, and they all praised the defence that Illugi had put up. They also told how tightly Grettir had held onto the short sword after he was dead, and they marvelled at this.

Just then a good many riders were seen approaching from the west; many of Asdis' friends had come, including Gamli and Skeggi of Melar. Ongul had intended to hold a court of confiscation on Illugi's possessions, for he and his men claimed them all. But when the reinforcements came, Ongul saw that there was nothing he could do.[1] Ospak and Gamli were very eager to attack Ongul, but the wiser men asked them to follow the counsel of their kinsman Thorvald and the other chieftains, and said that the greater the number of wise men dealing with Ongul's case, the worse it would be for him. The outcome was that Ongul rode away taking Grettir's head with him, intending to produce it at the Althing. He rode back home, and the situation seemed bleak to him, since most of the chieftains in the land either were related to Grettir and Illugi or were their kinsmen through marriage.

That summer Skeggi Short-Hand married Valgerd, the daughter of Thorodd Poem-Piece, so Thorodd supported Grettir's kinsmen in this matter.

84

When people rode to the Althing, Ongul had fewer supporters than he had hoped, for everyone condemned his deeds. Halldor asked

---

1 Men who were sentenced to outlawry forfeited all their possessions, and a court of confiscation was held within a fortnight of the passing of the sentence. But as Illugi had never been sentenced to outlawry, Ongul's proposed court of confiscation would have been unlawful.

him if they should take Grettir's head with them to the Althing, and Ongul replied that that was his intention.

'This would be very unwise,' said Halldor, 'for there will be plenty of enemies for you even if you don't stir up their grief by such reminders.'

They were already on their way, and intended to ride south across Sand, so Ongul had the head buried in a certain sandhill there which is now called Grettir's Dune.

The Althing was well attended. Ongul presented his case and praised his own deeds very much. He said that he had killed the greatest outlaw in the land, and demanded the money which had been put on Grettir's head. But Thorir gave the same answer as before. Then the Lawspeaker was asked to give a ruling. He said he wished to know whether there were any counter-charges which would disqualify Ongul from receiving the money – if not, Ongul would be entitled to the price which had been put on Grettir's head. Then Thorvald Asgeirsson called upon Skeggi Short-Hand to make the charges, and he indicted Thorbjorn Ongul, under the penalty of full outlawry, first for sorcery and witchcraft which had led to Grettir's death, and secondly for the crime of assaulting a dying man. At this point the assembly broke up into factions and there were few to support Ongul. The outcome was very different from what he had expected, for Thorvald and his son-in-law Isleif thought that to bring about a man's death by witchcraft was a crime punishable by death. At the suggestion of wise men, the conclusion of the case was that Ongul should go abroad the same summer and never come back to Iceland while there were any close kinsmen of Grettir and Illugi alive. Then it was adopted as law that all sorcerers should be outlawed.

When Ongul realized what his lot would be, he got away from the assembly, for it seemed likely that Grettir's kinsmen would attack him. He received nothing of the reward offered for the killing of Grettir, because Stein the Lawspeaker did not want it to be paid for such an evil crime. No compensation was paid for those of Thorbjorn's men who had been killed on Drang Isle: their deaths were balanced off against the killing of Illugi, although Illugi's kinsmen were not pleased with this. Then everyone rode home from the Althing, and all the claims which men had against Grettir were dropped.

Skeggi Gamlason – the son-in-law of Thorodd Poem-Piece and Grettir's nephew – rode north to Skagafjord; Thorvald Asgeirsson and his son-in-law Isleif, who later became bishop of Skalaholt, supported him in this. With the approval of everyone, Skeggi got a boat and sailed out to Drang Isle to fetch the bodies of the brothers, Grettir and Illugi. He brought them to Reykir in Reykjastrand, and buried them at the church there. It is a proof of Grettir's burial there that in the days of the Sturlungs,[1] when the church at Reykir was moved, Grettir's bones were dug up, and were found to be remarkably big. Illugi's bones were re-interred north of the church, but Grettir's head was buried in the church at Bjarg, where he was born.

Asdis stayed on at Bjarg, and she was so well liked that people did not trouble her, nor had they, even during Grettir's outlawry. Skeggi Short-Hand took over the Bjarg property after she died; he was considered a notable man, and many people are descended from him.[2]

85

Thorbjorn Ongul got a passage on a ship at Gasair, and brought with him everything he could. His brother Hjalti took charge of his estate, and Ongul gave him Drang Isle. Afterwards Hjalti became a great chieftain, but he does not come into this story again.

Ongul went to Norway, and continued to put on airs, for he thought he had done a great deed in killing Grettir. Many of the people who had not heard the circumstances and knew only what a famous man Grettir had been accepted this. Ongul took care to mention only those parts of his dealings with Grettir which were to his credit, and left out everything which was less glorious.

News of this came east to Tonsberg in the autumn, and when Thorstein the Galleon heard about the killings he became very thoughtful, for he had been told that Ongul was a strong and ruthless man. Thorstein called to mind what he had said to Grettir

---

1 The Sturlungs were one of the outstanding families in thirteenth-century Iceland: the most famous members of the family are the authors Snorri Sturluson and his nephew Sturla Thordarson.

2 *His son was Gamli, who was the father of Skeggi of Skarfsstead and of Asdis, the mother of the monk Odd.* This Odd (Snorrason) was a monk in the Benedictine monastery of Thingeyrar and lived in the second half of the twelfth century. He was a historian, and wrote a Latin *Life of King Olaf Tryggvason*, which survives only in vernacular versions.

long ago when they were comparing their arms. Thorstein kept track of Ongul's movements: that winter they were both in Norway, Ongul in the north and Thorstein south at Tonsberg, but neither had ever seen the other. However, Ongul came to hear that Grettir had a brother in Norway, and he thought this added to his difficulties in a foreign land, so he tried to work out what he should do.

At that time many Norwegians went out to Constantinople, where they became mercenaries. So Thorbjorn Ongul thought it a good idea to go there and win wealth and fame, while at the same time getting away from Grettir's kinsmen in Scandinavia. He made ready to leave Norway and travelled from land to land without stopping until he reached Constantinople. He became a mercenary, and stayed there for a while.

86

Thorstein the Galleon was a rich man and was held in much honour. He was told that Ongul had left the country to go to Constantinople. He wasted no time, but gave his estate into the charge of his kinsmen, and made ready for the journey. He started pursuing Ongul, and whenever he came to a place, Ongul had just left it, but Ongul remained unaware of him. Thorstein the Galleon arrived at Constantinople a little after Ongul, and was very eager to kill him, but neither of them could recognize the other. They both wanted to join the Varangian Guard,[1] and they were well received when it was known that they came from the north. At that time Michael Katalak was king in Byzantium.[2]

Thorstein the Galleon kept on the lookout for Ongul and tried to identify him, but he did not succeed because of the great number of people there. He used to stay awake at night, and was very unhappy about the situation, for he had suffered a great loss. Some time later the Varangians were sent on an expedition to restore peace in

---

1 The Varangian Guard was an élite corps of mercenaries, originally almost all Scandinavians, in the service of the Byzantine emperors.
2 Michael Catalactus ($\kappa\alpha\tau\alpha\lambda\lambda\acute{\alpha}\kappa\tau\eta\varsigma$, 'money-changer'), more formally known as Michael IV or Michael the Paphlagonian, was emperor from 1034 to 1041. See chapters 3 and 5 of *King Harald's Saga*, which was presumably known to the author of *Grettir's Saga*.

the country. It was their custom and law to hold an inspection of weapons before setting out, and so it happened this time. Once the inspection had been called, all the Varangians and others who intended to join the expedition had to attend and present their weapons.

Thorstein and Ongul were both there: Ongul was the first to present his weapons, and he was carrying Grettir's short sword. When he presented it, everyone admired it and said it was a splendid weapon, but added that it was badly flawed because of the piece broken out of the middle of the edge. They asked Ongul what had happened.

Ongul said this was a story worth telling. 'It begins out in Iceland,' he said, 'when I killed a champion called Grettir the Strong, the greatest and bravest warrior ever to have lived there, for no one could kill him until I came along. But since I was fated to overcome him, I vanquished him, although he was many times stronger than I. I struck his head with this short sword, and then a piece broke off the edge.'

The men who were present said that this Grettir must have had a hard skull, and they passed the short sword from one to another. From this Thorstein could see who Ongul was, and, like the others, he asked to look at the sword. Ongul willingly agreed, for everyone was praising his courage and valour, and he thought this man would do the same, since he had no idea that Thorstein or any other of Grettir's kinsmen were there. Thorstein took the short sword, and at once raised it up and struck at Ongul. The blow landed on his head, and it was so powerful that the sword went right down to his jaws. Thorbjorn Ongul fell dead to the ground. Everyone was speechless, and the king's steward arrested Thorstein at once and asked him why he had committed such a terrible crime at an inviolable assembly. Thorstein said that he was the brother of Grettir the Strong, and also that this was his first chance to take vengeance. Then many said that this strong man must have been very important since Thorstein had travelled so far from his home to avenge him. Those in authority were inclined to agree, but since there was no one present to testify on Thorstein's behalf, their law made it clear that anyone who killed a man forfeited his life. Thorstein was quickly given a hard sentence: he was to be incarcerated and kept in a dungeon until either he died or someone paid a ransom for him. When Thorstein came to the dungeon, there was another prisoner there already, who had been there for a long time, and was almost dead from misery. It was a foul, cold place.

Thorstein asked this man, 'How do you like your life?'

He replied, 'It is terrible, for no one is willing to help me, and I have no kinsmen to pay my ransom.'

Thorstein said, 'Many a chance can save a helpless man. So let's cheer up and find some amusement for ourselves.'

The other said that nothing could cheer him up.

'We'll try anyhow,' said Thorstein. Then he began to sing. He had such a splendid voice that there was hardly anyone to compare with him, and he sang his very best. The public street was close to the dungeon, and Thorstein sang so loudly that it rang from the walls; the man who had been half-dead found it a great pleasure. Thorstein went on singing until late in the evening.

87

There was a noble lady in the city called Spes; she was very rich and well born. She had a husband called Sigurd who was wealthy but of lower birth; she had been given to him in marriage for the sake of his money. They had little love for each other, and Spes felt that she had married beneath her. She was proud and high-spirited.

On the same evening that Thorstein was singing it happened that Spes was walking on the street near the dungeon where she heard a voice so beautiful that she thought she had never heard anything like it. She had a number of attendants with her, and she told them to go over and find out whom this splendid voice belonged to. They called out and asked who was so strongly locked up there, and Thorstein gave his name.

Then Spes said, 'Are you as outstanding in other things as you are in singing?'

He said that she was overpraising him.

'What have you done,' she asked, 'to deserve a painful death there?'

He said that he had killed a man to avenge his brother. 'But I could not produce witnesses to support me, and so I am kept here, unless someone is willing to ransom me, which I think very unlikely, since I have no kinsmen here.'

'What a great loss it would be,' she said, 'if you were to be killed. Was your brother whom you avenged so famous a man?'

He said that his brother had been twice as great a man as himself.

She asked what evidence there was of that.

Thorstein spoke this stanza:

Eight warriors failed
to pull the short sword
from brave Grettir's grip.
So then they were obliged
to cut off the hand
of my seafaring brother.

'What great glory!' said those who could understand the stanza.

When Spes heard this, she said, 'Would you accept your life from me, if that were possible?'

'Most certainly,' he said, 'provided that my companion who is kept here is also released with me. Otherwise we shall both stay here.'

She said, 'I think you will be a better bargain than he.'

'That may be so,' said Thorstein, 'but either we shall leave this place together or neither of us will go.'

She went to the Varangians and offered them money if they would release Thorstein. They were willing to do this, and by her influence and her wealth she managed to get both men released. When Thorstein came out of the dungeon he went to see Spes, who invited him to stay and kept him there in secret. But sometimes he used to join the Varangians on their expeditions, and always proved himself a man of great courage.

88

At this time Harald Sigurdarson[1] was staying in Byzantium, and Thorstein became friendly with him. Thorstein was now highly regarded, since Spes gave him plenty of money. Spes was greatly taken by his valour, and they fell in love with each other. She spent a lot of money, and kept up a large circle of friends. Her husband thought he noticed a change in her: her moods were different, and her behaviour, and also she was squandering their money. He began

---

1 Harald Sigurdarson (Harald Hardradi) later became king of Norway. He was killed in the battle of Stamford Bridge, in 1066. For an account of his life see *King Harald's Saga*.

to miss gold and treasures which were in her keeping. On one occasion Sigurd, her husband, had a talk with her and said that she was behaving very strangely. 'You show no respect for our property, but squander it in all directions. You act as if you were walking in your sleep, and you always keep away from me, wherever I am. I know for certain that something is going on.'

She said, 'I myself and my kinsmen told you before our marriage that I wanted to be independent, and free to use your money as I liked. That's why I don't stint. Is there anything else you want to say to me which would disgrace me?'

He answered, 'I am not entirely without suspicion that you are keeping someone whom you prefer to me.'

'I am not aware,' she said, 'that there is much to back this up, and indeed I think you are just trying to make up lies. I'm not going to talk with you any longer alone, if you make such outrageous charges.'

He said nothing further on that occasion.

She and Thorstein continued just as before and did not trouble to guard against malicious gossip, because she trusted in her shrewdness and her popularity. They often used to sit together enjoying themselves. One evening they were sitting in an upper room where her valuables were kept, and she asked him to sing a song, because she thought her husband was out drinking, as was his custom, and she locked the door. When Thorstein had been singing for a while, someone started ramming the door and shouting at her to open up. Her husband had arrived with a number of attendants. A little earlier she had raised the lid of a certain large coffer, and she was showing Thorstein her valuables. When she realized who had come, she refused to open the door, and whispered to Thorstein, 'Here is a quick solution: jump into the coffer and stay there quietly.'

He did so, and she put the lock on the coffer and sat down on the lid. Just then her husband stormed into the room, after they had broken the door.

The woman said, 'Why are you breaking in like this? Are you being chased by ruffians?'

Her husband answered, 'Splendid! Now you yourself will show what sort of woman you are. Where is that man who was straining his voice just now? You must think that his voice is better than mine.'

She said, ' "A wise man knows when to hold his tongue," and you should bear this in mind. You think yourself very cunning and you hope to make your lies stick, but the facts will speak for themselves. If you have spoken the truth, then find the man, for he's not likely to vanish through the walls or the ceiling.'

He searched the whole room but found nothing.

She said, 'Why don't you take him, since you're so certain he's here?'

He was silent then, and unable to understand how he had been tricked. He asked his companions if they had not heard the same sound that he did, but they realized that the woman was displeased, so they did not support him but only said that one often heard something which was not really there. With that the husband left the room, convinced that he knew the truth, although he had failed to find the man. For a long time after that he did not spy on his wife.

On another occasion, much later, Thorstein and Spes were sitting in a certain storeroom, where there was a lot of cloth, both cut and uncut, which belonged to her and her husband. She showed Thorstein many lengths of cloth, and they spread them out. When they least expected it her husband came with a number of men and started breaking into the room. But whilst they were doing this, she piled the cloth on top of Thorstein, and she was leaning against the pile when they entered.

'Will you deny this time that you have a man with you here?' her husband asked. 'There are people here who actually saw you together.'

She told them not to be so excited. 'You will have it your way, but leave me alone and don't push me about.'

They searched the whole room but found nothing and at last gave up.

Then the woman said, 'It is always good to turn out better than people expect, but you couldn't hope to find something which didn't exist. Now, my husband, will you admit your stupidity, and exonerate me from your wicked accusations?'

He said, 'Far from it, and I will not exonerate you, for I am convinced that my charge against you is a just one. You will have to do your best if you want to clear yourself.'

She replied that she did not mind in the least, and so they ended their talk.

Afterwards Thorstein stayed most of the time with the Varangians. Men say that he consulted Harald Sigurdarson, and it is thought that Spes and Thorstein would never have been able to find a way out if they had not had the benefit of his wise counsel.

After a while, her husband Sigurd mentioned that he was going away on some business. His wife did not try to stop him, and once he was away, Thorstein came and stayed with her all the time. Her house was built in such a way that it jutted out over the water, so there were some rooms which had the sea under them. Spes and Thorstein used to spend their time in one of these rooms. There was a small trap-door in the floor which no one else knew about, and they kept it open, in case it was needed in an emergency.

To return to the husband, he had not gone away at all but had been hiding in order to spy on his wife. And it happened one evening, when Spes and Thorstein were sitting in the room over the sea enjoying themselves, that her husband with a large number of people surprised them. He took several men up to the window of a room and told them to have a look and see whether he was telling the truth. Everyone agreed that he was, and that he must have been right on the previous occasions. They burst into the room.

When Spes and Thorstein heard the noise, she said to him, 'Now you must go down the trap-door, whatever happens after that. Give me a signal if you manage to get away from the house.'

He promised he would, and dived down through the floor. The woman kicked the trap-door shut, so that the floor appeared undisturbed. Her husband came in with his men, and they went around searching, but of course found nothing. The room was completely bare, with no furniture, but only the level floor and some benches. The woman sat there twiddling her thumbs; she paid no attention to them, and appeared as if nothing was the matter. Her husband was flabbergasted and asked his companions if they had not seen the man. They said they most certainly had.

The woman said, 'The old saying has once more been borne out: "Things happen in threes." This is true of you, Sigurd. On three occasions you have, I think, caused me annoyance. Are you any wiser now than you were to begin with?'

'This time I am not the only witness,' said her husband. 'Now you will have to prove your innocence, for I am certainly not going to put up with this humiliation.'

'You are asking for just what I wanted to offer,' said his wife, 'for I am looking forward to clearing myself of this charge. This accusation has become so well known that it would cause me serious embarrassment if I failed to refute it.'

'You shall also at the same time have to prove that you have not given away my money and treasures,' said her husband.

She answered, 'At the time that I clear my name I will clear it of all the charges you have brought against me. But you should bear in mind what the consequences will be. I want to go before the bishop tomorrow, as soon as I can, and ask him to decide how I may clear myself of these charges.'

Her husband accepted this and went away with his men.

180

Meanwhile Thorstein had swum out beyond the houses and had gone ashore where he wanted. He picked up a burning log and held it over his head so that it could be seen from her house. She had kept going outside throughout the evening and the night, for she was anxious to know if Thorstein had made it to land. When she saw the fire she realized that he had reached land, for they had earlier agreed on this signal.

The next morning Spes said to her husband that they must go to the bishop and discuss their case with him. Her husband was ready for that, and when they came before the bishop he repeated his charges against her. The bishop asked whether she had ever been accused in this way before, but no one claimed to have heard of such charges. Then the bishop asked what proofs he had to support his accusations, and the husband brought forth the witnesses who had seen her with a man in a locked room. The husband said that for this reason he suspected the man of having seduced her. The bishop said she could try to clear her name of this charge, if she wished. She replied that she wanted to, very much. 'I believe,' she said, 'that I can find plenty of women to swear with me to my innocence in this matter.'

Then the oath was drawn up, and a day fixed when she must come forth and swear to it. She went back home well pleased with herself, and met with Thorstein so that they could make their plans.

89

This day passed, and soon came the day when Spes was to swear her oath. She had invited all her friends and kinsmen. She dressed herself in her finest clothes, and had many elegant women in her retinue. It was a very rainy day, and the road was wet. They had to cross a certain muddy ditch before they could get to the church. By the time Spes and her retinue came to the ditch, a large crowd had gathered there, and also there were a number of poor men asking for alms, since this was on a main road. Everyone thought it their duty to greet her as warmly as they could, and to wish her well, because she had helped them on many occasions. Among the poor men was a certain old beggar; he was tall and had a long beard.

The women stopped at the brink of the ditch, for these courtly people thought it too muddy to cross. When the tall beggar saw Spes, who was more elegantly dressed than the others, he said to her: 'My lady, will you condescend to allow me to carry you across this bog? It is the duty of beggars like me to serve you the best we can.'

'How can you carry me,' she asked, 'when you can hardly support yourself?'

'But it would be proof of your humility,' he said, 'and I can do no more than offer you what I have. Everything will go better for you if you aren't arrogant to a poor man.'

'You can be sure,' she said, 'that if you don't carry me properly you can look for nothing better than to be flogged.'

'I will take the risk gladly,' he said, and scrambled into the ditch. She showed some misgivings about letting him carry her, but still she got onto his back. He stumbled along slowly, with the aid of two crutches, and when he was halfway across he began to sway in all directions. She told him to keep going. 'This will be the worst trip you ever made, if you drop me here,' she said.

The wretched tramp tried to struggle on, and was doing his utmost. By making his best efforts he got close to the bank on the other side, but then he stumbled and fell forwards, flinging her up on the bank, while he himself sank into the mud right up to his armpits. As he was lying there he grabbed at the lady, but he could not get a grip on her dress, and with his mud-covered hand he took hold of her knee and her naked thigh. She jumped to her feet, cursing him, and said that wicked beggars were always causing trouble. 'You ought to be whipped to shreds, except that you're already such a pitiful wretch.'

Then he said, 'We can't all be lucky. I thought I was doing you a favour, and I hoped you would give me some alms, but instead I get only threats and abuse, and nothing else.' And he seemed to take it very much to heart.

Many people felt sorry for him, but she said that he was full of tricks. Because people were pleading for him, however, she took out her purse, which contained a number of gold coins. She shook out the money, and said, 'Take this, old man. It would be wrong if you were not paid in full for my ill treatment of you. Now we can part, for you have had your reward.'

He picked up the gold and thanked her for her generosity.

Spes went to the church, where a great crowd had already gathered. Sigurd began vigorously and told her to clear herself of the charges he had made.

She answered, 'I care nothing for your charges. Who is the man that you claim to have seen in the room with me? It often happens

that some good man is near me, and I don't see anything shameful
in that. But I will swear an oath that I have never given gold to any
man and that I have never been physically defiled by any man, with
the exception of my husband – and that wicked tramp, who touched
my thigh with his dirty hand when he carried me across the ditch
today.'

Most people agreed that this oath covered everything, and that
she was not disgraced because a man had touched her by accident.
She replied that she had to include everything that had happened.
Afterwards she swore the oath which was just described, and many
people said that she was certainly living up to the proverb, 'Nothing
must be left out of an oath.' She replied that in her opinion wise
people would agree her oath was above suspicion. Her kinsmen said
it was an insult for women of high birth to have such charges brought
against them without redress, since it was punishable by death in
that country if a woman was found guilty of adultery. Spes asked
the bishop for a divorce, for she said she could no longer bear her
husband's false accusations. Her kinsmen supported her in this, and
with their backing and bribes she won a divorce. Sigurd got little
of the property and was forced to leave the country. Thus it turned
out, as is often the case, that the weaker must suffer defeat. There
was nothing he could do about it, although the truth was on his
side. Spes took over all their wealth, and was thought a paragon
among women. But when her oath was studied more carefully, it
seemed not to have been above suspicion, and it was thought that
some wise man must have dictated the terms of the oath to her. Then
it was discovered that the old tramp who had carried her was
Thorstein the Galleon. However, Sigurd got no redress, and he is
now out of the saga.

90

Thorstein the Galleon was with the Varangians while this affair was
being most talked about. He became so famous that hardly any
other man who had come there seemed comparable to him in valour.
Harald Sigurdarson held him in the highest honour, since they were
related, and it was thought that Thorstein had followed his advice.

Soon after Sigurd had been banished from the country, Thorstein proposed to Spes. She gave him a favourable answer, but referred the matter to her kinsmen. Family meetings were held, and it was agreed that she should make her own decision, so then the contract was made. Their marriage was a happy one, and they had a great deal of money. Thorstein was considered very lucky to have solved his problems in the way that he did.

After they had spent two years together in Byzantium, Thorstein told his wife that he wanted to go back to his estates in Norway, and she said that the decision was up to him. Then he sold their property, and got a good deal of money. They travelled with a fine retinue all the way from these distant parts to Norway. Thorstein's kinsmen gave them both a good welcome; it was soon evident that she was generous and magnanimous, and she became very highly thought of. Thorstein and Spes had several children; they stayed on their estates there and were very happy.

By this time King Magnus the Good[1] was the ruler of Norway, and Thorstein went to see him. He was well received, since he had become famous for having avenged Grettir the Strong. There is hardly an example known of an Icelander being avenged in Byzantium, apart from Grettir Asmundarson. It is said that Thorstein became King Magnus' retainer. Thorstein stayed quietly in Norway for nine years after his return there, and both he and his wife were held in high honour.

When King Harald Sigurdarson came north from Byzantium, King Magnus gave him half the kingdom, and for a time they were joint rulers of Norway. But the following summer King Magnus the Good died, and King Harald became the sole ruler. After the death of King Magnus many of his friends were very unhappy, for everyone had loved him. They also found it difficult to avoid clashes with King Harald, for he was harsh and revengeful.

By this time Thorstein was getting on in years, but he was still a vigorous man. This was sixteen years after the killing of Grettir Asmundarson.

1 King Magnus was the ruler of Norway from 1035 to 1046.

91

Many men kept urging Thorstein to go to King Harald and to give him his allegiance, but Thorstein had little to say about this. Then Spes said, 'I would like you not to go to King Harald, Thorstein, for we owe a larger debt to another king, and we must start thinking about that now. Our youth is well behind us, and we are getting on in years, but we have always lived more after our own desires than after Christian teaching or righteousness. I know that this debt of ours can be settled neither by our kinsmen nor by our wealth, but we must pay it ourselves. So I want us to change our way of life, and to journey from this country to the pope's palace, for I believe that this is the only way to save myself.'

Thorstein answered, 'Everything you say is as clear to me as it is to you. It is right and proper that you should make this decision, because you allowed me to make the decision when we were taking a much less promising path. We will do precisely as you suggest.'

This came as a great surprise to everyone. By this time Thorstein was sixty-seven years old, but still strong enough for anything he wanted to do. He invited all his relatives to come to see him, and he told them of his intention. Wise men approved, although they thought that their departure was a great loss. Thorstein said that it was by no means certain that they would return. 'I would like now to thank you all,' he said, 'for the way in which you took care of my property when I was away before. Now I want to ask you to take charge of my children's inheritance, and of my children themselves, and to bring them up to the best of your ability, for I have reached such an age that it is an even chance whether or not I will come back, even if I live. You must take care of everything I leave behind here, as if I should never return to Norway.'

They replied that everything would be in good hands if his wife remained there in charge.

Then she said, 'The reason that I went with Thorstein from Byzantium, my native land, leaving behind my kinsmen and my estates, was that I wanted us both to share the same fate. I have liked it here very much, but I have no desire to stay here in Norway, or in these northern lands, much longer, if my husband goes away.

We have always loved each other, and nothing has ever come between us. So now we shall go together, for we alone know about many things which have happened since our first meeting.'

When they had made all their arrangements, Thorstein asked some fair-minded men to divide his property evenly into two halves. His kinsmen were to take charge of one half, and this was intended for the children – who grew up with their father's relatives and became fine people; many of their descendants now live around Oslofjord. Thorstein and Spes took the other half and divided it: they gave some of it to churches for the good of their souls, and some they took with them. Then they set off on their journey to Rome, and many people prayed for them.

92

They travelled all the way to Rome and, when they came before the man who was appointed to hear confessions, they told him plainly everything that had happened and how they had contrived their marriage by trickery. They offered themselves humbly for any penance he wished to assign to them. Because it was their own wish to atone for their transgressions, without any pressure or compulsion from the leaders of the church, they were given the lightest possible penance. They received absolution for their past deeds, and were asked gently to provide wisely for their souls and to lead pure lives. They were thought to have conducted themselves with much wisdom.

Then Spes said, 'I think that this has gone very well, and that our problems have been happily solved. Now it is not misfortune alone we are sharing between us. It may happen that foolish people will follow the example we set when we were younger, so now we should end our lives in such a way as to set an example for good men. We must hire masons to build a stone hut for each of us, so that we may atone for our transgressions against God.'

Thorstein provided money for the building of the two stone huts, and also for the necessities of life. After their cells were ready and all the arrangements made, at an opportune time they terminated their worldly life together, of their own free will, in order that they might better enjoy eternal life together in the next world. They retired into two separate cells and lived there as long as God allowed them, and so they ended their lives. Most people agree that Thorstein the Galleon and his wife Spes were the luckiest of people, as it turned out. None of his children or descendants ever came to Iceland, as far as is known.

93

Sturla the Lawman has said that in his opinion there was never an outlaw as distinguished as Grettir the Strong. To support this claim Sturla gives three reasons. First, that Grettir was the most intelligent of them all, as can be seen from the fact that he lived as an outlaw longer than anyone else and could never be overcome while he remained in good health. Second, that he was the strongest man in the land during his time, and more successful than any other in dealing with ghosts and monsters. Third, that his death was avenged out in Byzantium, which has never happened for any other Icelander. Sturla also added the fact that his avenger, Thorstein the Galleon, enjoyed exceptionally good luck in the latter part of his life.

And so ends the saga of Grettir Asmundarson.

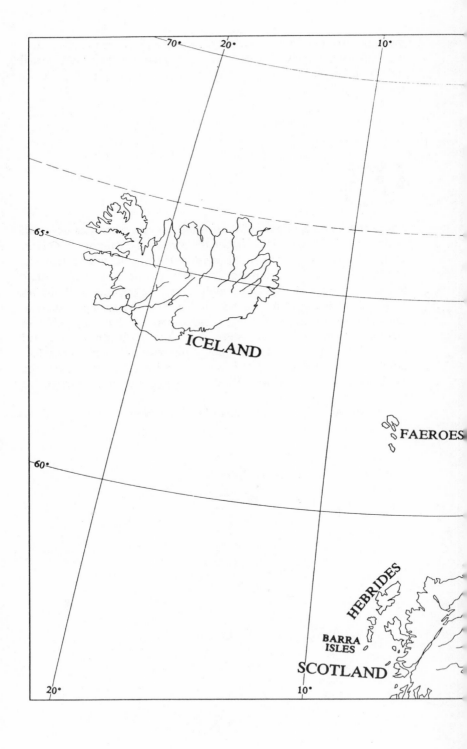

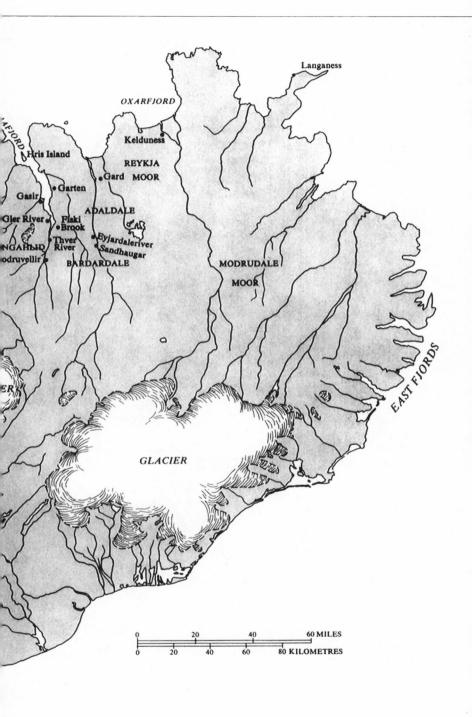

A note on the social and legal background of the saga

Most of the action of *Grettir's Saga* takes place in the first half of the eleventh century, some three centuries before the lifetime of its author. There is plenty of evidence to show that the author had a good historical sense: the first ten chapters describe the settlement of Iceland (c. 870-930); the introduction of Christianity into Iceland (1000) is mentioned in chapter 13, while the changes which it brought (and sometimes the slowness of these changes, as with the sorceress who contributes to Grettir's death) are clearly marked. By and large, the author describes Iceland as he imagines – not always very accurately – it to have been in the eleventh century. But his task was the easier because of the continuity and stability of Icelandic society: life in eleventh-century Iceland was in many ways very similar to life in fourteenth-century, or even eighteenth-century, Iceland.

The nature of the society was determined, above all, by the land. Though Iceland is bigger than Ireland, only the fertile lowlands – a very small part of the total area – are inhabitable. (Grettir, abnormally, spends much time in the barren interior, but this was a region outside society, fit only for those outside the law.) The most important crop, by far, was simply grass, which was used as fodder for sheep and cattle. In the summers, the farmers followed the Norwegian practice of moving animals to different pastures, usually on higher ground: hence the references in the saga to 'shielings,' a term used both for the summer grazing lands and for the huts built to accommodate the herdsmen and dairymaids. The settlers of Iceland came mostly from Norway where there were trees, for fuel and building, and large game, for food. In Iceland, the scrub trees which the first settlers found were never suitable for building and were, in any case, quickly depleted, while there were no indigenous land mammals at all. But, as a substitute, there was at least an intermittent supply of stranded whales and of driftwood; as a consequence, the 'driftage rights' were valuable, and occasionally, as in chapter 12, a source of controversy.

The original settlers of Iceland took up land in scattered areas and established farms similar to their Norwegian or Hebridean farms; the people who arrived later did the same. For centuries there were no towns or hamlets, nor were there any very rigid social classes. But it is possible to make some rough distinctions between different levels of society. To begin at the bottom, there were, in the earliest periods, slaves, but slavery died out during the twelfth century, and slaves do not figure in *Grettir's*

Saga. Next, there were servants, free men who sold their labour to others, and who were allowed to change their employer once a year (see, for instance, chapter 45). Above them were the crofters and tenants, men who were independent householders but too poor to pay tax. They do not figure prominently in *Grettir's Saga*, though by the fourteenth century they had become a very large segment of the population. The most important section of the society was constituted by the independent farmers, men like Grettir's father or his brother Atli. Though there were certainly differences of power and wealth between farmers, they were equal before the law and were, essentially, the citizens of Iceland. Finally, there were the *goðar* (sing. *goði*), or priest-chieftains. In the eleventh century there were forty-eight of these chieftains, as compared with about thirty-eight hundred tax-paying farmers. Chieftains were themselves farmers, but had also certain inherited duties and powers. The office had originally been partly a religious one, but by the eleventh century the chieftains had only legal and administrative functions. Each farmer had to be the supporter of one particular chieftain (an arrangement entered into by mutual consent), and had to accompany his chieftain to the annual meeting of the Althing and to other lawful assemblies. But it is important to emphasize that these chieftains did not form any sort of feudal ruling class: eleventh-century Iceland is best described as a confederation of free farmers.

Separate mention should be made of a few special classes. There were beggars, who, like outlaws, were outside society in that they had no legal domicile and were not members of a household. Then there were Christian priests, who were either employed by a farmer or were farmers themselves, and who were not required to be celibate. (It might be noted that in this translation 'Priest,' when it is part of a proper name, as with Snorri the Priest, translates *goði*, and does not mean that the man was a Christian priest.) Some men were traders, and spent at least part of their lives on trading voyages, mostly between Iceland and Norway, but they were usually also farmers. In Norway, besides kings and earls, there was the rank of a 'landed man', *lendr maðr*, a title used for a man who was given land, and local authority, by the king.

The Icelandic legal system is an important part of the background in *Grettir's Saga*, as it is in many of the sagas. There were three different types of legal assemblies, or *things*. Local assemblies dealt with issues between two litigants who belonged to the same district. Quarter assemblies (for judicial purposes Iceland was divided into four quarters) were established to cover cases where the litigants belonged to the same quarter, but to different local assemblies; in practice, however, they were not often held. The Althing, the open-air general assembly which was held for a fortnight every summer at Thingvellir in southwest Iceland, contained a legislative court, as well as four judicial courts, one for each quarter. About 1005 a 'Fifth Court' was added, which dealt with cases where the litigants were from different quarters, and which also functioned as a final court of appeal. The chieftains, as a body, constituted the legislative court, and they nominated the judges for the Quarter Courts and the Fifth Court (thirty-six judges for each court). They also elected the Lawspeaker of the Althing, who served for a three-year term. Down to the beginning of the twelfth century, before the laws were codified, the

Lawspeaker had the duty of reciting the laws from memory at the Althing, one third of them each year. He also acted as an arbiter when disagreements about legal points arose.

The Althing, however, had no executive powers, nor was there any public prosecutor. The kinsmen of a man who had been killed had the legal duty of prosecuting the victim's killer; if they were successful, they themselves had to enforce the verdict, though the community was supposed to give them support. Icelandic law provided for two types of penalties, fines and outlawry. A distinction was made between two types of outlawry, 'Lesser Outlawry,' and 'Full Outlawry.' The first penalty meant that the convicted person must, within three years from the time the sentence was passed, leave Iceland and spend the next three years abroad. He was inviolate, under certain restrictions, while he was in Iceland and when he was abroad, but if he failed to go abroad during these three years he became an outlaw for life. After three years abroad, he could return to Iceland and regain all his civic rights. Full outlawry, however, meant that the convicted man must stay out of Iceland forever, and that he could be killed with impunity, even abroad, by Icelanders. To help him was a serious offence, and hence Grettir had great difficulty in finding men to give him shelter. All of an outlaw's property was forfeited by a court of confiscation, and he was not even allowed a Christian burial. He usually had a price on his head of eight ounces of silver, which could be raised to twenty-four ounces if he committed a killing at the Althing, burned someone in a house, or was a slave who killed his master. According to *Grettir's Saga*, an outlaw who survived for twenty years would also regain his freedom, but this had no actual basis in law, as far as is known. The idea of outlawry is of course primitive and universal: a society takes a simple measure to rid itself of an undesirable element, and it becomes the duty of all the members of the society to assist in enforcing this measure.

Index of proper names

This is not an exhaustive index, but it is intended to contain the names of all the more important characters in the saga.

This book

was designed by

ELLEN HUTCHISON

under the direction of

ALLAN FLEMING

University of

Toronto

Press